Y0-AIO-618

E
185     Newman, Richard, 1930 –
N59
1996    Words like freedom

**DATE DUE**

Newman, Richard, 1930 –

E
185     Words like freedom
N59
1996

| DATE | ISSUED TO |
|---|---|
| FEB 2 1 2001 | |

AUDREY COHEN COLLEGE LIBRARY
75 Varick St. 12th Floor
New York, NY 10013

# Words Like Freedom

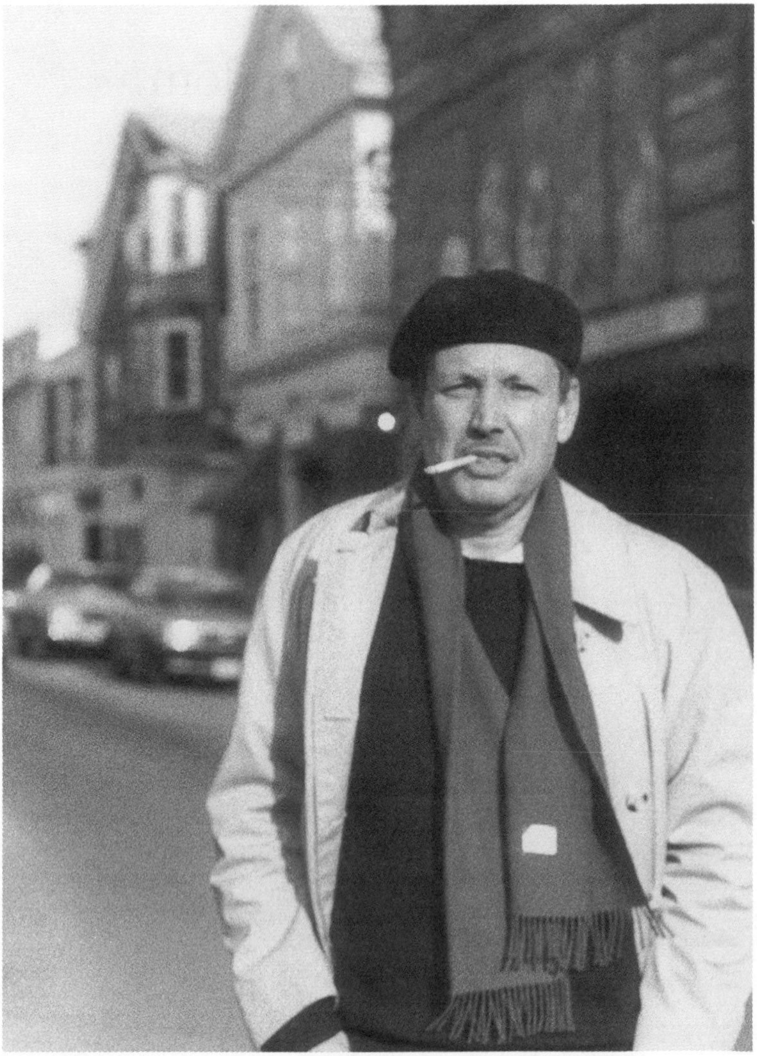

# Words Like Freedom

*Essays on African-American Culture and History*

*by*
Richard Newman

*Foreword by*
Nell Irvin Painter

LOCUST HILL PRESS
West Cornwall, CT
1996

© 1996 Richard Newman
All rights reserved

**Library of Congress Cataloging-in-Publication Data**

Newman, Richard, 1930—
    Words like freedom : essays on African-American culture and history / by Richard Newman : foreword by Nell Irvin Painter.
    215p.    cm.
    Includes bibliographical references and index.
    ISBN 0-933951-67-1 (lib. bdg. : alk. paper)
    1. Afro-Americans--History. 2. Afro-Americans--Intellectual life. 3. American literature--Afro-American authors. 4. Afro-American arts. 5. Afro-Americans--Religion. 6. Afro-Americans--Books and reading. I. Title.
E185.N59 1996
973'.0496073--dc20                                      95-52053
                                                                             CIP

Printed on acid-free, 250-year-life paper
Manufactured in the United States of America

For Belynda

"She is a friend to my mind. She gathers me. The pieces I am, she gathers them and gives them back to me in all the right order. It's good when you got a woman who is a friend of your mind."

—Toni Morrison, *Beloved*

O wrestlin' Jacob, Jacob day's a-breakin',
I will not let thee go!
O wrestlin' Jacob, Jacob day's a-breakin',
He will not let me go!
O, I hold my brudder wid a tremblin' hand,
I would not let him go!
I hold my sister wid a tremblin' hand,
I would not let her go!

—Traditional Spiritual

# Contents

Acknowledgments • *xi*
Foreword • *xiii*
Introduction • *xv*

## I. Writing

1. Words Like Freedom: Afro-American Books and Manuscripts in the Henry W. and Albert A. Berg Collection of English and American Literature • *3*
2. Henry Louis Gates, Jr.: The Scholar of African-American Culture Has Written a "Storytelling" Memoir of Growing Up in the South • *29*
3. Two Letters from Nella Larsen • *35*
4. Some Little-Known African-American Writers • *43*
5. Sara Lawrence-Lightfoot: "To Chart Different Journeys" • *47*

## II. Performing Arts

6. "The Brightest Star:" Aida Overton Walker in the Age of Ragtime and Cakewalk • *55*
7. Florence Mills • *77*
8. "East of Broadway:" Florence Mills at Aeolian Hall • *89*
9. The Lincoln Theatre: Once a Carnival of Merrymaking • *93*

## III. Religion

10. The Paradox of Lemuel Haynes • *101*
11. Black Bishops: Some African-American Old Catholics and Their Churches • *107*
12. An Interview with Sherry Sherrod DuPree • *149*

## IV. Reading

13. Vindicating the Race: Collectors of African-American Books • *157*
14. The First Printed Protest Against Slavery: George Keith's *Exhortation* of 1693 • *163*
15. Books and Writers of the Harlem Reniassance • *171*
16. Shaping the Future: New Guide and Database Will Range Across African-American History and Culture (with Henry Louis Gates, Jr.) • *181*
17. "Remarks Called For and Otherwise:" The Career of Charles F. Heartman, Bookseller (with Pamela J. Petro) • *187*

Index • *197*

About the Author • *215*

# Acknowledgments

*Words Like Freedom: Afro-American Books and Manuscripts in the Henry W. and Albert A. Berg Collection of American Literature.* New York: New York Public Library, 1989.

"Henry Louis Gates, Jr.: The Scholar of African American Culture Has Written a 'Storytelling' Memoir of Growing Up in the South." *Publishers Weekly* (June 20, 1994), 80–81.

"Two Letters from Nella Larsen." *Biblion: The Bulletin of The New York Public Library* 2:2 (Spring 1994), 124–29.

"Some Little-Known African-American Writers." *Research Library Notes* 3:4 (Fall 1991), 22–23.

"Sara Lawrence-Lightfoot: 'To Chart Different Journeys.'" *Publishers Weekly* (September 5, 1994), 80–82.

"'The Brightest Star': Aida Overton Walker in the Age of Ragtime and Cakewalk." *Prospects: An Annual of American Cultural Studies* 18 (1993): 465–81. In an earlier form this paper was read at the "African Americans in Europe" conference, Université de la Sorbonne Nouvelle, Paris, February 6, 1992.

"Florence Mills." *Notable Black American Women.* Jessie Carney Smith, ed. Detroit: Gale Research, Inc., 1992, pp. 752–56.

"'East of Broadway': Florence Mills at Aeolian Hall." *The Sonneck Society for American Music Bulletin* 20:3 (Fall 1994), 9–10. In an earlier form, this paper was read at the American Theatre in Higher Education conference, Philadelphia, August 4, 1993.

"The Lincoln Theatre: Once a Carnival of Merrymaking." *American Visions* 6:4 (August 1991), 29–32.

"The Paradox of Lemuel Haynes." Preface, *Black Preacher to White America: The Collected Writings of Lemuel Haynes, 1774–1833*, Richard Newman, ed. Brooklyn, NY: Carlson Publishing, Inc., 1990, pp. xi–xvii.

"Black Bishops: Some African-American Old Catholics and Their Churches." In an earlier form, a portion of this paper was read at "The Diversity of African American Religious Experience: A Continuing Dialogue" conference, Schomburg Center for Research in Black Culture, May 29, 1992. Another version was read at the Northeast Seminar on Black Religion, Barnard College, December 4, 1993.

"An Interview with Sherry Sherrod DuPree." *Newsletter of the Afro-American Religious History Group of the American Academy of Religion* 18:1 (Fall 1993), 5–8.

"Vindicating the Race: Collectors of African-American Books." *AB: Bookman's Weekly* 87:20 (May 20, 1991), 2089–92. An abbreviated version appeared as "A Heritage Preserved." *Orator* 1:1 (February 1993), 3–5. In an earlier form, this paper was read at a meeting of the Friends of the Library, Union Theological Seminary, November 8, 1990.

"The First Printed Protest Against Slavery: George Keith's *Exhortation* of 1693." *AB: Bookman's Weekly* 93:6 (February 7, 1994), 545–54.

"Books and Writers of the Harlem Renaissance." *AB: Bookman's Weekly* 91:7 (February 15, 1993), 621–28.

"Shaping the Future: New Guide and Database Will Range Across African-American History and Culture." (With Henry Louis Gates, Jr.) *Humanities* 15:3 (May/June 1994), 18–20.

"'Remarks Called For and Otherwise': The Career of Charles F. Heartman, Bookseller." (With Pamela J. Petro.) *American Book Collector* 7:10 n.s. (October 1986), 9–15.

# Foreword

Twenty-five years ago, as I was writing a dissertation on ordinary black southerners in the nineteenth century, I frequently encountered a question that Richard Newman has been answering all these years: How can you write black history in the absence of sources? Had I known him then, I would have had a ready answer: No problem, there's Dick Newman. He knows the sources.

Dick works the books—best-selling and obscure—the pamphlets, periodicals, reports, programs, in short, the raw material of history. Combing through lists and catalogues, he deciphers their signs like a reader of maps. An esoteric process? To a certain extent, it is. But his discoveries are fundamentally important: He knows that our history is documented, and he knows where those documents lie.

Had he never taken next steps, his inventory, of itself, would make a respectable life's work, an inestimable contribution to the field of African-American history. Happily Dick *has* taken next steps, also uniquely valuable, by addressing his readers as consumers of knowledge and as producers.

His delightful essays on popular culture and religion enrich the reader-consumer by reintroducing figures crucial to their era but subsequently drifted to the margins. He finds them all: bygone stars of ragtime, Harlem Renaissance novelists, bishops in obscure churches. Their rediscovery rounds out our understanding of their times and alerts us that many others, with fascinating stories of their own, wait in the shadows.

For fellow scholars—reader-producers of knowledge—Dick illuminates new and unexpected sources and associates who have published new books. Through his eyes we watch the making of new archives and the collection of materials that will undergird research in the future. We also meet the colleagues who are doing the work. Richard Newman guides our way to the scholarship of the twenty-first century, and I, for one, am grateful for that guidance.

> Nell Irvin Painter
> Edwards Professor of American
>   History
> Princeton University

# Introduction

The title of this book, *Words Like Freedom*, is taken from a line in Langston Hughes' poem "Refugee in America." He read the poem in 1943 at The New York Public Library in a series organized by May Sarton. The typescript of the poem is in the Library's Berg Collection, and I came across it in 1989 while I was going through Berg looking for African-American material. I wrote a bibliographic essay on my findings (the opening piece in this book) which later served as the catalogue of a Berg exhibition of its major black holdings. Both the catalogue and the exhibition were called "Words Like Freedom" and the essay was in print before I discovered in Arnold Rampersad's magisterial biography that Hughes himself had intended to write a book with that title.

I surveyed the Berg Collection because of my belief that The New York Public Library held many more African-American items than those separately catalogued and housed in the Schomburg Center, even though Schomburg is the largest and best collection of its kind in the world. Ignoring computers, I read every Berg catalogue card, and examined every item that might be by or about African Americans, broadly defined, including Abolitionist literature. There were some wonderful discoveries, including a broadside, printed on satin, the declaration of the first convention of the National Anti-Slavery Society meeting in Philadelphia on December 4, 1833. John Greenleaf Whittier was one of the signatories, and the broadside was catalogued under "Whittier" with no other access points. So African-American material does exist, waiting only to be found.

Throughout that project, I dealt with Berg's curator, my dear friend, the formidable Lola Szladits, coping as best I could with her curious beliefs; among them: people from India are also black, Al

Jolson was African American, and Mahatma was M.K. Gandhi's given name. I usually tolerated Lola's idiosyncrasies, but I had to be firm to maintain the integrity of the exhibition. We did in fact share a great deal, including dismay at the decline of The New York Public Library. "The barbarians are not at the gates," she was fond of saying; "They're on the second floor," that is, the Library's administrative corridor. Lola Szladits died March 30, 1980, and I still regret her passing.

It has been nearly ten years since I published another collection of essays: *Black Power and Black Religion*, issued also by Locust Hill Press and with an introduction by Robert A. Hill. Since that time, my research interests have expanded, particularly into the areas of African-American music—blues, jazz, and musical theater. I have been enormously fortunate over these last few years to have been able to work full-time across the whole spectrum of African-American life. I was invited by Jack Salzman and Robert O'Meally to join the Center for American Culture Studies at Columbia University to work as Managing Editor of the *Encyclopedia of African-American Culture and History*, a Macmillan publication of 1,500,000 words in five volumes.

Then Henry Louis Gates, Jr., invited me to join the staff of the W.E.B. Du Bois Institute for Afro-American Research at Harvard, first to be Managing Editor of the *Harvard Guide to African-American History*, then to be the Institute's Fellows Officer. This has been a wonderful place to work, given the Institute's annual group of visiting Fellows, some of the most creative and significant scholars in the field; a Department of Afro-American Studies, with members like Anthony Appiah, Henry Louis Gates, Jr., Evelyn Brooks Higginbotham, and Cornel West, now considered the country's best; and the library and other research resources of Harvard and Boston.

This book is appearing at a new, complex, and perilous time in African-American history. The moment, as Henry Louis Gates, Jr., has pointed out, is the best of times for the growing black middle class, and the worst of times for the large, entrapped, and abandoned black underclass. For these millions of men, women, and children, conditions are as bad as anything in the Great Depression, or perhaps even chattel slavery. Someone has even suggested that fewer black children are born into stable environments now than were before Emancipation.

*Introduction* xvii

In fact, nearly half of all African-American children are now born beneath an ungenerous poverty line. The accompanying statistics, compiled by Marion Wright Edelman's Children's Defense Fund, are so appalling as to be beyond belief: every 95 seconds, a black baby is born in poverty; every 69 seconds, a black baby is born to an unmarried mother; every six minutes, a black baby is born at a low birth rate (under five and a half pounds); every 43 minutes, a black baby dies. For those who survive, the CDF figures provide no encouragement. Every 46 seconds in the school day, a black child drops out of school. Every four hours, a black child is murdered.

And we continue to deal with effects rather than causes. California, long the symbolic embodiment of utopian America, now spends more money annually on prisons ($3.7 billion) than it does on education ($3.5 billion). This means an average expenditure of $25,000 on each incarcerated inmate, and an average of $8,000 on each undergraduate student in the state's university system. California's population is 13 per cent African American but 31 per cent of all prisoners are black, while the freshman class at Berkeley is 6 per cent black. Incidentally, the annual salary for a University of California assistant professor is the same as that of a San Quentin prison guard.

Something is deeply wrong.

The Second Reconstruction of the 1960s was an enormously hopeful period. Just as in the 1860s, it was widely assumed that access to the ballot was empowering enough to solve the black community's ills and fulfill its social needs. The Black Power Movement offered an affirmative self-consciousness to instill pride to promote personal motivation and to fuel group self-reliance. Many African Americans have undoubtedly benefited from the dismantling of segregation and the opening up of American society. But for those trapped in dead and decaying urban neighborhoods, the chief external hope today is the same as it was 100 years ago: a concerned, active, progressive federal government. The Compromise of 1877 ended the national government's protection and support of the freedpeople; the reactionary Reagan-Bush-Gingrich destruction of the New Deal withdraws national commitment to poor people, a disproportionate number of whom are black.

Actually, the situation is even worse. The current right-wing government in this country has not merely abandoned the urban poor, it has labeled them as the enemy and targeted them for destruction, while narrowing the definition of "true" Americanism. If we thought America had grown wise enough not only to perceive but to celebrate its multi-ethnic history and diverse character, we could not have been more mistaken. Patrick Buchanan's speech at a Republican National Convention calling for a military "re-taking" from "them" of city streets, block by block, effectively ended any restrictions on public discourse. Magazines played up the pseudo-scientific "bell curve" as if it were serious scholarship instead of white supremacy propaganda. And writers like Dinesh D'Souza command a national audience for racist rhetoric.

So the fact that we now live in a country building more prisons than schools is undergirded by a re-emergence of discredited beliefs and theories about race. It is hard to know what to do effectively in the 1990s when we are living in a replay of the "nadir" of the 1890s. We must keep the faith, stay the course, work wherever and whenever we can for a more just country and a more free society, and continue to seek innovative ways for change. In the midst of all this, we should not underestimate the African-American community's own internal wisdom, courage, and willingness to struggle for freedom and advancement.

Arthur Schomburg, the bibliophile, pointed out that black activism, which was, in fact, often the dangerous and pioneering work of self-liberation, was one of the major discoveries of his lifetime of collecting the lost records of the black past, and it was evidence enough to contravene prevailing views of white benevolence. There was, for example, an African-American anti-slavery organization in Boston before Garrison founded the *Liberator*. Free blacks were teaching the freedpeople at the end of the Civil War before the American Missionary Association arrived on the scene. In our own time, African Americans will continue to find ways to work against both personal and institutional racism, as they always have, and this effort must not be minimized.

The essays collected here in *Words Like Freedom* are, one hopes, another building block, however small, in the edifice of a living, positive tribute to African-American history and culture. I certainly received a great deal of help, support, and assistance in writing these pieces, and I want to pay my debts and acknowledge those to whom I am grateful and appreciative.

*Introduction* xix

First of all, my friend Nell Painter was gracious enough to write the foreword, even though it meant taking precious time from the finishing touches of her forthcoming biography of Sojourner Truth. Truth is a monumental figure, and few historians are big enough to take her on. But Nell Painter, like Truth herself, is a woman of strength, character, and steadfastness, and her definitive book will transform our understanding of the most important African-American woman of the nineteenth century.

As this book was in production, Nancy L. Grant, a friend and colleague, died of cancer at the age of 46 in St. Louis where she was Associate Professor of History at Washington University. We knew each other at the Du Bois Institute where she was a Fellow, and in the Institute's Black-Jewish Working Group, of which she was an active member. I found Nancy an ideal scholar: a cool, careful, sane, and eminently fair-minded thinker, researcher, writer, and lecturer. Behind her shy exterior was, I slowly came to discover, an extraordinary person. She was a woman of total honesty and integrity, who always told the truth and did the right thing.

She was also a person of extreme personal reticence and privacy. She let me into her life just enough for me to experience her sly wit and to let me know we shared identical views on most subjects. She was a wonderful person of great achievement and even greater promise. I looked forward to continuing our friendship over the years ahead, as well as to her continuing contributions to African-American studies. Our conversations helped to shape this book and I anticipated sharing it with her. But she left us too soon.

The following are librarians, scholars, colleagues, friends (or some combination), or just people I want to thank for one reason or another: Alice Adamczyk, Jean-Claude Baker, Tom Bechtle, Esme Bhan, Alisa Bierria, Elsa Barkley Brown, Lucile Bruce, Nancy Burkett, Randall K. Burkett, Ralph Carlson, Kenneth Carpenter, Jacob Chernofsky, Yvonne Chireau, David Cronin, Stephen Crook, James P. Danky, Thadious Davis, Mary Diaz, Sherry Sherrod DuPree, Nancy Fairley, William P. French, Milton McG. Gatch, Henry Louis Gates, Jr., Carol V.R. George, Enid Gort, Cheryl Greenberg, Lisa Gregory, Betty K. Gubert, Lisa Hacken, Lee Hancock, Marguerite Harrison, Susan Herner, Robert A. Hill, Richard Hoffman, Jean Blackwell Hutson, Jennifer James, Glenderlyn Johnson, Bruce Kellner, Joanne Kendall, Victoria King, Diana Lachatanere, Philip McBlain, Sharon McBlain, Helen MacLam, Genette McLaurin, Elizabeth Maguire, Francis O. Mattson, Philip Milito, Irene Monroe, Pamela J. Petro, Warren Platt, Albert Raboteau, Edwin Redkey, Marcia R. Sawyer, Betty Shabazz, George Shepperson, Shelah Stein, Sybil Steinberg, Patricia Sullivan, James M. Washington, Jill M. Watts, Judith Weisenfeld, Dorothy Porter Wesley, Cornel West, Preston Williams, Andre Willis, Deborah Willis, David Wills, Mary Yearwood, and Gay Young.

My greatest debt is to Belynda Blair Bady, to whom *Words Like Freedom* is lovingly dedicated.

Richard Newman
Boston, Massachusetts
Fall 1995

# Part I
# *Writing*

"Words are your business, boy. Not just *the* Word. Words are everything. The key to the Rock, the answer to the Question."

—Ralph Ellison

# Words Like Freedom
*Afro-American Books and Manuscripts in the Henry W. and Albert A. Berg Collection of English and American Literature of the New York Public Library*

The Henry W. and Albert A. Berg Collection of English and American Literature of The New York Public Library is a collection of books, manuscripts, correspondence, and ephemera. Breathtaking in its riches, the Berg Collection is resplendent with the written and printed works of great figures in Anglo-American literature— a roll call of such names as Dickens, Thackeray, Conrad, Hawthorne, and Whitman. The Collection includes T.S. Eliot's original typescript of *The Waste Land* with Ezra Pound's autograph corrections; Alice Liddell's own copy of *Alice's Adventures in Wonderland* with Lewis Carroll's presentation inscription; two copies of what collectors consider the most desirable American book, Edgar Allan Poe's *Tamerlane*; Virginia Woolf's manuscript diaries and notebooks; and a host of other treasures.

The private collections of Henry W. and Albert A. Berg, W.T.H. Howe, and Owen D. Young form the basis of the present Berg Collection. Although they did not restrict their acquisitions to classic authors, Afro-American writing had no priority in their collecting. Also, when the Schomburg Center for Research in Black Culture became part of The Research Libraries within The New York Public Library system in 1972, it was assigned the responsibility—and the prerogative—of acquiring material by and about people of African descent.

As every researcher learns, however, not everything is as it seems, and large library collections always yield surprises. The Berg Collection is no exception. It has a small but significant body of Afro-American material even if it came by an indirect route or was acquired on the basis of some other factor. This essay examines black literature, broadly defined, a cache little known because the Berg Collection's specialization has made it an unlikely place to search for black material.

## The Nineteenth Century

Perhaps the Berg Collection's most extensive and strongest Afro-Americana is its archive of material by white authors who were actively engaged in the Abolitionist movement. One spectacular item is a broadside printed on satin, the *Declaration of the Anti-Slavery Convention Assembled in Philadelphia, December 4, 1833*, issued that year in Philadelphia by J.R. Sleeper. The proclamation of the organizing meeting of the National Anti-Slavery Society, the broadside declares the sentiments of the convention, and is embellished with biblical quotations and the image of a subdued lion.

The sixty signatories from ten states include John Greenleaf Whittier and William Lloyd Garrison of Massachusetts, Samuel J. May and Simeon S. Jocelyn of Connecticut, and Beriah Green and Lewis Tappan of New York. Whittier (1807–1892) was a member of the committee selected to write the declaration, but the actual text was composed by Garrison (1805–1879), the radical founder of the *Liberator*, who believed in moral principles over political action, pacifist nonresistance, and disunion with the slave South.

### *Lydia Maria Child*

Child (1802–1880), a popular and successful Boston novelist, was an early convert to the Abolitionist cause and in 1833 published *An Appeal in Favor of That Class of Americans Called Africans*. Dedicated to Samuel J. May, it was an early anti-slavery work printed in America in book form; the Berg Collection has a copy of the first edition. The Unitarian minister William Ellery Channing (1780–1842) was so impressed with the book that he walked from Boston to Roxbury to thank Mrs. Child for writing it. She had, however, taken up a difficult cause. The directors of the Boston Athenaeum were so impressed with her novels they sent her a free admission ticket; on reading her *Appeal*, they withdrew it.

Mrs. Child had no reason to be surprised; in the *Appeal*'s preface she wrote, "I am fully aware of the unpopularity of the task I have undertaken; but although I *expect* ridicule and censure, I cannot *fear* them." The Collection also has a presentation copy from Whittier to Mrs. E.P. Whipple, of the first edition of the *Letters of Lydia Maria Child*, edited by Whittier and published in Boston by Houghton, Mifflin in 1883. The *Letters* contains an appendix by Wendell Phillips (1811–1894), actually the text of his remarks at Mrs. Child's funeral. She was "the outgrowth of New England theology, tradition, and habits," he wrote, "the finest fruit of these." So was Phillips himself, an aristocratic Bostonian who was perhaps the ablest radical anti-slave agitator.

## *John Greenleaf Whittier*

Whittier is the best-represented New England Abolitionist in the Berg Collection, which has two copies of his *Poems Written During the Progress of the Abolition Question in the United States Between the Years 1830 and 1838*, published in Boston by Isaac Knapp in 1837. One copy of the rare first issue of the first edition contains the inscription "Amanda A. Warford from A.J. Passon, 1845"; the other copy is of the second issue of the first edition and has Samuel Aaron's autograph.

This small book of twenty-one poems in ninety-six pages includes engravings of the well-known anti-slavery images of a kneeling black man and a kneeling black woman with the mottoes "Am I not a man and a brother" and "Am I not a woman and a sister." The book itself consists of such poems as "The Yankee Girl," in which Whittier typically contrasts a sturdy freedom-loving New Englander with a slave-owning Southern planter. Whittier addresses the planter:

> Full low at thy bidding thy negroes may kneel,
> With the iron of bondage on spirit and heel;
> Yet know that the yankee girl sooner would be
> In fetters with them, than in freedom with thee!

Also in the Collection are three copies of Whittier's *Narrative of James Williams, an American Slave Who Was for Several Years a Driver on a Cotton Plantation in Alabama*, a biography published in New York in 1838 by the American Anti-Slavery Society. One copy is a first issue of the first edition, another is a second issue, and the third is a copy of the periodical in which the narrative also appeared, the *Anti-Slavery Examiner*, no. 6 (1838). The Examiner dramatized its Abolitionist message by reprinting advertisements for escaped slaves from Southern newspapers. No. 6 reprints a letter to the *Constitutionalist* dated December 20, 1836, from a coroner in Aiken, South Carolina. The coroner reported on the inquest dealing with the dead body of a runaway named Sam who "came to his death by his own recklessness. He refused to be taken alive." The coroner concluded, "The boy was apparently above 35 or 40 years of age."

Whittier's two-page poem "The Branded Hand" was inspired by an actual event. A white Floridian named Jonathan Walker attempted to bring his slaves to the free North. He was apprehended by Southern authorities and his hand branded with the letters "SS" for "Slave-Stealer." Whittier praised Walker's courage and in his poem transformed the letters to stand for "Salvation for the Slave." The poem was printed in the *Anti-Slavery Bugle*, no. 9 (1845), and was reprinted in a separate pamphlet as a tract along with James Russell Lowell's (1819–1891) "Lines on Reading of the Capture of Certain Fugitive Slaves Near Washington."

Whittier's essay *Justice and Expediency, or, Slavery Considered with a View to Its Rightful and Effectual Remedy* appeared in the *Anti-Slavery Reporter*, vol. 1, no. 4 (September 1833). Whittier also published it as a pamphlet at his own expense. The Berg Collection has three copies, one of the second edition, first issue, and two of the second edition, second issue. The Collection also has a copy of the rare Whittier broadside *For Frémont and Freedom! Campaign of Fifty-Six*, published in New Haven in 1856. It consists of seven militant poems supporting John C. Frémont (1813–1890), the first presidential candidate of the fledgling Republican Party. Despite Whittier's efforts, Fremont lost to the pro-Southern James Buchanan (1791–1868).

At the death of Charles Sumner (1811–1874), Massachusetts' great anti-slavery senator, Whittier composed an ode entitled "Sumner" for the commemorative service held at the Music Hall in Boston on June 9, 1874. The Berg Collection has a copy of the third proof of the poem, its most complete form, and also a copy of the printed book with John A. Spoor's bookplate.

Also in the Collection is a copy of a poem, "A Legend of the Lake," that was not included in Whittier's collected works, but did appear in several printed versions. One, the eight-page, undated pamphlet held by the Berg Collection, was produced in the printshop at Hampton Institute, the school for blacks established in Virginia following the Civil War. It is a handsome example of the work of a black press.

In the Berg Collection's seventy-five Whittier letters, there are numerous references to his Abolitionism. Writing to Lydia Maria Child at the close of the Civil War, he said, "How strange that we should have lived to see the end of slavery! Is it not a great privilege? But what of those—the noble and generous men who have fallen in the way—do they share our joy?" Writing in 1875 to John Bright, a leader in the British anti-slavery cause, to introduce William Chaflin, a former governor of Massachusetts, Whittier can think of no higher recommendation than to describe Chaflin (who once actually purchased a slave in Missouri in order to set him free) as "a life-long abolitionist and friend of Sumner and Lincoln."

Writing to an unnamed correspondent in 1879 who was considering writing a book on John Brown (1800–1859), Whittier the Quaker could not condone Brown's violent methods, but he did say, "There can be no doubt as to the place which John Brown must forever hold among the heroic and self-sacrificing confessors of Truth and Freedom. His death was as sublime as that of Socrates."

## *John Brown*

Brown was the Calvinist zealot who consecrated his life to the destruction of slavery. He believed that to redeem America from this sin, "the sum of all villainies," it would be necessary "to purge this land with blood." After successfully engaging in a holy war in Kansas to save it as a free state, Brown felt called to instigate a black uprising in the Slavocracy itself. In 1859 with a small band of followers he seized the federal arsenal at Harper's Ferry in Virginia. He was captured and sentenced by a hysterical South to be hanged.

An extraordinary document among the Berg Collection's manuscripts is John Brown's last letter, written on December 2, 1859, just an hour before his execution. That morning, after reading his Bible and sending his will to his wife, Brown said, "I am now ready." It was 11 a.m. and a thousand armed men surrounded the Charlestown, Virginia, jail. Informed he had one more hour, Brown said, "I will write another letter." He wrote a single page to Lora Case of Hudson, Ohio, one of his oldest friends. They had been boys together in Sunday School.

Case, a "liberty-loving hater of slavery," had sent Brown a message of support after the old revolutionary's conviction and sentence. In his unsophisticated penmanship Brown spelled out in reply his last words:

> Such an outburst of warm hearted sympathy not only for myself; but also for those who "have no helper" compel's me to steal a moment from those allowed me; in which to prepare for my last great change to send you a few words. Such a feeling as you manifest makes you to "*shine* (in my estimation) in the midst of this wicked; and perverse generation as a light in the world."... Pure and undefiled religion before God ... is as I understand it: an *active* (not a *dormant*) principle.

Brown said farewell to Aaron Stevens, one of his followers, who replied, "Good-bye, Captain, I know you are going to a better land." "I know I am," Brown said. Brown was escorted to a wagon where he sat on his own coffin as he was driven to the gallows.

Three copies of the first edition of Stephen Vincent Benét's *John Brown's Body*, published by Doubleday in 1928, are in the Berg Collection. One is number 95 of a limited, signed edition of 201 copies.

### Henry David Thoreau

At two o'clock, the hour of John Brown's execution, throughout the Abolitionist communities of the North, businesses closed, flags flew at half-mast, church bells tolled, and memorial services were conducted. In Concord, Massachusetts, it was a springlike day and "Services for the Death of a Martyr" had been organized at the Town Hall by Henry David Thoreau (1817–1862). Amidst the hymns and prayers, Thoreau read Sir Walter Ralegh's "The Soul's Errand" and a long passage from Tacitus, translated for the occasion by Ralph Waldo Emerson (1803–1882) (but later re-translated by Thoreau for publication). "Let us honor you," Thoreau read, "by our admiration, rather than by short-lived praises, and, if nature aid us, by our emulation of you." Bronson Alcott read from Plato, and Emerson from John Brown's own letters and speeches.

*Words Like Freedom*

Six copies of the handbill announcing the Concord service (and fragments of three other copies) survive because Thoreau, ever the thrifty Yankee, later used the backs of them to make nature notes. They are now part of an unpublished 411-page manuscript by Thoreau entitled *The Dispersion of Seed*. The broadside contains an unsigned seven-verse dirge, which includes the lines:

> Today beside Potomac's wave,
> Beneath Virginia's sky,
> They slay the man who loved the slave,
> And dared for him to die.

Thoreau knew Brown well. They had shared a meal in Thoreau's home when Brown was in Concord garnering money and support. After dinner Emerson dropped by and the three spent an afternoon talking. When Brown was arrested and tried, Thoreau addressed his fellow townsfolk on October 30, 1859, in "A Plea for Captain John Brown." In a speech biblical in its righteous anger, Thoreau spoke eloquently of the condemned revolutionary, comparing him to Cromwell and Christ.

A page of pencilled notes for this speech survives in the Berg Collection as one leaf of a 600-page unpublished manuscript entitled *Notes on Fruits*. In Thoreau's hand are the Words "I am here to plead his cause with you. I plead not for his life but for his character—his immortal life; and so it becomes your cause wholly, and is not his in the least." Thoreau's speech first appeared in print in journalist James Redpath's *Echoes of Harper's Ferry*, published in Boston in 1860. The Berg Collection's copy of the first edition is a presentation copy to Mary M. Brooks "with the high regards of her friend William Lloyd Garrison."

Various essays by Thoreau condemning slavery and supporting John Brown are in his *A Yankee in Canada, with Anti-Slavery and Reform Papers*, published in Boston by Ticknor and Fields in 1866. The Berg Collection has five copies of the first edition, one of them a presentation copy from Thoreau's sister Sophia to the younger William Ellery Channing (1818–1901), as well as a copy of *Anti-Slavery and Reform Papers*, edited by the English reformer Henry S. Salt and published in London in 1890.

The essay of Thoreau that has made the most difference to people of color worldwide is his 1847 lecture "Civil Disobedience," which influenced both Mohandas K. Gandhi and Martin Luther King, Jr. There is in the Berg Collection a copy of its first publication, an essay entitled "Resistance to Civil Government," which appeared in *Aesthetic Papers*, edited and published in Boston in 1849 by Elizabeth Palmer Peabody (1804–1894). One of the Peabody sisters of Salem, she was the feminist author and reformer whose sisters married Nathaniel Hawthorne and Horace Mann.

## Harriet Beecher Stowe

If John Brown demonstrated to the North, even to nonresistants like Thoreau, that only armed conflict could bring down the Slave Power, Northern minds and hearts had been turning against slavery through the influence of a novel by Harriet Beecher Stowe (1811–1896) called *Uncle Tom's Cabin*. The daughter, sister, and wife of Congregational ministers, Mrs. Stowe also believed she was doing God's work. Now considered sentimental and melodramatic, even a euphemism for black subservience, her novel nonetheless made an extraordinary impact in its day. Now it is chiefly remembered as a publishing phenomenon; no other book ever created such a sensation, and it became the best-selling novel of the nineteenth century.

*Uncle Tom's Cabin* was published in two volumes by John P. Jewett of Boston on March 20, 1852, in an edition of 5,000 copies. They sold out in two days. In the next eight weeks, sales climbed to 50,000. Three power presses worked twenty-four hours a day and over one hundred binders labored to try to meet the demand. By September 30, American sales were at 150,000 and by the end of the year reached 300,000. In Britain, forty pirated editions eventually numbered a million and a half copies. The book was translated into forty languages with combined sales of over four million. In a letter of June 1853, the author described the book's extraordinary success by listing translations into such languages as Wallachian, Welsh, and Low Dutch (for readers in Batavia in the Spice Islands).

There were *Uncle Tom's Cabin* songs (twenty in 1852 alone), thirty pro-slavery novels written in response, and dramatic presentations all over the world well into the twentieth century. In the American South, copies were publicly burned, and Southern courts imprisoned people for possessing the first novel profoundly to criticize American society.

The first edition of *Uncle Tom's Cabin* became highly desirable to collectors, but in the publisher's rush to produce a second 5,000 copies, he had neglected to differentiate between the first and second issues. Of the eighty-six known copies that can be identified as of the first issue, five are in the Berg Collection, the largest number in any library. One of these has R.B. Adam's bookplate; another bears Mrs. Stowe's inscription to Charles Kingsley (1819–1875), the English clergyman, accompanied by a presentation letter dated March 20, the very day of publication.

The Berg Collection has additional copies of Mrs. Stowe's classic, including another 1852 imprint, although from the 110th thousand, with the signature of S.A. Diffenderffer, and two copies of the London edition of 1852 issued in thirteen parts with twenty-three illustrations by George Cruikshank. One set was bound in one volume by Zaehnsdorf for John Wanamaker. There is a copy of the London 1852 third edition with Charlotte Cushman's autograph. There is a copy of the 1892 edition illustrated by E.W. Kemble, one of 250 large-paper copies, with a presentation inscription to J.D. Mille in which Mrs. Stowe quotes Scripture: "The Spirit of the Lord is upon me because he has anointed me ... to preach deliverance to the captives." This copy also includes an original signed sketch of a black man by Kemble on the verso of the title page, and DeWitt Miller's autograph.

Among the ephemeral material relating to *Uncle Tom's Cabin* are an eight-line statement of 1895 in Mrs. Stowe's hand noting that the characters Uncle Tom and George Harris are fictional; a six-line holograph quotation dated 1893 from Chapter 12: "Not one throb of anguish, not one tear of the oppressed is forgotten by the Man of Sorrows"; and an eight-line holograph motto from Chapter 40: "Deem not the just by Heaven forgot." This is dated 1866.

Related items include a two-page incomplete manuscript by William Makepeace Thackeray (1811–1863) ridiculing the English Emancipation League, an organization founded by Mrs. Stowe to protest American slavery. There are three copies of E.E. Cummings' (1894–1962) *Tom*, a ballet based on *Uncle Tom's Cabin*, published by Arrow Editions in 1935. One is the dedication copy to Cummings' wife, Marion Morehouse Cummings, who suggested the idea. Another is an inscribed presentation copy from Cummings to his mother. The book has a frontispiece drawing of Uncle Tom by Ben Shahn.

Mrs. Stowe's profound opposition to human slavery is reflected in numerous pieces of her correspondence: letters which also reveal something of the New England Abolitionist network.

Charles Sumner wrote to Mrs. Stowe in 1852: "You have at this moment a marvellous power, which the enemy will try to break down, by cavil and criticism. Your pamphlet will carry a knowledge of the legalized enormities of slavery where nothing else could carry them.... I rejoice in your devotion to the cause."

Several letters with cryptic references suggest either secret anti-slavery meetings or participation in the illegal Underground Railroad which spirited escaped slaves to freedom in Canada. James Russell Lowell (1819–1891) wrote to Mrs. Stowe in 1857: "Mr. Phillips tells me that you are kind enough to say that it would be agreeable to you if our proposed conference upon a certain affair were to take place in Andover [Mrs. Stowe's residence]." Wendell Phillips wrote to her in 1860: "No doubt the fraternity will gladly avail themselves of such an opportunity.... Congratulations between us all in the rapid ripening of events."

Before they had ripened so decisively, Mrs. Stowe wrote a four-page letter in 1853 to Cassius M. Clay (1810–1903), the Kentucky anti-slavery leader: "For many years I have been an enthusiastic admirer of the spirited and manly course you have pursued in your native state. What more glorious sight to God and angels than a man *without fear*—devoted to the emancipation of his country! I say emancipation for slavery is a *bond* galling to both races.... All true lovers of America speak the word slavery in a deprecatory tone—and true lovers have a right to be heard for love's sake."

### Abolitionist Literature

Among the Berg Collection's additional Abolitionist literature is James Russell Lowell's *A Fable for Critics*, published in 1848. There are three copies, one of which belonged to Thomas Wentworth Higginson (1823–1911) and has a presentation inscription from Lowell, Higginson's notes, and Lowell's textual corrections. Higginson was one of the most radical Abolitionists, a supporter of John Brown, a commander of black troops in the Civil War, and the confidant of Emily Dickinson.

*The Constitution. A Pro-Slavery Compact; or Extracts from the Madison Papers* was edited by Wendell Phillips and published in New York by the American Anti-Slavery Society in 1856. The Berg Collection's copy of the third edition belonged to William Lloyd Garrison, has his signature, and is marked throughout by him. At

Garrison's death, a *Tribute to William Lloyd Garrison at the Funeral Services, March 28, 1879* was published in Boston. It contains remarks by Samuel May, Lucy Stone, and Theodore Dwight Weld, poems by Whittier and Lowell, and the report that a black quartet sang the hymn "Awake My Soul, Stretch Every Nerve."

*The North Star: The Poetry of Freedom by Her Friends*, issued in Philadelphia in 1840 by Merrihew and Thompson, is a small book of twenty-seven poems by John Quincy Adams, Elizur Wright, Jr., James T. Fields, Whittier, and others. The Collection's copy is dated Germantown 1841 and has the label of Philadelphia's Anti-Slavery Book Depository pasted in.

Eleven of the fifteen editions of *The Liberty Bell* "by Friends of Freedom," an annual gift book published for the fund-raising Massachusetts Anti-Slavery Fair (1839–46) and the National Anti-Slavery Bazaar (1847–58), are here. Maria Weston Chapman was editor. The books, enhanced by ornate bindings, contain poems and essays by such well-known literary personalities as Elizabeth Barrett Browning, Emerson, Longfellow, and Lowell, as well as political figures Abby Kelly, Frederick Douglass, Charles Lenox Remond, Garrison, and Phillips.

The most interesting *Liberty Bell* is the 1853 volume since it is a presentation copy from Anne Warren Weston to William C. Nell (1816–1874), the black Bostonian publisher of Douglass' paper *North Star* and author of *The Colored Patriots of the American Revolution*. Among other literary annuals and gift books are *Liberty Chimes*, published by the Providence, Rhode Island, Ladies' Anti-Slavery Society in 1845, and two copies of *The American Anti-Slavery Almanac for 1847*. This includes Lowell's first "Biglow Paper," as well as poems by George Moses Horton, the North Carolina slave.

Other anti-slavery publications include *Liberty or Slavery: The Great National Question, Three Prize Essays on American Slavery*, issued by the Congregational Board of Publications in 1857; two presentation copies by Garrison of his *Selections from the Writings and Speeches*, published in Boston in 1852; seven numbers of the *Annual Report* of the Massachusetts Anti-Slavery Society, four of which are presentation copies from Edmund Quincy to Cassius Clay; Daniel Webster's *Speech ... on the Subject of Slavery, Delivered in the U.S. Senate on Thursday, March 7, 1850* with Moses Stuart's rejoinder, *Conscience and the Constitution*.

Finally, the Collection has a copy of *A Full Statement of the Reasons Which Were in Part Offered to the Committee of the Legislature of Massachusetts, on the 4th and 8th of March, Showing Why There Should Be No Penal Laws Enacted, and No Condemnatory Resolution Passed by the Legislature, Respecting Abolitionists and Anti-Slavery Societies*, published by the Massachusetts Anti-Slavery Society in 1836. Samuel May, Samuel Sewall, Ellis Gray Loring, and Garrison are among the signers, and the pamphlet contains Whittier's poem "Stanzas for the Times."

## *Joel Chandler Harris*

Harris (1848–1908) was a white Southern journalist, humorist, and Negro-dialect author who wrote during the late nineteenth century for the *Atlanta Constitution*. He is now perceived as an expropriator and exploiter of the black folk tradition, and his chief character, Uncle Remus, is seen as even more the stereotypical "darky" than Harriet Beecher Stowe's Uncle Tom. While this is undoubtedly the case, two things can be said in Harris' defense. He did hear folk tales from slaves on the Putnam County, Georgia, plantation where he grew up, so his stories did have a basis in authentic Afro-American folk culture with its African retentions and American Indian influences. Also, Harris committed these oral tales to writing and thus helped to preserve them, even if they must now be read carefully as the products of a white Southerner with all the conscious and unconscious racism of his time and place.

The Berg Collection has extensive Harris holdings. There are sixty-seven manuscript pages: Chapters 7 through 16, all that remain of the original manuscript, of *Nights with Uncle Remus: Myths and Legends of the Old Plantation*. These chapters include "African Jack," "Brother Fox Says a Grace," "Why the Alligator's Back Is Rough," and "Brother Rabbit and His Famous Foot." The Collection has a 1900 edition of the printed book with Harris' essay on black folklore, a long presentation inscription from the author, and his signature on the half-title page.

In addition to several Harris letters, there are the five-page manuscript "Uncle Remus at the Telephone," the sixty-six-page manuscript *The Baby's Christmas*, and the one hundred forty-eight-page manuscript *Daddy Jake the Runaway; or The Runaway Negro* with an autographed portrait of Harris inserted. Several "darky" illustrations are included in *Drawings by A.B. Frost*, published by Fox, Duffield & Co. in New York in 1904, along with poems by Wallace Irwin and an introduction by Harris.

Further titles by Joel Chandler Harris include four copies of the first edition of *Uncle Remus; His Songs and His Sayings: The Folk-Lore of the Old Plantation*. This has illustrations by Frederick S. Church and James H. Moser, and was published in New York by Appleton in 1881. There is also a copy of the 1891 edition, inscribed by Harris, as well as a copy of a new and revised edition of 1899 with 112 illustrations by A.B. Frost. This copy is inscribed with a poem by the author to Horace Ransom Bigelow Allen at the request of Ivy Lee and also includes Harris' monogram label.

Other Harris books, all first editions. are *Mingo and Other Sketches in Black and White*, published by J.R. Osgood in Boston in 1884; *Free Joe and Other Georgia Sketches*, Charles Scribner's Sons, New York, 1887; *Little Mr. Thimblefinger and His Queer Country* with illustrations by Oliver Herford, issued by Houghton Mifflin in Boston in 1894 and inscribed by Harris to DeWitt Miller; and *Sister Jane. Her Friends and Acquaintances*, Houghton Mifflin, Boston, 1896.

In addition, the Collection includes *The Story of Aaron* illustrated by Oliver Herford, published in Boston by Houghton Mifflin in 1896, with Louis Martin Antisdale's bookplate; *The Tar Baby and Other Rhymes of Uncle Remus* illustrated in color by A.B. Frost and E.W. Kemble, published in New York in 1904 by Appleton, with E.W. Kemble's autograph; and *Uncle Remus Returns* illustrated by A.B. Frost and J.M. Conde, published in Boston by Houghton Mifflin in 1918.

A memorial tribute to Harris entitled *"Uncle Remus," Joel Chandler Harris as Seen and Remembered by a Few of His Friends ...* was compiled by Ivy Lee and privately printed in 1908. The Berg Collection's copy is number 5 of 300. It is signed by Ivy Lee and bears, as well, a presentation inscription from him to R.B. Allen. The book includes photographs of Southern blacks including contemporaries of George Terrell, supposedly the model for Uncle Remus.

Joel Chandler Harris with his stories of post-Reconstruction blacks still loyally serving their white masters is little read today. But Uncle Remus is a permanent fixture in popular American fiction, and in the animal tales the thinly veiled accounts of the triumph of the weak over the strong do have redeeming social value.

Brer Rabbit is, after all, as Robert A. Bone suggests, "one tough bunny."

## The Twentieth Century

### Paul Laurence Dunbar

The earliest prominent black poet in the Berg Collection is Paul Laurence Dunbar (1872–1906). The son of former slaves, he was an elevator operator in Dayton, Ohio, despite his high school education. His poems came to the attention of William Dean Howells, the leading literary critic of the day, who reviewed them favorably in *Harper's Weekly* and so established Dunbar's reputation. Howells preferred Dunbar's Negro dialect poems to the ones he wrote in standard English, a view not shared by Dunbar's middle-class black readers. In fact, his dialect poems are without equal, in part because they are sympathetic to their subjects.

The Berg Collection has first editions of two volumes of Dunbar's poems—*Lyrics of Lowly Life*, introduced by Howells and published in New York by Dodd, Mead in 1896, and *Lyrics of Love and Laughter*, published by Dodd, Mead in 1903—and a collection of short stories, *Folks from Dixie*, issued by Dodd, Mead in 1898. The Collection holds one Dunbar manuscript, the two-page dialect poem "Lover's Lane," which appeared in his *L'il Gal* in 1904.

### Booker T. Washington

At the beginning of the century the most prominent and powerful Afro-American was Booker T. Washington (1856–1915). The principal of Tuskegee Institute in Alabama, Washington advocated accommodation rather than opposition to the resurgent white South; industrial training in preference to liberal arts education; and black economic self-sufficiency instead of political action. Washington's philosophy won him white support, and his resultant power won him black support, except from activists and intellectuals. He is represented in the Berg Collection by *The Future of the American Negro*, published in Boston by Small, Maynard in 1899 and inscribed to A.P. Strout, and by three typed letters from 1901 and 1902 to T. Fisher Unwin, the London publisher. Unwin had entertained the Washingtons in England, and urged "The Wizard of Tuskegee" to write another book.

## William Stanley Braithwaite

The Berg Collection has fifty-three letters, mostly manuscript, from Sara Teasdale (1884–1933) to William Stanley Braithwaite (1878–1962), the black poet, critic, and anthologist. They date from 1912 through 1926. The letters are embarrassingly flattering and full of unsubtle requests for favors: will Braithwaite criticize her work? write a blurb for her new book? include her in his newest annual poetry anthology? "I am very proud that you think my work deserving of so high an honor," Teasdale wrote in 1912 after Braithwaite reviewed her favorably in the *Boston Evening Transcript*. A few months later she coyly inquired, "I wonder if it will bore you to see a piece of blank verse...?"

Teasdale and Braithwaite developed a friendly personal relationship, they visited each other's homes, and in 1915 Teasdale sent a Valentine's Day gift to Braithwaite's daughter Fiona. But most of her letters inform him of the existence—and availability—of her newest poems, or keep up the requests. "It would help tremendously to have a letter from America's foremost critic of poetry and I shall be eternally grateful," she wrote later the same year.

The Collection also includes letters from Braithwaite to various correspondents. On July 15, 1918, he wrote to Gladys Cromwell, asking permission to include four of her poems in his *Anthology of Magazine Verse for 1918*. Braithwaite's July 28, 1923, letter to Padraic Colum (1881–1972) at the MacDowell Colony concerns Seumas O'Sullivan's books, Joseph Campbell's poems, and other literary matters. Colum wrote the introduction to *The Poems of Seumas O'Sullivan*, published in 1923 by the B.J. Brimmer Company in Boston, the publishing firm of which Braithwaite was president.

Also in the Berg Collection is a typed letter of September 7, 1917, from Alain Locke (1885–1954) to Padraic Colum. Professor of philosophy at Howard University and the first Afro-American Rhodes Scholar, Locke wrote from Boston where he was studying at Harvard for the year. Responding to Colum's inquiry about his writing a book on the Negro in literature, Locke replied: "I have had more leisure to keep in touch with literary things.... Mr. Braithwaite and I have often spoken of you."

## The Harlem Renaissance

The Harlem Renaissance was an explosion of black creativity in literature, art, music, and dance that burst into national prominence in the 1920s. Several of its writers are represented in the Berg Collection, thanks to the generosity of Carl Van Vechten (1880–1964).

James Weldon Johnson (1871–1938) was multi-talented: a poet, novelist, musician, editor, professor, U.S. consul in Venezuela, and, preeminently, a civil rights activist in the National Association for the Advancement of Colored People (NAACP). The Collection has a copy of the first edition of his *The Book of American Negro Poetry* "With an Essay on the Negro's Creative Genius," published by Harcourt, Brace in New York in 1922. In 1927 Johnson wrote *God's Trombones*, a collection of sermons in verse, published in New York by Viking Press. The extraordinary illustrations are by Aaron Douglas (1899–1979), perhaps the most brilliant artist of the Renaissance. At his request, Johnson was buried holding a copy of *God's Trombones*. The Berg Collection has a copy of the first edition.

Countee Cullen (1903–1946) is represented in the Collection by first editions of two of his books of poems: *Color*, published in New York by Harper in 1925, and *Copper Sun*, issued by Harper in 1927. A conservative and skillful lyric poet, Cullen was a disciple of Keats who avoided racial themes as much as possible and did not choose to be thought of as a black writer. Claude McKay (1889–1948), the Jamaican-born poet and novelist, was also a classicist in style, but he was more racially conscious than Cullen and went out of his way to emphasize in his writing the "lower" forms of black life. The Berg Collection has James Weldon Johnson's autographed copy of the first edition of McKay's poems *Harlem Shadows*, introduced by Max Eastman and published in New York by Harcourt, Brace in 1922.

## Langston Hughes

The largest archive in the Berg Collection of material by and about a black writer consists of the seventy-four-page carbon typescript of Langston Hughes's (1902–1967) play *Mulatto*, with accompanying correspondence and documents concerning Hughes's dispute over production of the play and his difficulties in receiving royalties. Acquired from the American Play Company, this archive comprises 483 items in 624 pages dating from June 1935 through May 1941, including thirty-three letters and telegrams from Hughes. Known as "the poet laureate of Harlem," Hughes was the first black author to make his living, however precarious, from writing. He worked in a variety of literary forms and was a leading figure of the Renaissance. Hughes's creativity was drawn from the vital folk tradition of the black masses—language, images, blues, jazz—and he raised the racial folk form to literary art.

Written in 1930 and produced at the Vanderbilt Theatre in New York in 1935, Hughes's *Mulatto* was the first play on miscegenation addressed to a white audience by a black writer. It ran for a year and was the longest-running Broadway play by an Afro-American until Lorraine Hansberry's *A Raisin in the Sun* (1959). Martin Jones, the white producer, altered the text, humiliated Rose McClendon and the other black cast members, and used every possible device and subterfuge to deny Hughes his royalties.

Jones admitted hating Hughes, and threatened to close the play unless he waived his royalties "until the show shows a profit." Since everyone except Hughes was being paid, including Jones, Hughes naively wondered why Jones was keeping the play running. The *Mulatto* files consist of letters, telegrams, notes, statements, complaints, legal orders, playbills, accounts, telephone messages, and cancelled checks. The bulk is correspondence to and from the American Play Company, the Dramatists Guild, the American Arbitration Association, and numerous other participants in the dispute, including Hughes's attorney, Arthur Spingarn of the NAACP.

Additional Hughes material in the Berg Collection consists of letters and cards to Muriel Rukeyser, Frances Steloff, and Louis Untermeyer; a 1967 program of the memorial service for Hughes at St. Mark's Methodist Church; and a file of letters to May Sarton, dated 1943, concerning Hughes's reading his poetry in a series at The New York Public Library, with accompanying typescripts of Hughes's "Refugee in America" and "The Ballad of Margie Polite." The deceptively simple "Refugee in America," one of his Library readings, was published in the November 1943 issue of the *Bulletin of The New York Public Library* with an introduction by Sarton:

> There are words like *Freedom*
> Sweet and wonderful to say.

> On my heartstrings freedom sings
> All day everyday
> There are words like *Liberty*
> That almost make me cry.
> If you had known what I knew
> You'd know why.

## Carl Van Vechten

If any white person is identified with the Harlem Renaissance it is Carl Van Vechten, critic, novelist, dance reviewer, photographer, and arbiter of societal trends and tastes. He befriended a number of talented blacks, wrote articles on behalf of black culture, and used his influence to bring black writers to the attention of publishers. He also guided fashionable white tourists to the most daring Harlem nightspots; Andy Razaf in his lyrics to "Go Harlem" invited people to "go inspectin' with Van Vechten."

The Collection has a copy of the printed program for the *Exercises Marking the Opening of the James Weldon Johnson Memorial Collection of Negro Arts and Letters Founded by Carl Van Vechten* at Yale in 1950, and a copy of the printed resolution from the president and fellows of Yale thanking him for his gift.

Carl Van Vechten was also a friend of The New York Public Library, and the Berg Collection's first curator, John D. Gordan, honored him in 1950 with an exhibition—the first for a living donor.

Van Vechten presented to the Collection a large number of his photographic portraits, some two dozen of which are of black subjects. Many of these are significant literary figures, including William Stanley Braithwaite, Countee Cullen, Chester Himes, Zora Neale Hurston, LeRoi Jones (Amiri Baraka), Claude McKay, Ann Petry, Margaret Walker, John A. Williams, and Richard Wright.

Other portraits are of Owen Dodson, W.E.B. Du Bois, C.L.R. James, Charles S. Johnson, James Weldon Johnson, Willard Motley, Roi Ottley, George S. Schuyler, William Gardner Smith, and Walter White. There are also performance photographs of Gertrude Stein's opera *Four Saints in Three Acts*.

In a program note for *Four Saints in Three Acts*, Van Vechten wrote, "It was genius on Virgil Thomson's part to choose a Negro cast to sing this music and these lovely words." Directed by John

Houseman, the original cast included Beatrice Robinson Wayne as St. Theresa I, Edward Matthews as St. Ignatius, John Diggs as St. Chavez, and Bruce Howard as St. Theresa II. Eva Jessye, later the choral director for *Porgy and Bess*, was Choir Mistress.

The Berg Collection has several of Van Vechten's copies of programs and fliers for various productions of the opera, first performed in Hartford, Connecticut, in 1934, as well as a copy of *Four Saints in Three Acts; an Opera by Gertrude Stein and Virgil Thomson, Scenario by Maurice Grossner, Complete Vocal Score*, published in 1948 by Music Press and Arrow Music Press in New York.

## Eugene O'Neill

It has been said that American theatre "came of age" with the production by the Provincetown Playhouse in 1920 of Eugene O'Neill's (1888–1953) *The Emperor Jones*. This expressionistic American play concerns a black ex-Pullman car porter who proclaims himself emperor of a West Indian island. Blacks had heretofore been portrayed on the stage largely as comic figures, but *The Emperor Jones* offered a spectacular Negro part. It was brilliantly filled by Charles Gilpin (1878–1930), who had a long history in black theatre but was running an elevator at Macy's at the time he was cast in the role. The Berg Collection has a signed and numbered copy of the published play, issued by Boni and Liveright in 1928 with illustrations by Alexander King; a presentation copy, it is inscribed to Dr. Albert A. Berg from Mr. and Mrs. J.L. Kaluschines.

The Collection also has a five-page holograph essay on *The Emperor Jones* by George Cram Cook, founder and director of the Provincetown Players, in which he pays extraordinary tribute to Gilpin: "Here is a man who for years has had within himself the power to mount to the top of the ladder, and there has been no ladder, none upon which circumstances permitted a man of his race to set foot. Eugene O'Neill made the ladder." The critics agreed on the quality of Gilpin's performance, with the *New Republic* ranking him one of the greatest actors of the American stage. Following *The Emperor Jones*, however, Gilpin returned to Macy's elevators.

In 1924 the Provincetown Players produced O'Neill's *All God's Chillun Got Wings*. The Berg Collection has a one-page manuscript fragment by O'Neill of the play's outline, headed "Naturalism with Expressionistic background," along with Carl Van Vechten's copy of the play, published by Boni and Liveright in 1924, inscribed to him by O'Neill. The production starred Paul Robeson (1898–1976) as a black intellectual married to an inferior white woman, played by Nancy Blair. There was much public criticism of the play's portrayal of an interracial marriage, especially of the scene in which Blair kissed Robeson's hand. Mixed marriages are "a crime against the future of our people," the *New York Times* reviewer said.

Although they produced jobs for black actors, O'Neill's plays were not well received by black people. *The Emperor Jones* was criticized because it suggested that blacks when free are as exploitative as whites. *All God's Chillun* was criticized because blacks felt they had more important issues with which to concern themselves than interracial marriages. Loften Mitchell, the black theatre historian, commented that O'Neill's "efforts in dealing with Negroes appear more sincere than skillful."

## Marc Connelly

On February 26, 1930, Marc Connelly's (1890–1980) play *The Green Pastures* opened at the Mansfield Theatre in New York. It was a smash hit and won that year's Pulitzer Prize. The unlikely plot consisted of a series of biblical stories as supposedly interpreted by a group of simple Southern Negroes. The original manuscript had disappeared until one day, years later, Connelly ran across it by chance in his backgammon table. The Berg Collection bought the 113-page, heavily edited *Green Pastures* typescript, the Exodus scene of which was typed by Dorothy Parker. The Collection also has a copy of the first edition of the published play, issued in New York by Farrar and Rinehart in 1930, and two copies of a limited edition of 550, published also by Farrar and Rinehart in 1930, printed on large paper and signed by Connelly and the illustrator, Robert Edmond Jones. This version was the first to contain both the text of the play and the spirituals which constituted the music.

*The Green Pastures* provided work for a number of talented but little-known and underemployed black actors including Jesse A. Shipp as Abraham, Wesley Hill as Gabriel, Tutt Whitney as Noah, and, especially, Richard B. Harrison (1864–1935), who played "De Lawd." Born in Canada of fugitive slave parents, Harrison read

Shakespeare to Negro audiences for forty years. He was past sixty, however, before he was given a chance on a Broadway stage, and had to be coached in Negro dialect by a white actor who had played "darky" roles.

The play was in fact a patronizing caricature of black life. Langston Hughes called it "a naive dialect play about a quaint funny heaven full of niggers." Despite the stereotypes, the cast managed to infuse *Green Pastures* with dignity, and Hal Johnson's choir contributed authentic music from the black folk tradition. After a Broadway run of 640 performances, the play went on the road. A final irony was its appearance at the National Theatre in Washington, D.C., a house that did not allow blacks in the audience.

## Muriel Rukeyser

Among the Muriel Rukeyser (1913–1980) papers is the carbon typescript of an unpublished, undated four-page article entitled "Women and Scottsboro," to which Rukeyser made several manuscript corrections including the addition of a subtitle, "An eye-witness." This is reportage based on the second Scottsboro trial, held in 1933, during which the nineteen-year-old Rukeyser caught typhoid fever in an Alabama police station. She had been detained by local police for "contempt of court" after she was seen talking with black reporters.

The Scottsboro case began in 1931 when nine black youths riding an Alabama freight train in search of work were arrested at random and charged with raping two white prostitutes. They were summarily tried and condemned to death.

The "Scottsboro Boys," as they came to be known, were defended by the International Labor Defense Fund, a Communist organization, and there was worldwide protest against their obvious frame-up. One of the prostitutes later admitted she lied, and joined the defense. After years of trials, appeals, public agitation, political machinations, and bitter struggles between Communists and non-Communists over control of the defense, the convictions were finally overturned. The last Scottsboro Boy was freed in 1950.

"Women and Scottsboro" contrasts Ada Wright and Janie Patterson, mothers of two of the Scottsboro Boys, "who have seen the slow sacrifice of their sons to a deepening class struggle," with the two prostitutes who are, Rukeyser says in a crossed-out line, "[c]ompletely cheap, completely tough, ready to be used for anything." Rukeyser extended the contrast: "Behind one pair stand ... all conscious women workers—behind the others are grouped the ignorance and vulgarity of the bourgeoisie and the prejudice of the group that used to be referred to delicately as 'the flower of Southern womanhood.'"

Muriel Rukeyser described the women present in the Decatur, Georgia, courtroom: Carol Weiss King, one of the I.L.D. lawyers; Mary Heaton Varse of the *New Republic*; and the black working women of the town. Many of the issues of the Scottsboro case, Rukeyser said, were tied to the problems of women: unemployment, prostitution, "the old cry of 'rape!' whenever a Negro is to be persecuted." Therefore, she concluded, women must help in the fight to free the Scottsboro Boys as well as help to solve the problems that led to their trial.

The Berg Collection has the manuscript and typescript drafts of *Theory of Flight*, Muriel Rukeyser's first book, a volume in the Yale Series of Younger Poets published in New Haven by Yale University Press in 1935. Her involvement with the Scottsboro case is reflected in "The Trial," a section of the poem which includes the lines:

> Nine dark boys spread their breasts against Alabama,
> schooled in the cells, fathered by want.
> Mother: one writes: they treat us bad. If they send us
> back to Kilby jail, I think I shall kill myself.

## Richard Wright

Richard Wright (1908–1960) was probably the finest and most significant Afro-American writer to emerge after the Harlem Renaissance. A product of Southern racism and poverty, Wright was an expatriate, a disillusioned Communist, and an existentialist thinker as well as the author of brutally realistic novels. The Berg Collection has a copy of the first edition of his *Native Son*, introduced by Dorothy Canfield Fisher and published in New York by Harper and Brothers in 1940, and a copy of the first edition of his autobiographical *Black Boy: A Record of Childhood and Youth*, issued by Harper's in 1945.

Also in the Collection is a copy of the French periodical *L'Arbalète*, no. 9 (Autumn 1944), which includes Wright's "Le départ de 'Big Boy,'" translated by Marcel Duhamel and introduced by Paul Robeson. A bit of Wright ephemera is Carl Van Vechten's copy of the one-page broadside "A Steinian Catechism," a 1946 advertising flier in question-and-answer form in which Wright endorsed Gertrude Stein's *Brewsie and Willie.* Wright and Stein were friends, and her writing, he said, reminded him of his grandmother's dialect speech with its biblical influences.

## The Present

The Berg Collection holds the eighteen-page signed and corrected typescript of James Baldwin's (1924–1987) first published short story, "Previous Condition," which concerns a black actor who is evicted by a white landlady and his subsequent dream of violence. The story appeared in *Commentary* in October 1948 and was included in Baldwin's *Going to Meet the Man,* a collection of stories issued in 1965. The book was not particularly well received, most critics suggesting that Baldwin's fiction was not so strong as his essays. The Collection also owns a Baldwin letter from Istanbul to Alfred Kazin dated 1961 in which Baldwin explains why he left New York.

In 1967 Cecil Woolf and John Bagguley published *Authors Take Sides on Vietnam;* the Berg Collection has the contributors' original statements. Baldwin wrote: "I am against U.S. intervention ... because we are deluded in supposing we have the right or the power to dictate the principles under which another people should live." Nobel laureate Wole Soyinka (born 1934) contributed the statement: "It has become quite obvious that the solution lies solely in the hands of the American people, not in world opinion. And Mohammed Ali (formerly Cassius Clay) has taken the lead."

The Herbert Mitgang Papers include a folder of more than fifty pieces of correspondence between the *New York Times* staff member and Alan Paton (1903–1988), the white South African author of *Cry, the Beloved Country.* In 1968 Mitgang invited Paton to write the first of several articles for the *Times.* Paton's manuscript "The Yoke of Racial Inequality" includes a paragraph inadvertently omitted from the published essay. In it Paton called Western exploration, colonization, exploitation, and slavery "catastrophic for the rest of the world." He continued: "But we Westerners are only now beginning to understand the cost of it, and the depth of the traumatic wound that we inflicted on the non-Western world."

An extensive collection of correspondence and papers of Kay Boyle (born 1903) recently acquired by the Berg Collection includes her draft of a statement on Angela Davis, and six letters from Sonia Sanchez. There is also an exchange with Julian Bond inviting him to write the introduction to the letters of George Jackson, one of the Soledad Three prisoners.

If one widens the circle of search in the Berg Collection, there are many other items touching on Afro-Americans. Among the Countess of Blessington's papers are twenty pages of documents relating to Captain George Maclean, acting commandant of Cape Coast Castle in the Gold Coast, now Ghana. He was accused in 1834 by Lieut. I.I.H. Burgoyne of owning a slave, selling him to the Dutch governor for export, and causing the death by flogging of another slave imprisoned in Accra for theft.

The Collection has numerous letters from William Wilberforce (1759–1833), the father of the British anti-slavery movement, as well as Senator Charles Sumner of Massachusetts. In a lighter vein is a postcard picturing Josephine Baker (1906–1975), sent by Clive Bell to Sir Edward Marsh on December 12, 1930.

Several conclusions can be drawn from the fact that the Berg Collection holds a larger and more important collection of Afro-Americana than might be thought. As has been mentioned, large library collections always produce surprises. Also, an item acquired for one reason—for example, a poem because it is by Whittier—may well fulfill another criterion as well, that is, be an important piece of anti-slavery literature.

Finally, as more people begin to question the Eurocentric bias of our literary heritage, it is becoming possible to perceive a tradition that is only now beginning to emerge. These minority writings were blurred and overlooked by the dominant forces within society. As Henry Louis Gates pointed out recently in *The New York Times:* "The teaching of literature is the teaching of values, is the teaching of an aesthetic and political order in which none of the members of the black community, the minority community of color or the women's community, were ever able to discover the reflection or representation of their images or hear the resonances of their cultural voices."

It was once asserted that Afro-Americans had no cultural history. Then it was conceded that they did have, but it was unrecorded and irretrievable. We now know that careful search in fact yields a rich and diverse black cultural heritage, including a literary one. The Henry W. and Albert A. Berg Collection of English and American Literature holds some of the pieces of that tradition.

# Henry Louis Gates, Jr.:
## *The Scholar of African-American Culture Has Written a "Storytelling" Memoir of Growing Up in the South*

The name of Henry Louis Gates, Jr.—universally known as "Skip"—seems to turn up everywhere. In university circles, he is the whirlwind 43-year-old chairperson who has transformed Harvard's Afro-American Studies Department into the country's most exciting black academic program. He is the author of *The Signifying Monkey* (Oxford, 1988), a scholarly *tour de force* which links black vernacular expression to literary criticism, and which won an American Book Award. Ishmael Reed calls the book "the Rosetta Stone of the American multicultural Renaissance."

As an editor, Gates's name is attached to a variety of publications, including a dozen new volumes in *African American Women's Writings*, a reprint series forthcoming from Macmillan of previously neglected early 20th-century authors and titles. His literary criticism is well represented in *Figures in Black* (1987) and *Loose Canons* (1992), both from Oxford. Perhaps best known are Gates's frequent forays as cultural critic. He appears regularly in the *New Yorker* and on the *New York Times* op-ed page with sharp, insightful essays on such topics as black-Jewish relations, the First Amendment, filmmakers Allen and Albert Hughes and even the televised *Superman* series.

Gates's 1994 book, issued by Knopf, is something unexpectedly different. *Colored People* is a revealing memoir of his coming-of-age in Piedmont, a small West Virginia town, in the 1950s and '60s. "I've always wanted to be a storyteller," Gates commented to *Publishers Weekly* in his office overlooking Cambridge's Harvard Square. " Storytelling was a natural part of the village culture where I grew up." Inspired by James Baldwin and Ralph Ellison,

Gates says he wanted to write something accessible, "a book people can read from," like a novel or poem.

*Colored People* is not one good story, but a whole repository of them, recounted as if the reader were sitting around the table with Skip after dinner while he entertained with one wonderful anecdote after another of small-town black life, especially life "when white people weren't around." The stories are nostalgic and bittersweet, and they are all delivered in an African American verbal style where mastery of words is a cultural commonplace. They are alive with gestures, dialect and italicized words.

There are tales of high school sex, adolescent religious zeal and eccentric relatives. "But I want to do more than amuse," Gates says. "I'm trying to recollect a lost era, what I call a sepia time, a whole world that simply no longer exists." The book is in fact addressed to Gates's two teenaged daughters. "I wanted them to know what it was like, not just my life, but our life as a people."

Piedmont in Gates's day was a town of 2500 people, 380 of whom were black. Although he shared some cultural affinities with the urban male blacks who matured quickly and angrily on inner-city "mean streets," Gates never found his true self there. "I wasn't a city kid and we never thought of ourselves as poor," he explains. "There's a spectrum of black experience just as there is of black views and opinions."

The town's African Americans created their own space, partly as a counterweight to segregation, and they created their own language of indirect communication, partly for the same reason. In *Colored People*, Gates opens the door and admits white readers into the black world—not only through his narrative account but also via that special language which provides its own access. In "talking the talk," as the black phrase has it, Gates has exchanged the formal language of the literary critic for the double-edged "signifying" speech of black America.

Was this a hard book to write? "Yes and no. Actually, the words themselves just came." Gates was at Bellagio, the Rockefeller conference center in Italy, using his August vacation to start work. To evoke old times, he took along CDs of the music of his childhood and youth. The first morning there, he recalls, he looked out the window, and the spectacular view of lake and mountains took him back to West Virginia. "I started writing and wrote 20 pages a day. At the end of the month I had a manuscript, but I'd lost 10 pounds."

Yet the facility with which he completed the initial draft was misleading. "Only the writing was easy. The editing was very difficult," Gates observes. There was trauma, he says, in revisiting some corners of his youth, primarily the anxious fear that he had somehow been responsible for his mother's illness and death. Working through submerged memories made rewriting a task far more tangled than the usual polishing of prose, almost a kind of therapy. Also, the text had to be freed as much as possible from adult perspectives and intellectual emendations. "I wanted these events to live again and these stories to tell their own truth," Gates says.

According to Elizabeth Maguire, Gates's longtime friend and Oxford University Press editor, the task of Gates's writing is usually to build up layers of scholarship, but *Colored People*, in contrast, strips layers away in order to regain a child's perspective on a family and a town. "The great thing about this book is Skip's bravery," Maguire says. "He's opened himself. He's moved from academic discourse to become a writer who honestly deals with gritty physical sensibilities, all the sounds and smells of real life."

Gates informs readers that his father was a loader in the town's paper mill during the day and worked as a janitor at night, and that his mother was a domestic in white people's houses. "He's the leading academic in his field, but he's able to put aside the intellectual to speak in another voice," according to Maguire. "He's exposed himself by showing the warmth and loving intimacy of a black family that most of mainstream America knows nothing about."

*PW* asks Gates how he managed the difficult feat that Thomas Wolfe claimed one could not do: to "go home again." In response, he says: "I worked very hard to eliminate the distances from that time and that place, and in the telling to get rid of the baggage that's been added to my life since then." Coming to terms with his own past was an emotional struggle, he confesses. He also had to decide how many private family details to disclose. His publisher's lawyers did point out that the book was addressed to his children and suggested he cut some of the spicier accounts of Piedmont's sex life.

Aside from personal family information, does *Colored People* reveal too much intimate information about the lives of African Americans as a people? Gates looks thoughtful. "You've got to understand that this book is not about Every-Negro, but about a frozen time in Piedmont, West Virginia. There are cultural and ethnic particularities here. I'm not telling secrets, I'm sharing experiences of universal rituals with a larger audience."

One chapter excerpted in the *New Yorker*—about straightening hair in his mother's kitchen—elicited a letter from A'lelia Bundles, the great-great granddaughter of Madam C.J. Walker. "She was the first black woman millionaire, who got rich with her 'hot comb' technique for what's now euphemistically called 'hair relaxing,'" Gates observes. Her descendant congratulated Gates on capturing the humor attending that ambivalent rite.

A more controversial dimension of *Colored People* is Gates's take on desegregation. Having begun public school just as integration was inaugurated, he experienced the breakdown of the old, racially segregated society. He argues, though, that important black community institutions were weakened in the process and that local events like the annual Colored Picnic, a ritual gathering which helped shape and define a special and unique culture, were abandoned in the drive for integration. "That's not why we marched!" he says with conviction. "Not to destroy a culture." He mentions with some satisfaction that local folks a few years ago reestablished the famous picnic that was the center piece of black Piedmont's collective social life.

*Colored People* takes Gates through high school when he leaves Piedmont for New Haven, Conn., and Yale. The memoir's parameters now seem obvious, but Ashbel Green, Gates's editor at Knopf, says they were not so distinct when the manuscript first arrived. Gates had written some account of life after Piedmont, but it was finally decided not to include those chapters. Green says he doesn't know yet whether they will turn up in a sequel. "We have a multi-book contract with Skip, and we're working on several projects, but I'm really not sure yet what's coming next."

How did Gates get from there to here, from Piedmont to Harvard? He graduated *summa cum laude* from Yale in 1973, and went on to Clare College at Cambridge University in England, where his tutor was Wole Soyinka, subsequently the first African to become a Nobel laureate in literature. Gates received an M.A. in

1974 and a Ph.D. in 1979, and he held teaching positions at Yale, Cornell and Duke before moving to Harvard three years ago.

He came to public attention as the recipient of a MacArthur Foundation "genius" award which recognizes and supports individuals of unusual ability and promise. Gates also received considerable publicity when he turned up a copy of *Our Nig*, a virtually unknown 19th-century novel, and established the identity of the author as Harriet Wilson, a woman of color. Reissued by Random House in 1983, *Our Nig* helped launch a movement for the reclamation of the African American literary heritage.

While he was a graduate student, Gates worked as a European correspondent for *Time* magazine and involved himself in an incident that's reported in another new Knopf book this season, David Leeming's biography, *James Baldwin*. Planning to do an article on American expatriates, Gates brought Josephine Baker to Baldwin's house in France for dinner in August 1973. In an historic moment, Baker and Baldwin looked back over their lives and careers as exiles from the promised land. *Time* rejected the article, calling the principals "passé," but the dinner party became the catalyst for Baldwin's last work, a play called *The Welcome Table*, in which Gates appears as one of the characters.

At Harvard, Gates is eloquent in articulating his vision for African American studies. As cornerstones of the doctoral program he intends to build at the university, he has hired academic superstars Cornel West and Evelyn Brooks Higginbotham. When Higginbotham arrives in Cambridge next fall, she will be the only black woman with tenure on the Harvard College faculty, a sign both of Gates's commitment to women of color in the academy and of his power to effect change at Harvard. Through the W.E.B. Du Bois Institute for Afro-American Research, of which he is director, Gates plans to edit the *Encyclopedia Africana*, a massive research and reference project first envisioned by Du Bois himself in 1910, and now reconceived in electronic format.

Beyond the mechanics of these various enterprises, Gates, the student of culture, sees black studies transforming the academy intellectually and making a real impact on national life. "This is all about redefining the very meaning of America," he says with animation. "Anglo-American regional culture is simply not universal. We're helping to create a new cultural consciousness, one that's pluralistic and diverse." Gates sees the current breakthrough of

African American studies into school curriculums as pointing the way towards a new racial, gender, ethnic and sexual inclusiveness which will make for a more free, honest and humane society.

Perhaps Henry Louis Gates, Jr. appears to be everywhere at once because he is: giving a lecture, writing an article, hosting a conference, sitting on a committee, receiving an honorary degree—in as many parts of the country and all in the course of a week. Gates's energy, like his optimism and enthusiasm, is apparently without limit. He has reinvented himself since Piedmont, but *Colored People* is his trip back to his roots, and he permits his readers to share the journey.

# Two Letters from Nella Larsen

Nella Larsen was a major novelist of the Harlem Renaissance, but little is known about her life.[1] No collection of Larsen papers or manuscripts survives, and there are relatively few Larsen letters in American libraries.[2] The Schomburg Center for Research in Black Culture, however, has two holograph letters from Larsen to Edward Wasserman. Dated just after the appearance of her first novel, *Quicksand*, in 1928, they deal largely with the most spectacular African American social event of the decade, the wedding of Countee Cullen and W.E.B. Du Bois's daughter Yolande.

Nella Larsen was born in 1891 in Chicago to a black West Indian father and a Danish mother. Following her husband's death, her mother married a white man, and Larsen began a life of uncomfortable marginality between the races, one of many autobiographical motifs that appear in her fiction. As if trying out alternate identities, Larsen briefly attended Fisk, the black university in Nashville, and then the University of Copenhagen. She trained and worked as a nurse, and in 1919 married Elmer S. Imes, a black physicist with a Ph.D. from the University of Michigan.[3]

Larsen began work as a librarian at the 135th Street Branch of The New York Public Library in September 1921, one of the first African Americans hired by the Library in a deliberate effort to integrate the branch staff in a neighborhood rapidly becoming black. As a center of the new cultural renaissance, the library was one of the first places Langston Hughes visited when he arrived in Harlem the same month Larsen began working there.[4] She attended the Library School of The New York Public Library from 1922 to 1923, worked also at the Seward Park Branch, and in October 1924 returned to 135th Street in charge of the children's room. She resigned on January 1, 1926, when she published her first short story.[5]

Carl Van Vechten introduced Larsen and her work to Alfred A. Knopf, who published *Quicksand* to substantial critical praise. Larsen's sophisticated handling of the themes of class and caste, identity, sexuality, and the interior life of the black bourgeoisie made her central character Helga Crane a modern urban woman in search of meaning, and revealed Larsen herself as a writer of the first rank. Her second novel, *Passing*, at first called *Nig*, was published the next year, and in 1930 Larsen became the first black woman to receive a Guggenheim award for creative writing.

An unsubstantiated charge of plagiarism, and a divorce in which there was public talk of her husband's liaison with a young white woman, apparently destroyed Larsen's confidence; in any case, several new novels were begun but never finished. She moved to the Village and then literally disappeared into the Lower East Side. One of the most gifted writers of the Harlem Renaissance, Larsen worked unrecognized in several hospitals in Manhattan for thirty years. She died in 1963, forgotten and unknown, her books long out of print.

The Schomburg Center's letters were written, however, when Larsen was living well as a society matron in Harlem and just about to be hailed as a major novelist.[6] The first letter, of two pages, was written from "Home," 236 West 135th Street, on "Thursday," April 5, 1928, and postmarked the same day. The envelope is present. The text reads:

> Dear Eddie:
> Are you going to the Cullen–Du Bois wedding? I'm asking a few of the thousand and one invited guests to come by here for a cocktail before proceeding to the solemnities. Please come if you can. Come even if you are not expected at the wedding. It is at six o'clock on Monday the ninth. Any time between four and five-thirty you can wet your whistle at 236 West 135th Street.
> We haven't seen you for years. Not since your grand birthday party. Do you still look the same?
> Until Monday then.
>
> Nella Larsen Imes

Larsen's correspondent, Edward Wasserman, was born in 1896, the son of Edward Wasserman, Sr., and Emma Seligman of the wealthy Seligman banking family.[7] His birthday was February

11, probably the date of the party Larsen mentions where she last saw him. Wasserman inherited a fortune and lived a bohemian life in New York, counting Zora Neale Hurston, Carl Van Vechten, Ethel Waters, and Blanche Knopf among his friends.[8] His East 30th Street residence, with its round bed large enough for several people, was popular in homosexual circles for all-male racially mixed parties. In the 1930s, Wasserman moved to Paris, where he became an art dealer, Roman Catholic convert, drug addict, world traveler, and sometime escort to Alice B. Toklas after Gertrude Stein's death.[9] Wasserman and Larsen were good friends; he wrote a letter of support when she was nominated for a Harlem Award for Distinguished Achievement Among Negroes, and they met regularly at those social events frequented by what Zora Neale Hurston called the "niggerati."

The party to which Larsen invited Wasserman was to precede one of black America's most prestigious and theatrical productions, the wedding of Countee Cullen and [Nina] Yolande Du Bois. Cullen was the brilliant young poet, as full of promise as of achievement, probably Harlem's best-known literary figure. Du Bois was the daughter of the race's most distinguished leader, and Dr. Du Bois personally orchestrated the wedding ceremony, perceiving it as "a pageant symbolic of the beauty and power of the new breed of American Negro."[10]

Larsen was not exaggerating when she spoke of "the thousand and one invited guests." In fact, 1,300 select people received the coveted invitations. Another thousand, less fortunate folk, gathered on the street outside Salem Methodist Episcopal Church on Seventh Avenue at 128th Street, whose minister and Countee's adoptive father, Frederick Asbury Cullen, performed the ceremony. There were sixteen bridesmaids, all graduates of Eastern colleges, friends from Baltimore where Yolande was teaching at Douglass High School. The groom's ushers included Langston Hughes, Arna Bontemps, and Robert C. Weaver. Canaries sang in gilded cages and Dr. Du Bois was only at the last moment restrained from having a thousand doves released to the heavens.[11]

Yolande Du Bois may have been the daughter of one genius and now the wife of another, but she herself was, in David Levering Lewis's phrase, "outstandingly ordinary—a kind, plain woman of modest intellectual endowment" (201). This was not, though, the reason why the Cullen–Du Bois marriage was a disaster, however brilliant the wedding had been. There were immediate problems of compatibility, particularly sexual compatibility, for which even Dr. Du Bois blamed his beloved daughter. Soon Countee Cullen departed for Paris, not in the company of his wife, but with the best man, the handsome Harold Jackman, schoolteacher, bon vivant, and an intimate member of Wasserman's circle.[12] Countee and Yolande were formally divorced in 1930.

Whether or not he was invited to the famous wedding, Edward Wasserman did not come to Nella Larsen's prenuptial party. On April 16, she wrote him a two-page letter from "Home Sunday":

> Dear Eddie:—
> We were terribly disappointed that you didn't get here last week. And I was furious with myself for mentioning the damned wedding to you because it turned out that we didn't go. People kept coming in and then deciding not to go on to the wedding, so we were here until eight o'clock. Then we went out to dinner. It was very amusing too because the sandwiches kept getting fewer and fewer, and I kept rescuing them from hungry guests and saying firmly 'You'll have to leave some for Eddie Wasserman and someone else.' Then when you didn't appear they accused me of trying to save the food.
> I do want to see your review. Will you have a copy? I'm too poor to subscribe to a clipping bureau. Besides, What's the use? It seems that your review will be the only notice I'll have. I would like to see that.
> Elmer says hello.
>
> > Sincerely,
> > Nella Larsen Imes

*Quicksand* was published on March 20. At the time of Larsen's letter, only one review had appeared, a very positive unsigned piece in *The New York Times Book Review* of April 8. Since Larsen had access to the *Times*, that could hardly be the review by Wasserman she asks to see, although her tone seems to suggest the review had already been published. Larsen sounds a bit coy about reviews in general and Wasserman's in particular: one wonders if her whole purpose in inviting Wasserman to her party was to find out what he'd said about her book. If, when, and where Wasserman's review actually appeared remains something of a puzzle. It is possible to trace at least twenty-two reviews of *Quicksand* following the one in the *Times*, none of which is signed by Wasserman but eight of which are unsigned.[13]

Du Bois thought Larsen the best Negro writer since Charles W. Chesnutt. The *Times*'s anonymous reviewer saw that *Quicksand*'s story of Helga Crane was finally about not race or class but the interior tragedy of an individual life. The book, the reviewer wrote, "has a dignity few first novels have, and a wider outlook upon life than most negro [sic] ones." So little is known about the details of Nella Larsen's life that even the small pieces of the story provided by these letters are welcome.

## Acknowledgment

I am grateful to Thadious M. Davis, Berry Gubert, Bruce Kellner, and Shelah Stein who read a draft of this essay and made suggestions for its improvement.

## Notes

1. Arthur P. Davis, *From the Dark Tower: Afro-American Writers 1900 to 1960* (Washington, D.C.: Howard University Press, 1981) notes on p. 94: "Of all the New Negro authors, Nella Larsen is the most elusive in the matter of biographical details...." Mary Helen Washington subtitled an article on Larsen "Mystery Woman of the Harlem Renaissance" in *Ms.* 9 (Dec. 1980): 44–50.

2. None of the standard guides lists any Larsen manuscripts or correspondence. However, Margaret Perry in *The Harlem Renaissance: An Annotated Bibliography and Commentary* (New York: Garland Publishing, Inc., 1982) points out that there are Larsen letters in the James Weldon Johnson, Carl Van Vechten, Dorothy Peterson, and Langston Hughes papers, all in the James Weldon Johnson Collection in the Beinecke Library at Yale. Some of the more important of these are discussed in William Bradford Clark, "The Letters of Nella Larsen to Carl Van Vechten: A Survey," *Resources for American Literary Study* 8 (Fall 1978): 193–99. David Levering Lewis, *When Harlem Was in Vogue* (New York: Alfred A. Knopf, Inc., 1981), 333, mentions Larsen letters in the Walter White Papers in the Library of Congress. There is at least one in the Carl Van Vechten Papers in the Rare Books and Manuscripts Division, The New York Public Library. There may well be others elsewhere.

3. There is no book-length biography of Larsen, though Professor Thadious M. Davis of Brown University is preparing one for Louisiana State University Press. In the meantime, the best biographical sketch is Davis's "Nella Larsen" in Trudier Harris and Thadious M. Davis, eds., *African-American Writers from the Harlem Renaissance to 1940, Dictionary of Literary Biography* (Detroit: Gale Research Co., 1987), 51: 187–92. A shorter but excellent updated essay by Davis is in Bonnie Kime Scott, ed., *The Gender of Modernism* (Bloomington: Indiana University Press, 1990), 209–16. I am indebted to Elyse Demaray for calling this to my attention. Davis also has an excellent essay, "Nella Larsen's Harlem Aesthetic," in Amrijit Singh, et al., eds., *The Harlem Renaissance: Revaluations* (New York: Garland Publishing, Inc., 1989), 245–56. Many new studies of black feminist writers and writing devote space to Larsen.

4. Everyone mentions the centrality of the 135th Street Branch Library as meeting place and sponsor of readings, lectures, programs, art exhibits, and little theatre in addition to performing the basic purposes of a library. This needs to be developed into a book or major article, especially dealing with the library's extraordinary staff, which included Regina Anderson Andrews, Catherine Allen Latimer, and Ernestine Rose.

5. *Library School of The New York Public Library Register, 1911–1926* (New York: The New York Public Library, 1929), 44.

6. On May 20, 1928, the Women's Committee of the NAACP held an autograph party for Larsen where she was introduced by James Weldon Johnson, according to Ann Allen Shockley, *Afro-American Women Writers, 1746–1933: An Anthology and Critical Guide* (Boston: G.K. Hall & Co., 1988), 434. On May 23, an interview with Larsen appeared in the New York *Amsterdam News* on p. 6: Thelma E. Berlack, "New Author Unearthed Right Here in Harlem."

7. Eddie Wasserman's distinguished pedigree is spelled out in [George S. Hellman], *The Family Register of the Descendants of David Seligman* (Baltimore: Norman T.A. Munder and Co., 1913), 53. See also "Sorting Out the Seligmans," *The New Yorker* 30 (Oct. 30, 1954): 34ff., and Stephen Birmingham, *Our Crowd: The Great Jewish Families of New York* (New York: Harper & Row, 1967), 259.

8. *The New York Times*, Feb. 7, 1914, 3.

9. Undated letter from Bruce Kellner to Richard Newman (January 1991) and Richard Newman interview with Bruce Kellner, New York City, January 8, 1991. For Wasserman and Alice B. Toklas, see Edward Burns, ed., *Staying On Alone: Letters of Alice B. Toklas* (New York: Liveright, 1973), 244, 323, 373.

10. Blanche E. Ferguson, *Countee Cullen and the Negro Renaissance* (New York: Dodd, Mead & Co., 1966), 100.

11. Arnold Rampersad, *The Life of Langston Hughes, Vol. I: 1902–1941; I, Too, Sing America* (New York: Oxford University Press, 1986), 162.

12. What W.E.B. Du Bois was probably incapable of imagining was not lost on others. Thirty-five years later Langston Hughes was still amused by "that wonderful [Baltimore] *Afro[-American]* headline: 'Groom Sails with Best Man.'" Charles H. Nichols, ed., *Arna Bontemps–Langston Hughes Letters, 1925–1967* (New York: Dodd, Mead & Co., 1980), 459.

13. The unsigned reviews are New York *Amsterdam News* (May 16), *Saturday Review of Literature* (May 19), Pittsburg (Mo.) *Bulletin* (June), Boston *Transcript* (June 20) which was undoubtedly written by William Stanley Braithwaite, *Times Literary Supplement* (July 26), Cleveland *Open Shelf* (July 28), *World Tomorrow* (November), and *Book a Week* (1928). Wasserman sent Larsen a copy of his review; she thanked him for it in a letter (held by a private collector) dated April 23. Presumably he sent a manuscript copy.

# Some Little-Known African-American Writers

In 1977 Robert Hemenway published his biography of Zora Neale Hurston, a modest enough event except that it set Hurston on the road from obscurity to the extraordinary popularity she now commands. That same year J. Lee Greene published his biography of Anne Spencer, but no such public recognition or attention followed, and Spencer remains a little-known African-American writer.

Of course Spencer (1882–1975) was a poet rather than a novelist, her style was classical rather than in the black folk tradition, her private life was less dramatic than Hurston's, and she has only scattered poems in print and no book to her credit. But Spencer was also a writer of the first rank, and she represents a number of black writers whose work, despite its quality, continues to go largely unnoticed.

Anne Spencer's mother was the illegitimate daughter of a white aristocrat and a slave woman; her father, who had Seminole blood, operated a saloon because he was too independent to work for a white man. Spencer lived her adult life in Lynchburg, Virginia, but she was in touch with black intellectuals and activists from "way down here in the 'total immersion' belt." The librarian of a segregated branch, she managed to fight the system by walking or hitching rides on grocery wagons rather than use Jim Crow public transportation.

Spencer did not publish her first poem until she was nearly forty years old, and of the many she did write only a few survive either in print or manuscript. One of her verses runs:

> Lady, Lady, I saw your heart,
> And altared there in its darksome place

> Were the tongues of flame the ancients knew
> Where the good God sits to spangle through.

Unlike Spencer, who is known to scholars and who may yet be rescued from oblivion by current interest in the Harlem Renaissance and black women writers, there seems little chance for Gerard Shyne ever to be read or become known. But he was a short story writer of masterful ability with an exquisitely tuned ear for language and a gift, not unfamiliar in the black community, for telling an outrageous tale.

In his seven published stories, Shyne is unequalled in representing lower-class vernacular black speech. The nuances, vitality, imagery, creativity are all here, artless and effortless, in line after perfect line. There is constant talk of ten to six, Peter Rabbit, toe-twinkling, pompom, and hooty-skooty, all euphemisms of the time for sex. And in one or another of its many possible manifestations, the plots are in fact all about hooty-skooty, too. The dialog is coarse and crude, direct and honest, irreverent and satirical, vulgar and low-down, vibrant and alive. It is also very, very funny.

Shyne (1917–1991) was born in Brooklyn, orphaned as a child, and lived his youth in a variety of boarding houses all over the borough. A rooming house and its lodgers are the setting and cast for his ribald stories. From 1946 to 1974 he laboriously worked toward a bachelor's degree at Columbia's School of General Studies, aided by the G.I. Bill. For 25 years a post office custodian, Shyne was too shy to come to the party his friends gave when his collection of stories was published in 1979.

It may not be too surprising that Shyne wrote only one book and remains unknown, but it does seem unlikely that anyone could publish some thirty books and still be virtually undiscovered. That is the case, however, with Edgar Mittelholzer (1909–1965), the Guyanese novelist. He was a dark-complected child in a light-skinned family and his novels are obsessed, as was Mittelholzer himself, with color and class, their subtle interconnections and endless fine distinctions.

He wrote incessantly from childhood on and assaulted editors with manuscripts. Many of the novels are at best mediocre, particularly several long historical ones set in British Guiana and researched in part in The New York Public Library. But *Corentyne Thunder*, the first novel to explore Guyanese peasant life, is very good, and one book of Mittelholzer's, *Shadows Move Among Them*, is absolutely brilliant.

*Shadows* is an adroit, ingenious, slightly hallucinatory fantasy about a Utopian colony in the British Guianese jungle, not far from where Mittelholzer's paternal grandfather ran a Lutheran mission. The story is an attack on the pretensions of the colonial middle class, especially its sexual and religious hypocrisy, but underneath are Mittelholzer's own personal themes of heredity and environment, race and status, blood and jungle.

One reason *Shadows Move Among Them* is so good is that everything turns out to be somewhat different than it first appears, and the subsequent exposure of levels of reality is great fun. Another reason is that one of the central characters, the child Olivia, is totally captivating, and ranks with such appealing little girls of fiction as Addie in Joe David Brown's *Addie Pray* and Jeanette in Jeanette Winterson's *Oranges Are Not the Only Fruit*. Mittelholzer said he was willing to be judged by *Shadows*; if he is he establishes himself as an impressive novelist.

## *Bibliography*

Greene, J. Lee. *Time's Unfading Garden: Anne Spencer's Life and Poetry*. Baton Rouge: Louisiana State University Press, 1977.

Hemenway, Robert. *Zora Neale Hurston: A Literary Biography*. Urbana: University of Illinois Press, 1977.

Honey, Maureen, ed. *Shadowed Dreams: Women's Poetry of the Harlem Renaissance*. New Brunswick: Rutgers University Press, 1989.

Mittelholzer, Edgar. *Corentyne Thunder*. London: Eyre & Spottiswood, 1941.

Mittelholzer, Edgar. *Shadows Move Among Them*. Philadelphia: J.B. Lippincott Co., 1951.

Shyne, Gerard H. *Under the Influence of Mae*. New York: Inwood Press, 1979.

# Sara Lawrence-Lightfoot:
# "To Chart Different Journeys"

It is not easy to invent a new literary genre, but that is what Sara Lawrence-Lightfoot seems to have done in her latest book, *I've Known Rivers: Lives of Loss and Liberation*, published by Addison-Wesley/Merloyd Lawrence. The work, which was chosen as a BOMC main selection, is the product of her lengthy interviews with six middle-class, middle-aged, African American men and women, but the portraits Lawrence-Lightfoot sketches of her subjects are not biography or sociology, or even oral history or therapy, though they sometimes appear to lean in those directions.

Rather, Lawrence-Lightfoot's accounts contain elements of all these traditional ways of understanding human lives, but their combination, plus her own controlled participation in the process, adds up to a literary species she calls "storytelling." In fact, Lawrence-Lightfoot sees herself as a kind of human archaeologist, practicing qualitative research in which she evokes and shapes a penetrating narrative from the stories related by each of her subjects. The results, she believes, push beyond conventional boundaries to a deeper level of authenticity in the explication of personal lives.

Lawrence-Lightfoot talks about the creation of her new book with *Publishers Weekly* in her office in the Graduate School of Education at Harvard where she is the second African American woman in the history of Harvard University to be granted tenure. Statuesque, with a commanding presence, a well-modulated, mellifluous voice and a dazzling smile, she has the ability to mesmerize an audience—be it students, readers on her book tours or her *PW* interviewer. She is elegant in flowing purple garb and a mass of heavy African jewelry. A collection of Masai necklaces decorates the wall behind her desk. Lawrence-Lightfoot's talk is elegant, too, as she describes how she conceived and carried out her storytelling project.

## Early Inspiration

The idea germinated, she says, at her family's dining-room table, where, as a child, she was intrigued by the quality and intensity of her parents' and their guests' conversations. The talk itself was often beyond her reach, she recalls, but she recognized lively minds at work, saw real communication taking place and understood that something really important was happening. "I wanted to recreate that environment," she explains, "and I wanted to participate in it myself."

It is easy to appreciate the appeal of her family's table talk. Her father, Charles Lightfoot, was a sociologist, and her mother, Margaret Morgan Lawrence, triumphed over extraordinary odds to become a distinguished Harlem psychiatrist and the subject of her daughter's previous book, *Balm in Gilead: Journey of a Healer*. The book won a 1988 Christopher Award for "literary merit and humanitarian achievement," was a *Los Angeles Times* Book Prize finalist and a *New York Times* Notable Book of the Year. In his *New Republic* review, Robert Coles saw in it the virtue of storytelling rather than "abstract argument or theoretical assertion."

*Balm in Gilead* is an account of two journeys. The external one is Margaret Morgan's pilgrimage from a middle-class black family in Mississippi to Cornell University in 1932, where, as an African-American undergraduate, she was forced to live off-campus. At Columbia Medical School (Cornell refused to admit her), she had to promise she would not object if a white patient refused to be examined by her. The inner journey is the account of the pain of racism, the necessity of its repression and control and the battle to keep anger from exploding and destroying one's life, a victory not everyone achieves.

In interviewing her mother for *Balm in Gilead*, which has in the short time since it was published become something of a classic, Lawrence-Lightfoot found herself challenging the traditional "boundaries between daughter, inquirer and narrator." That experience was clearly her preparation for *I've Known Rivers* where all the protective and defensive fences come down, and men and women tell stories that draw readers into the immediacy of their lives.

PW asks Lawrence-Lightfoot how she proceeded once she had made the basic decision to cross the lines of conventional sociology. "First of all, I decided to focus on middle-aged people," she explains. "Developmental work on babies and adolescents has already been done, and in our culture mid-life is a moment of mature self-reflection. Many things are behind us, we are at our full power, and we are free to shape the second half of our lives." The specific value of her project, Lawrence-Lightfoot feels, was that "deep storytelling," as she calls it, on the part of middle-aged men and women would provide a real lens on the world, and she means everyone's world, not just the worlds of her subjects.

**Life Journeys**

The people whose stories Lawrence-Lightfoot elicited compose a spectrum of African American middle-class life, but they all have in common a dramatic rise above their origins combined with a need to remain in touch with their roots. Katie Cannon is a highly educated professor of theology; a child of North Carolina sharecroppers, she faced the trauma of writing her first letter to her illiterate father. Charles Ogletree is a top criminal-defense lawyer who never lost a case in 10 years as a public defender in Washington, D.C., but who is haunted by the memory of a childhood friend who is in jail for life.

Toni Schiesler, a research chemist and former nun, was conceived in rape. Tony Earls is a psychiatrist whose research is enriched by the jazz improvisation of native New Orleans. Cheryle Wills is a glamorous and successful entrepreneur, who owns television stations and the largest funeral home in the country and is involved in community activism. Orlando Bagwell is a documentary filmmaker (*Eyes on the Prize*) who perceives both beauty and ugliness in history and events.

**A Double Choice**

Lawrence-Lightfoot says she chose her subjects "not because they are famous, but because they are known in their particular communities and fields as being very good at what they do." She went about selecting them with the knowledge that both they and she would be making an unusual commitment. "I very much wanted people from different walks of life, from different geographical origins and different social class backgrounds. I wanted to chart different journeys, and I wanted to do it in depth, with richness and subtlety and detail. I chose the people, but in a way, they chose me. These storytellers had to commit to a lot of time, and to a relationship that was trusting and penetrating. I worked about a year with each one, at various rhythms depending on the way they wanted to work and the time they had in their schedules."

It was not an easy project to set in motion. She talked to many more people than her eventual six subjects; some couldn't commit to the project because it required too much energy and time or was too invasive of their privacy, or because temperamentally they were not suited for such introspection "Those who said yes were ready for the extraordinary and ambitious journey we took," Lawrence-Lightfoot says.

The author believes that two stories go on simultaneously in *I've Known Rivers*. One traces the lives of the men and women who related them. "The other," she says, "chronicles the developing relationship between me and the storytellers. My voice is revealed—and quite purposely so—in the text, in showing how intimate the development of our relationships became. Each one is idiosyncratic and personal."

Because of this enhanced portrayal, Lawrence-Lightfoot is convinced that hers is the first book that has set out to recreate a life journey refracted through the listener's perceptions. "People tell stories, not to walls, but as part of a developing relationship with the listener," she emphasizes.

For the participants in *I've Know Rivers*, it was a life-enhancing experience. Katie Cannon, now on the faculty of Temple University in Philadelphia, reflects that she didn't worry about revealing too much. "My real story is about me and my family," she says. "They're plain folks in North Carolina. They can't understand who I am or what I'm doing with my life or why I'm different from them. I've had to separate myself from my family in order to maintain my own integrity. My participation in *I've Known Rivers* was so intensive and so important it became part of a crisis in my life. But I've gone through that now, and because I've paid that price, it's easier for me to try to reconnect with my family."

## A Deep Soul

According to Cannon, Lawrence-Lightfoot's ability to bond with her subjects is remarkable. "Sara has a gift," she says, "and a deep soul. She was surely a soul-sister to me all the way through the journey we took together. And it was an I-Thou rather than an I-It relationship. Sometimes we even cried together. But don't misunderstand me, Sara is strong. There's an old black saying that describes her: 'She doesn't take any tea for the fever.'"

Strength of character, empathy and self-possession are characteristics Lawrence-Lightfoot possesses in abundance. In addition to the knowledge she absorbed at home, she was educated at Swarthmore College, the Bank Street College of Education in New York and Harvard University, where she took a doctorate in the sociology of education. She was invited to join the Harvard faculty the year she completed her degree there, a highly uncommon academic occurrence.

She is that rare writer who has negotiated the publishing path without an agent and with a felicitous relationship each time out. *Beyond Bias: Perspectives on Classrooms*, which she wrote with Jean V. Carew, was aimed at an academic audience, appropriate for Harvard University Press. When she was ready to bring out *Worlds Apart: Relationships Between Families and Schools*, she remembered that many of the volumes in her parents' library were published by Basic Books. "I knew it was a serious trade press filled with good academic writers who cared about both the academic community and the wider world," she recalls. She was happy with the editing at Basic and the careful way the book was publicized, and she went on to repeat the experience with *The Good High School: Portraits of Character and Culture*, five years later.

A prestigious MacArthur Foundation Award provided the opportunity to write *Balm in Gilead*. The book was a significant departure from her earlier works; "it was both more biographical and more literary, and I had the expectation of a wider audience." Although Basic was "enthusiastic" about it, she says, she felt "they wanted to turn it into a piece of social science and I wanted it to be social history." So she looked elsewhere, her curiosity piqued by the good things she had heard about Addison-Wesley's Radcliffe Biography Series edited by Merloyd Lawrence.

While she remained unagented, Robert Licht, who was known as a "book lawyer," helped her sell the book there, and again her expectations were fulfilled. Merloyd Lawrence's editing is "exquisite," she says, and their association has been "productive and wonderful." Thus she was motivated to stay with Addison-Wesley with *I've Known Rivers*, though several other houses were interested.

### A Langston Hughes Poem

The title of *I've Known Rivers* comes from an early poem by Langston Hughes. He wrote of the Euphrates, the Congo, the Nile and the Mississippi, the great waterways along which Africans and people of African descent have lived their lives over the centuries. Speaking on behalf of the African Americans who are their heirs, Hughes wrote, "My soul has grown deep like the rivers." Sara Lawrence-Lightfoot indeed captures the stories of "deep-souled folk," and she truly shows her readers real "lives of loss and liberation."

She has brought an even deeper mission to her book, however. She is eager that readers experience the paradox that has always intrigued her, that in the particular lies the general. As she and her subjects "move closer and go deeper into their lives, readers from every walk of life can experience universal feelings and relate to them in a universal way. I think that readers in their middle years will feel a special resonance with this work," she says, with the same conviction that has led her to raise her expectations, and her standards, with each book she writes.

# Part II
## *Performing Arts*

"On Sundaies in the afternoon, their musick plaies and to dancing they go."

—Richard Ligon, 1657

# "The Brightest Star":
# Aida Overton Walker in the
# Age of Ragtime and Cakewalk

I

A golden period of African-American music and dance flourished from the mid-1890s until the First World War. Minstrelsy had been the country's leading vernacular entertainment for half a century, but it was now in decline. Its sentimentality and nostalgia appeared passé and rustic in the more sophisticated and urbanized Gilded Age. An old order was breaking up and a new, looser, freer order taking its place, one that called for a faster beat.

What made the turn of the century a glorious moment musically was the happy confluence of ragtime, a new black rhythm, with the cakewalk, an old black plantation dance. The result was a national craze not to be seen again until two other lower-class black cultural phenomena, jazz and the Charleston, made exactly the same explosive impact on the 1920s and came, also, to define an era. As Eric Hobsbawn points out, this music and dance, this black folk art of the 1890s, was poised to transform bourgeois culture from below, a complex process that continues, internationally, to the present.[1]

For African Americans, the most important benefit of the Ragtime Age was that they themselves had access to the stage in significant numbers. They could earn money, perform unique aspects of their own culture, and begin to counter the crude racism of minstrelsy. Aida Overton Walker was the leading black woman singer and dancer throughout this period, and Alain Locke gave special credit to her and her cakewalk for advancing the new authenticity.[2]

A beautiful, graceful, sensuous, dark-skinned woman, Aida Walker (1880–1914) was at the center of this outburst of black creativity because of her own enormous talent. Carl Van Vechten said the cakewalk of Aida and her husband George W. Walker was one of his great memories of the theater, and he said so in an essay that recalled as comparable highlights the dancing of Isadora Duncan and Nijinsky.[3]

As a singer, Aida's Walker's voice was a rich, low-pitched, velvety mezzo-soprano with a natural sob. She electrified audiences with the vaudeville and musical theater songs she made famous: "Miss Hannah from Savannah," "I Don't Like No Cheap Man," "That's Why They Call Me 'Shine,'" "A Rich Coon's Babe," "I Want to Be the Leading Lady," and "Why Adam Sinned."

Walker's preeminence was well certified by everyone who heard her sing and saw her dance. The New York *Dramatic Mirror* said she was "the best Negro comedienne of today."[4] Sterling Brown called her "the most talented Negro soubrette and dancer of her time."[5] James Weldon Johnson wrote that she was "beyond comparison the brightest star among women on the Negro stage."[6] *Variety* said she was "easily the foremost Afro-American stage artist."[7]

In comparing Walker with her two best-known successors, Tom Fletcher thought she surpassed them both by combining the outstanding qualities of each: Florence Mills's ability and dedication with Josephine Baker's style and sexuality.[8] Twenty years after her death and following the flowering of the Jazz Age and the Harlem Renaissance, the New York *Amsterdam News* still said, "The late Aida Overton Walker, Bert Williams and George Walker stand preeminently as the foremost artists of the stage among Negroes, and have never been equalled."[9]

Ada Wilmore Overton was born at 13 Cornelia Street in Manhattan on Valentine's Day, February 14, 1880, the second child of Moses and Pauline Whitfield Overton. Her father was a waiter. A contemporary *City Directory* lists the Overtons' address as 112 Thompson Street, then an African-American neighborhood known as Coontown or Little Africa, just south of Washington Square in Greenwich Village.[10]

Little is known of Ada's early life, but she seems to have soon taken to music. Bruce Nugent tells the story that as a child she followed a hurdy-gurdy man blocks away from her home, then on

30th Street, singing and dancing to everyone's pleasure, including the musician's because he took in more money with her participation.[11] A grammar-school classmate recalled that at age nine Ada would never play the usual children's games but insisted on practicing her dance steps.[12]

She may have appeared in earlier shows, but it is known that Ada at fifteen or sixteen was a member of "Black Patti's Troubadours" for at least one season. Black Patti, or Madame Sissieretta Jones, was a concert singer of remarkable ability and success, called "The Black Patti" in deference to Adeline Patti, the noted white singer of the day. After a brilliant European tour, Mme. Jones's managers created an all-black traveling show. Written by Bob Cole in the minstrel tradition, it combined farce with serious music.

Ada appeared in two numbers during the show's first half, Cole's skit called "At Jolly 'Coon'-ey Island." One was with a fellow singer named Davis performing "The Three Little Kinkies." The other was as a member of a quintella doing "4–11–44." Ada was also one of the "chorus of forty trained voices" that accompanied Black Patti in the Troubadours' second part, "The Operatic Kaleidescope," which featured selections from grand and comic opera.[13]

Ada's life changed in 1898 when Stella Wiley, a friend from the Troubadours, invited her to pose dancing the cakewalk for an American Tobacco Company trade-card photograph. The male dancers in the foursome were two young comedians named George Walker (1873–1911) and Bert Williams (1874–1922), hopeful entertainers recently come to New York from California. They billed themselves "The Two Real Coons" to take advantage of the popular interest in black music, dance, and comedy and to suggest, even with self-deprecation, that black people were better portrayers of African-American ethnic entertainment than were white imitators.

Williams and Walker incorporated into their vaudeville routines the lively new syncopated ragtime music with its origins in black saloons and sporting houses and recently introduced with great success by Ben Harney at Tony Pastor's music hall. They combined ragtime with popular high-stepping cakewalk dancing then being performed by the elegant black team of Dora Dean and Charles Thompson.

Williams and Walker were soon on their way to becoming the leading figures of the new entertainment as they merged these song and dance elements with their own humorous sketches: Walker played the sharp dude and Williams the comic "darky." Ada Overton joined the Williams and Walker troupe as a dancer, and she and Walker were married on June 22, 1899, by the Rev. Hutchins C. Bishop, rector of St. Philip's Episcopal Church.

Off stage as well as on, George Walker was the stylish, urban "Jim Dandy" sport and hustler, with his extravagantly elegant clothes, gold teeth, and confident sexuality. Off stage, he was generous, honest, entrepreneurial, and, unlike Williams, a shrewd businessman. It was said that he spent more time with his tailor than with his wife. Walker's extramarital affairs were legendary and included liaisons with Jeanette Foster, "The Chocolate Venus," and Eva Tanguay, who was white, the famous "I Don't Care Girl," who became the highest-paid woman in vaudeville.

Ada Walker worked with the Williams and Walker company and took advantage of the cakewalk fad by dancing in local competitions and teaching the steps to wealthy and fashionable white men and women. Because of its improvised promenading movements, syncopated ragtime was the perfect cakewalk accompaniment. Wearing fancy dress, the dancers folded their arms across their chests, threw back their heads, arched their entire bodies backwards, and strutted.

Presumably, the cakewalk originated as a plantation dance when slaves imitated, exaggerated, and, in fact, satirically mocked and mimicked formal white cotillions. The name comes from the cake awarded as a prize in cutting contests to the couple receiving the most audience applause. Blackface minstrelsy had incorporated the cakewalk in its grand finales as the walk-around. This means that when the dance reemerged in the 1890s, it was performed by blacks imitating whites who had been imitating blacks imitating whites.[14]

When the cakewalk craze was at its height in 1903, a white newspaper made the unusual move of interviewing Ada Walker. The headline ran: "Cakewalk in Society / Gotham follows Paris in Adopting the Fad / Product of Slaves Now the Craze of Fashion / New York 400 Falls Under Spell of the Willowy Dance / Ada Overton Walker Leads Young Women in the Mazy Steps / Graceful Young Negress Teaches the Art of Terpsichore / Cheerfulness the Keynote of the Fascinating Pastime."

Walker explained to her white readers that they should keep their shoulders back and cultivate elasticity. She described various cakewalk steps such as the swan's bend, driving tacks, shooting the chute, and the kangaroo. "The cakewalk is a dance peculiar to our people," Walker pointed out, as she urged New York aristocrats to try to emulate what she called the flourish and grace, the easy swing of black dockworkers unloading cotton.[15]

With Ada Walker leading the dancers, the Williams and Walker troupe, billed as the Senegambian Carnival, took over from Ernest Hogan the lead in the 1898 Eastern tour of *Clorindy, or The Origins of the Cakewalk*. By Will Marion Cook and Paul Lawrence Dunbar, *Clorindy* was one of an important series of all-black musical theater productions of the decade that marked the movement away from minstrelsy. In a slow but discernible progression, these shows created more black autonomy over black theater in all its dimensions and clearly blunted the more extreme and vulgar manifestations of racism, although stereotypical images did continue. These shows included Bob Cole's *A Trip to Coontown*, John Isham's *Oriental America* and *Octoroons*, and Sam T. Jack's *The Creole Show*.[16]

A foundation existed, then, for Williams and Walker's bold decision to create their own full-length ragtime musical with an all-black cast. The producers were Seamon and Hurtig, who were white and who had access, as blacks as yet did not, to theaters, but the production itself was entirely African-American. Williams wrote the songs and Walker the book, Jesse A. Shipp directed, and Will Marion Cook led the orchestra.

Originally called *A Lucky Coon*, the title was changed to *4–11–44* and finally became *The Policy Players*. It opened in 1899. There was a story line, but the plots of these shows were thin and largely a device to hold together elements of song, dance, and comedy. The plot of *The Policy Players* concerned a winning combination in the illegal lottery or numbers game, and the first scene opened in a betting parlor on Thompson Street where Ada had lived as a child. The numbers enterprise was so popular and widespread that Claude McKay later called it "the greatest industrial phenomenon in Harlem."[17]

Ada had a major role in the show. In a sister act, she and Grace Halliday portrayed "Honolulu Belles," and Ada introduced a novelty dance. She sang Williams and Walker's "I Don't Like No Cheap Man." She also choreographed *The Policy Players'* dance numbers, which made her one of the first recognized black women choreographers, if not the first, and apparently one of the first women to receive program credit, as she did on their next show, *Sons of Ham*.[18] Opening in 1900, *Sons of Ham* was Williams and Walker's first real success and their first revue to appear on Broadway. Again produced by Seamon and Hertig, it was staged by Jesse A. Shipp, lyrics were by Alex Rogers, music was composed by Will Marion Cook, and Shipp, Williams, and Walker wrote the script—an extraordinary constellation of African-American talent.

Ada Walker played Carolyn Jenkins, a student at Riske College. She sang "I Want to Be the Leading Lady," and a number that became one of her standards, "Miss Hannah from Savannah," which she concluded with a showstopping eccentric dance. When the road company of *Sons of Ham* later played Washington, D.C., Ada taught "Miss Hannah from Savannah" to a local extra added attraction, a five-year-old ghetto child named Florence Mills. Ada Walker became Mills's heroine and role model and Mills's own career in the 1920s almost exactly paralleled that of Walker's in the 90s.[19]

At this early stage in her career, Walker did not receive the uniform praise from the critics that she was later to enjoy. The *New York Telegraph* reviewer thought she read badly in *Sons of Ham* and was afraid to use her full voice, but "she is commencing to acquire some skill in facial byplay" and he saw her emerging as a major "dark soubrette." The show itself, however, was a "new departure," he thought, and "something new in this class" of revue, an advance over the old Octoroon productions.[20]

Other reviewers also saw that something was different about the Williams and Walker ragtime musicals. The *Indianapolis Freeman*, for example, noted that chicken stealing and crap games were conspicuously absent.[21] Many of the traditional darky elements of minstrelsy were still present, but they had been perfected to an artistry that transcended the conventional coon show and the racism that informed it.[22]

In large part, the change was due to the genius of Bert Williams. He became, it can be argued, the greatest comedian in the history of the American stage, second not even to Chaplin. The darky role that he played was so alien to him that he had to learn the accent and imitate the stereotypical mannerisms, but he perfected the part to such a degree that it can be said that he "transformed racist stereotyping into authentic black humor," as Henry Louis Gates, Jr., said of Amos 'n' Andy.[23]

Ironically, if Williams raised the darky character to an art form, which he did, he probably contributed to its perpetuation. At the same time, he elevated authentic black themes to a new height and widened the audience for an authentic African-American ethos. A few years later, Williams and Walker's *Abyssinia* received this comment from Alan Dale, a major New York critic and the reviewer for the *New York American*: This "is a coon show in name only; in reality, it was a most serious near-grand opera for which we were totally unprepared."[24]

In speaking of Will Marion Cook's compositions for the same show, the *Boston Evening Transcript* said, "Musical comedies with real music are rarities, but this is one.... The composer has succeeded in lifting Negro music above the plane of the so-called 'Coon song' without destroying the characteristics of the melodies."[25] Whatever the ambiguities, then, Williams and Walker and their company did succeed in demonstrating more authentic African-American culture, presenting it with great ability, and having it appreciated by a wide audience of both blacks and whites.

In 1901, Ada appeared briefly in New York apart from the Williams and Walker troupe in a short-run comic opera called *The Cannibal King*. Music was by Will Marion Cook and Willis Accooe, with lyrics by Bob Cole and J. Rosamond Johnson. The text of these shows was sometimes fluid and improvised, but it would be instructive to reconstruct the African themes that run through many of them. This was especially true of the Williams and Walker productions. African motifs, however comic, were deliberate attempts on George Walker's part to replace American darky elements with what he called "native African characteristics."[25]

Williams and Walker came to their full maturity with *In Dahomey* in 1902. Ada herself was now second in popularity and importance only to the two principals. Again, music, lyrics, and libretto were by blacks. Ada played Rosita Lightfoot, "a troublesome young thing." Wearing a white Swiss dress plaited and bordered with yellow satin, she sang "Why Adam Sinned" and "A Rich Coon's Babe." At the New York Theater on Broadway between

44th and 45th Streets in early 1903, one could see *In Dahomey* for prices ranging from twenty-five cents to one dollar.

With a thousand people seeing the ship off, the cast of *In Dahomey* sailed to London, where the show opened at the Shaftesbury Theater in the West End on May 16, 1903. There was only moderate success at first, but then came a royal command for an afternoon lawn-party performance at Buckingham Palace on June 23 to celebrate the ninth birthday of the Prince of Wales. While the royal family watched approvingly from lawn chairs, Ada sang and performed a solo dance on the parquet floor that had been laid on the grass. She met and was complimented by the king and queen, and Edward VII, who had an eye for attractive women, gave her a diamond brooch.

Royal patronage made *In Dahomey* a hit for 250 performances over eight months, though the British were at first so bewildered by the show it was necessary to play "God Save the King" at the end to indicate it was over. The *Star* found Ada "black but comely," and the *Times* thought the singing "rich" with "snap" and "dash" and particularly liked the vivacious dancing. When asked what it was like to meet Edward VII, George Walker simply said, "He treated me as one king should another."[27]

Back in New York, Ada was involved in a minor racial incident with the city's high society. Mr. and Mrs. Robert L. Hargous gave a party at Delmonico's in honor of Lady Paget, the American-born wife of General Sir Arthur Paget. Ada and George Walker were brought in to entertain. Hargous surprised everyone by personally introducing Ada to his guests and joining her in leading a cakewalk. He then invited her to waltz. At this point, the *New York Sun* reported, "a number of women guests thought it was time to leave, and the party did break up shortly afterward."[28]

There was much talk of the matter in social circles. Either Robert Hargous crossed the color line by treating a black woman virtually as a guest and equal, or several wives present resented their husbands' attentiveness to the glamorous and exotic Ada: "Many gentlemen treated her with courtesy," someone noted. The *New York Times* elected to interpret the resentment as a kind of public relations achievement: Hargous's "action made Mrs. Walker ... a fad of the season," it said.[29]

The Williams and Walker successes continued with the large and lavish *Abyssinia* of 1906. Ada played the role of Miram. Again she created, arranged, and rehearsed the dancing, and appeared with a group called the Nine Abyssinian Maids performing "The Dance of the Falasha Maids" and "Menelik's Tribute to Queen Tai Tu." She sang "I'll Keep a Warm Spot in My Heart for You" and "The Lion and the Monk (Die Trying)." A number of important black women dancers, including Anita Bush and Lottie Gee, first got their start under Ada's direction.

It was about the time of *Abyssinia* that Ada changed her name to Aida and on occasion hyphenated Overton-Walker. She probably felt the prominence she had achieved warranted a more appropriate identity, though Carl Van Vechten wondered with tongue in cheek if the alteration were at the insistence of a numerologist.[30] One white reviewer condescendingly described the name change and her appearance:

> Those shaded show girls in 'Abyssinia' are led by Aida Walker who used to be Ada Overton. Is the change from 'Ady' to 'I-e-da' meant to mark a musical advance by Williams and Walker from negro [sic] melody to operatic music? Aida is a lively lightweight, impish, sprightly, and coquettish. Her complexion is a half-tone and her hair hesitates between Marcel waves and Afric kinks.[31]

The last Williams and Walker revue was *Bandanna Land* of 1907. With Williams's pantomime poker game and George Walker's hit song "Bon Bon Buddy, the Chocolate Drop," *Bandanna Land* showed them at the height of their power and popularity. As in *Abyssinia*, the production was entirely under black control and, again Aida choreographed the dances. The continued progress of these revues was noted in the *Dramatic Mirror*: "With all its savor of a minstrel performance, the piece comes very close to being opera comique."[32]

Aida played Dinah (later changed to Susie) Simmons, one of the female leads. With a half-dozen "Kinky Girls," she sang Mord Allen's "Kinky" in Act 1 and "It's Hard to Love Somebody When Somebody Don't Love You" in the second act. In Act 3, Aida "and Girls" danced "Ethiopia," her own creation that included a ragtime parody of *The Merry Widow*.

After four months on Broadway, *Bandanna Land* traveled to a number of major cities, undergoing, as usual, a good many changes along the way. Aida added "The Sheath Gown in Darktown" to Act 2 and appeared wearing an example of the smart new fashion.

Somehow a Salome dance found its way into the third act, and Walker was apparently the first black woman to perform this "modern" dance. There was public anxiety, especially in Boston, about the display of John the Baptist's head and Aida Overton Walker's body. The *Sunday Herald* assured concerned readers, however, that there was nothing offensive about the Baptist's head,[33] and another paper explained that although Aida appeared to be scantily clad, she was in fact actually wearing bronze trunks over what the paper delicately referred to to as "her frame."[34]

Aida's controversial "Salome" was followed on stage by Bert Williams's imitative burlesque in which he wrapped himself in gauze and removed his oversize shoes for dancing. The head of John the Baptist that magnetically mesmerized the dancer was replaced in his parody by a large watermelon.

*Bandanna Land* was George Walker's last performance. With an advanced case of syphilis, he began missing cues and lines. He then started stuttering and finally had to leave the road show. He died January 6, 1911, in a sanitarium. The troupe went on, Williams appearing alone, and Aida poignantly singing George's numbers, particularly "Bon Bon Buddy," dancing his cakewalk strut, and wearing his flashy clothes. Bruce Nugent called her "probably the first and certainly the best" male impersonator.[35]

Williams continued without his partner and offered Aida the female lead in Shipp and Rogers' *Mr. Lode of Koal* in 1909, but she refused. They went separate ways, and Williams was invited by Florenz Ziegfeld to become the first—and only—black to appear in the *Follies*. Aida accepted a starring role in Cole and Johnson's *The Red Moon* in 1909. With the revue's American Indian theme, she played the role of Flaming Arrow and performed "Wildfire," billed as an aboriginal dance. She continued with her group of female dancers, she still did George Walker numbers in male clothes, and she introduced new songs, like "Phoebe Brown," billed as "a Spanish-coon melody."

In 1910, Aida joined S.H. Dudley and his Smart Set Company in *His Honor the Barber*. A musical comedy in three acts and seven scenes, the book was by Edwin Hanaford, a white man, with music by James T. Brymn, who was black. It was produced by the Southern Enchantment Company. Blacks were not relegated to the balcony but had seats in alternate sections throughout the theater.[36] Dudley played Raspberry Snow, a barber whose ambition was to shave the President of the United States, a goal that he achieves in a second-act dream sequence.

Walker sang "That's Why They Call Me 'Shine'" and "Golly, Ain't I Wicked." She performed a popular song-and-dance number called "Porto Rico" that generated several encores. For this sinuous dance, she wore "a marvelously audacious creation of pink shimmering Salome silk trimmed with satin, silver, and green networked spangles inlaid with brilliant jewels."[37] The *Dramatic Mirror* lauded the performance, especially "her impersonation of a Negro 'chappie' ... which is the real hit of the play."[33] This, of course, was her George Walker number.

William Hammerstein decided in 1912 to revive a performance of the once faddish Salome dance at his Victoria Theater on Broadway and 42nd Street, the country's leading vaudeville emporium. With a flair for publicity he kept secret for weeks the identity of the dancer while encouraging speculation to center on such well-known names as Lady Constance Roberston and Ruth St. Denis.

When Hammerstein revealed the name of Aida Overton Walker as his choice for the part, he also announced this as the first time a black woman was to play the role as well as the first time a black woman would do a "classic" dance on stage. This, of course, was not the theatrical history that Hammerstein's public relations agents claimed since Walker had danced her version of Salome in *Bandanna Land* four years earlier.

The Victoria Theater's "Salome" was a spectacular production with elaborate scenery, a symphony orchestra of thirty-six pieces, and special music composed by James Reece Europe. Wearing a bespangled but modest costume that left bare only her feet and shoulders, Aida began her nine-minute performance at the top of a flight of stairs. The daring aspects, real or imagined, of the dance had to be presented in a way that could be billed as artistic, so she added some shoulder shrugging and snakelike jerks of her hands and arms to give an Egyptian-Oriental flavor to her performance. *Vanity Fair* remarked on her pantherine movements and langorous grace.[39] In the main, reviewers were cynical of Hammerstein's hype, but *Variety* exhorted, "It was some 'Salome' boys, and catch it while it's going."[40]

Aida Overton Walker maintained an active professional life in vaudeville and appeared in many benefits for black causes and in an important show at Chicago's Pekin Theater in 1913. Her last appearance was at Hammerstein's in the summer of 1914. With a new "ballroom" partner, J. Lackey Grant, she danced the maxixe, a sensual Afro-Brazilian dance, the hesitation tango, the Southern drag, and the jigeree. These last two, as *Variety* pointed out, involved "considerable hip gyrating and swaying."[41]

In September, she was confined to bed with what *Variety* called kidney congestion and the *New York Times* said was a nervous breakdown.[42] She died at home, 107 West 132nd Street, on Sunday night, October 11, 1914. She was 34 years old. Funeral services were conducted by Dr. Bishop of St. Philip's Church, who had married her and George Walker. She left no real estate and only $250 in personal property.[43]

Carl Van Vechten lamented her passing by saying that she danced as few white women have danced. He remembered that appreciative blacks in her audience had been heard to exclaim "Ain't she loose!" and he confessed he could not recall her performances without crying. Since her time, "The dancing is becoming Broadwayized and sophisticated," Van Vechten wrote, and "the singing is fast losing its essential style."[44]

Aida Walker herself was fully conscious of her art and of its sources. In 1905, she wrote,

> There are characteristics and natural tendencies in our people which make just as beautiful studies for the stage as to be found in the make-up of any other race, and perhaps far better.... Unless we learn the lesson of self-appreciation and practice it, we shall spend our lives imitating other people and deprecating ourselves.[45]

Solidly grounded in a vital and dynamic black folk culture, Walker's racial art was of such quality as to transcend race. The particularity of ragtime and cakewalk struck such a responsive vernacular chord as to become universalized in American popular culture and beyond. Besides the inherent appeal of the material itself, one reason was the genius of Aida's own awesome talent. Reviewing *Bandanna Land*, the *Brooklyn Eagle* critic wrote, "But art knows no color line and it is simple justice to say that our stage has no white ... singing soubrette with the grace and distinction of style ... of Aida Overton Walker."[46]

## II

Aida Walker sang a range of contemporary show tunes, ballads, ragtime ditties, and popular Tin Pan Alley numbers, songs beginning to constitute an emerging modern and highly commercialized entertainment industry. She also sang "coon songs," a genre of enormously popular songs of the day that combined peppy ragtime syncopation with supposedly humorous darky-dialect lyrics. Coon songs created a musical craze that engulfed the country: over a thousand titles were published around the turn of the century, and Fred Fisher's "If the Man in the Moon Were a Coon" sold three million copies in sheet music in 1905.

For fifty years, beginning in the 1840s, minstrelsy had been America's predominant vernacular entertainment, but minstrelsy began to decline in the 1880s, perhaps because a post-Civil War society entering the more sophisticated, more urban Gilded Age called for a music more appropriate to the time. Up to then, both words and music of popular songs were romantic and sentimental. With ragtime providing a jaunty tempo, lyrics now became tougher, slangier, sexier, more lower-class, more impudent.

In terms of African Americans specifically, minstrel ballads had portrayed them as rural, aged Southern darkies plaintively longing for the old master and yearning for the old plantation. Coon songs in contrast were about younger, sassier, flashily dressed, citified blacks. Mammy and Uncle Ned were replaced by sharp dudes with saucy yaller gals on their arms. The chief objects of coon songs' humor were all the familiar racist stereotypes, which they in fact helped implant in the culture. To judge from lyrics and sheet-music art, blacks are wooly haired, physically hard-headed, eye-rolling, thick-lipped, big-footed, malaprop-speaking, lazy, superstitious, crap-shooting, chicken-stealing, watermelon-eating, razor-wielding, constantly dancing buffoons.

Using one or more of these stock descriptors, coon songs often made sport of the supposed pretentiousness of black people trying to act like whites, and so the songs' role in protecting white preserves and reinforcing social control is obvious. The hostility interwoven with the supposed humor of coon songs is very real, an element of the violent white reaction in the 1880s and 1890s to the modest black gains of Reconstruction and the successful white crusade to reduce African Americans, though technically free, to political submission, economic servitude, and social inferiority. It is ironic that this massive oppression of blacks occurred precisely when black singing and dancing were beginning to infiltrate and even subvert white middle-class popular culture.

The ragtime music of coon songs is clearly an African-American creation, born probably in the black bordellos of St. Louis. The negative images of black people so bluntly articulated in coon-song lyrics may in fact exert at the same time a kind of subtle attraction. The sharp, hedonistic urban black—Jim Dandy as opposed to Jim Crow, George Walker in contrast to Bert Williams—is privately, secretly, perhaps even unconsciously, admired for his audacious, style-setting, masculine self-possession, for what we would now call his coolness. He is, in a circa 1900 manner, even hip. This is surely a very early instance of the American black man as model and folk hero, but it is hardly the last. The phenomenon is repeated in the jazzy life-style emulated by whites in the 1920s, in Norman Mailer's "white Negro" in the 1950s, and in the disrespectful rappers and hip-hoppers of the 1990s.

Within this context, one real function of coon songs was to introduce sexuality into popular music. Songs in black dialect could get away with a suggestive sexuality as yet unthinkable if linked with whites, especially, of course, white women. Through the 1890s, songs about white women carried such saccharine titles as "She's a Sweet Little Snow White Blossom" and "She Kissed Him for His Mother." But coon songs about black women were able to abandon such sweetness and light for earthier themes and a more visibly sexual flavor: "The Warmest Colored Girl in Town," "I Wants Ma Honey Boy Now," and "My Black Mammy Did, Did She?"

As a transition from white female asexuality, these less restrained lyrics rather quickly evolved into popular white love songs and spread across the culture, first among the new urban proletariat and then to the bourgeoisie. It was now possible to connect white women with sexuality as songs originally about supposedly more erotic black women were absorbed and deracinated in the mainstream. Some of the better known transitional numbers are those where the darky element was minimal in the beginning and has now been lost or forgotten—with only a trace of dialect remaining: "Hello, Ma Baby," "For Me and My Gal," "Put Your Arms Around Me, Honey."

Another facet of this prism is that it now also became possible in lyrics to link black people with romance. Aida Walker herself spoke feelingly on this issue. Interviewed as the only African-American actress with a national reputation, she discussed the special problems that blacks faced in the entertainment world, and pointed out that because of white prejudices, she had never seen on the stage a hint of a serious love story involving blacks.[47] But now Bob Cole and J. Rosamond Johnson produced romantic songs like "Tell Me, Dusky Maiden" and "Under the Bamboo Tree" (which was in fact a syncopated version of the spiritual "Nobody Knows the Trouble I See").

In the main, however, what can be most clearly posited about the coon songs of the period is their blatant and vulgar racism. Typical titles include "Mammy's Little Pumkin Colored Coon," "I'se Your Nigger if You Wants Me, Liza Jane," "Pickaninny Nigs," and the most notorious of all, Ernest Hogan's "All Coons Look Alike to Me." These songs sound indefensible in any way, yet it would be a mistake not to look carefully at their lyrics, particularly those most closely identified with Aida Overton Walker.

In *The Policy Players*, Walker sang "I Don't Want No Cheap Man," with words and music by Williams and Walker, arranged by W.H. Tyers, copyrighted in 1897 by Joseph W. Stern and Company, with the copyright renewed in 1924 by Lottie Williams, Bert Williams' widow. The lyrics are:

> Miss Simpson had always been considered de finest gal in town,
> She was de envy of all de men dat lived for miles around.
> Last week, Bill Johnson took her out to see de minstrels at de hall,
> He bought de seats in de gallery, and she didn't like that at all.
>
> *Chorus*
> She said, "I don't like no cheap man
> Dat spends his money on de 'stalments plan;
> Dat's de reason I always carry with me
> 'Nuf money for what I want.
> I got a sweet disposition as anyone,
> But 'sakes a live,' I hate to be done
> In front of de people dat's sitting here, too.
> You's a cheap man, and you won't do!"

While it would be easy to read too much into this comic song, it is also the case that Miss Simpson clearly presents herself as an independent and self-reliant woman. She carries her own money so that she is not financially dependent—unless she chooses to be—on one of her men friends. She is a proud person with a firm and positive sense of self who is embarrassed in front of others by her male companion who is so miserly he buys only gallery seats. As a result, he is unacceptable, and Miss Simpson bluntly tells him so.

The same theme is expressed more vigorously in "A Rich Coon's Babe" published by Howley, Haviland, and Dresser in 1902. The lyrics are by Clare Kummer, a white woman who was, rather surprisingly, the grand-niece of Harriet Beecher Stowe. The words read:

> Yo' ain't de first dat's axed me fo' ma han,
> I wants to marry if I can find de man;
> But tho' I like yo' face, I ain't lookin' for a place
> To cook an' take in washing understand?
> I ain't a-goin' to marry just fo' love,
> Dere's other little things I'se got to have;
> You say I am a peach, but de fruit am out of reach,
> Unless yo' got de money fo' to give.
>
> *Chorus*
> For I was raised to be a rich coon's baby,
> My mudder taught me fo' to be a lady;
> I don't know a-how to cook, or sew, or save,
> But you can hab me if you got de money,
> If you haben't I can't be yo' honey,
> For I'se only raised to be a rich coon's babe.

Here is an even stronger assertion of a black woman's independence and self-reliance. The speaker is not unwilling to marry; in fact, she probably knows that it is a social necessity. But she is exercising her prerogative to be selective. She may have to sell out, but she is not going to sell cheap. She is not going to marry merely for love, and, most of all, she is not going to marry if that means the dumb drudgery of household work. She is aspiring and ambitious and, if she must barter herself in marriage, she is not going to trade for anything less than economic well-being.

With the lyrics' aggressive self-confidence combined with the exaggerated dialect, the words were undoubtedly received by white audiences only as a large joke. The singer's affirmation of her autonomy and freedom from control was likely seen as an aspect of the black pretentiousness that constituted such a major theme in coon songs. But surely this message of self-reliance was neither lost on the performer, nor unconscious on the part of the author, a member of the country's most distinguished white abolitionist family.

The opposition to sexist convention is even stronger in "Miss Hannah from Savannah" written by Cecil Mack (Richard C. McPherson) and Thomas Lemonier for *Sons of Ham* and copyrighted by Joseph W. Stern Company in 1901. This is the statement of a young black woman who has just moved from South to North. She anticipates an encounter with Northern black society because she has heard it is high toned and imitative of whites. If anyone should try to approach her with such false claims, she warns, "Ah'll tell 'em who I am." And just who is she? The chorus reads,

> My name's Miss Hannah from Savannah,
> Ah wants all you folks to understand-ah;
> Ahm some de blue-blood ob de land-ah,
> I'se Miss Hannah from Savannah!

Unconcealed here is Miss Hannah's (when African Americans were not designated as "Miss") strong sense of identity and self-worth. Perhaps it was amusing for a white audience to see and hear a self-assured black woman assert her personal dignity, her family's distinction, and her pride of place, but she avers them all nonetheless. It is not a misstatement to suggest that the same thread runs through all of these songs, nor an overstatement to suggest that Miss Hannah's confidence is even more and more clearly a self-affirming feminist statement than the others.

Another song identified with Walker was "I Want to Be the Leading Lady" with music by Harry Von Tilzer and lyrics by George Totten Smith, written in 1901 and sung in the second act of *Sons of Ham*. The words read,

> I want to be the leading lady,
> I want to play the real star part.
> Make no mistake now; I know how to act.
> Just give me a chance
> And you'll see it's a fact.

On the surface, this is the statement of the flirtatious soubrette who wants the chief role in a play. If, however, it is about black life in white America, the speaker is confident of her self-worth and her ability to take her full place in society, and she promises successful results. She speaks as an equal, with no hint of servility even though she is a petitioner, and she assures the person to whom she is speaking, who is in a position to grant her request, that she knows what she's doing and needs only the opportunity to demonstrate it.

Walker also sang "That's Why They Call Me 'Shine,'" a song that retains its popularity and continues to be recorded. The lyrics, again, were by Cecil Mack, the music was by Ford Dabney, and it was copyrighted in 1910 by Shapiro, Bernstein and Company. The words are

> 'Cause my hair is curly
> 'Cause my teeth are pearly
> Just because I always wear a smile
> Like to dress up in the latest style
> 'Cause I'm glad I'm living
> Take troubles smiling, never whine
> 'Cause my color's shady
> Slightly different, maybe
> That's why they call me "Shine."

Here the theme is race rather then the place of women. The message is that black physical and cultural characteristics are neutral if not positive qualities. "Shady" color is only "slightly different," with a "maybe" added to cast doubt on any physiological difference whatsoever. The distinction between these lyrics and those of many coon songs was not lost on black commentators. R.G. Doggett believed that this song "embodies the spirit that every Negro should possess," that is, to be called a derogatory name does not detract from positive realities, and one should be able to rise above racial slurs which, while ill-intended, are without meaning.[48]

Without more investigation, it is difficult to know what and how much is actually going on in coon songs. The racism masked as humor in titles like "Koonville Koonlets" and "When They Straighten All the Colored People's Hair" is clear enough. The major impact of coon songs in the creolization of American vernacular culture is also clear, although not always recognized or acknowledged. Not every critic is so insightful as Roger Lane, who writes, "The coon song, then, not only changed the nature of the

Afro-American influence on popular culture but began the process of changing the nature of the culture itself."[49]

These songs identified with Aida Overton Walker, however, have a different aspect yet. "Shine" is almost a song of social protest in its antiracism. The others noted here seem to have an interior and internal dimension. When Walker sings "I'se Miss Hannah from Savannah," to whom is this feminist affirmation being made? If it is not to an insensitive and even uncomprehending white audience, then perhaps it is to herself as an assertion of her own autonomy and integrity in the literal midst of a sexist and racist world. Perhaps, even, like the double meanings of the spirituals and slave songs, it is a message, a secret message to those who have ears to hear.

## Notes

1. E.J. Hobsbawm, *The Age of Empire* (New York: Vantage, 1987), p. 237.

2. Alain Locke, "The Negro in the Arts," *United Arts: International Magazine of Asian Affairs* 5 (June 1953): 177–81.

3. Carl Van Vechten, "Terpsichorean Souvenirs," *Dance Magazine* 31 (January 1957): 16–18.

4. May 8, 1911, quoted in Allen Woll, *Black Musical Theatre: From Coontown to Dreamgirls* (Baton Rouge: Louisiana State University Press, 1989), p. 55

5. Sterling A. Brown, "The Negro on the Stage" (1940), in *The Negro in American Culture*, Carnegie-Myrdal Study, The Negro in America, Unpublished study, Schomburg Center for Research in Black Culture, New York, p. 37.

6. Brown, "Negro on the Stage," p. 36.

7. *Variety* 36 (October 17, 1914): 13.

8. Tom Fletcher, *100 Years of the Negro in Show Business* (New York: Burdge, 1954), p. 18.

9. New York *Amsterdam News*, December 22, 1934. For biographies of Williams, see Mabel Rowland, ed., *Bert Williams, Son of Laughter* (New York: English Crafters, 1923); Ann Charters, *Nobody: The Story of Bert Williams* (New York: Macmillan, 1970); and Eric Ledell Smith, *Bert Williams: A Biography of the Pioneer Black Comedian* (Jefferson, Mo.: McFarland, 1992). Unfortunately, there is as yet no biography of George Walker.

10. *Trow's New York City Directory, Volume XCIII, for the Year Ending May 1, 1880* (New York: Trow City Directory, 1879), p. 1174.

11. Richard Bruce Nugent, "Marshall's: A Portrait," *Phylon* 5 (Fourth Quarter 1944): 317.

12. *New York Mirror*, August 7, 1909.

13. Henry T. Sampson, *The Ghost Walks: A Chronological History of Blacks in Show Business, 1865–1910* (Metuchen, N.J.: Scarecrow, 1988), p. 120.

14. Terry Waldo, *This Is Ragtime* (New York: Hawthorn, 1976), p. 25.

15. Unidentified clipping dated March 29, 1903, Theater Division, Performing Arts Research Center, New York Public Library.

16. These musicals are of great importance and have been little dealt with. John Graziano is presently engaged in a study that will spell out their history, correct the errors that have crept into the literature, and place them in their proper perspective.

17. Claude McKay, *Harlem Glory: A Fragment of Aframerican Life* (Chicago: Charles H. Kerr, 1990), p. 64.

18. Barbara Cohen-Stratyner, *Biographical Dictionary of Dance* (New York: Shirmer, 1983), p. 920.

19. Richard Newman, "Florence Mills," in *Notable Black American Women*, ed. Jessie Carney Smith (Detroit: Gale, 1991), pp. 752–56.

20. *New York Telegraph*, September 20, 1901. Quoted in Sampson, *Ghost*, p. 238.

21. *Indianapolis Freeman*, December 14, 1901. Quoted in Sampson, *Ghost*, p. 241.

22. *Detroit Free Press*, February 3, 1902.

23. *New York Times*, November 12, 1989, sec. 2, p. 40.

24. *New York American*, February 23, 1906.

25. Quoted in Maud Cuney-Hare, *Negro Musicians and Their Music* (Washington, D.C.: Associated Publishers, 1936), pp. 159–60.

26. Charters, *Nobody*, p. 69.

27. Jeffrey T. Green, "*In Dahomey* in London in 1903," *Black Perspective in Music* 2 (Spring 1983): 23–40. See also the unsourced clipping "King Edward and the Negro Opera" in the Vertical File, Schomburg Center for Research in Black Culture, New York Public Library.

28. Brown, "Negro on the Stage," p. 36.

29. *New York Times*, November 26, 1905, p. 9.

30. Bruce Kellner, ed., *'Keep A-Inchin' Along:' Selected Writings of Carl Van Vechten about Black Arts and Letters* (Westport Conn.: Greenwood, 1979), p. 31.

31. Unsourced clipping, Harvard Theater Collection.

32. *Dramatic Mirror*, February 25, 1908, p. 3.

33. Boston *Sunday Herald*, September 6, 1908.

34. Unsourced clipping, Harvard Theater Collection.

35. Nugent, "Marshall's," p. 317. The role of transvestism in racial as well as sexual identity, and their combination, is a theme that needs study. See "Black and White TV: Cross-Dressing the Color Line," Chapter 11 of Marjorie Garber's *Vested Interests: Cross-Dressing and Cultural Anxiety* (New York: Routledge, 1992), pp. 267–303.

36. *Variety*, May 13, 1911.

37. R.G. Doggett, "The Late Aida Overton Walker: The Artist," *Colored American Review* (January 1916): 17.

38. *Dramatic Mirror*, May 8, 1911.

39. August 3, 1912.

40. *Variety*, August 9, 1912.

41. *Variety*, August 7, 1914, p. 15; and *Variety*, May 8, 1914, p. 14.

42. *New York Times*, October 12, 1914, p. 9; and *Variety*, October 17, 1914.

43. *New York Times*, October 27, 1914, p. 5.

44. Kellner, *'Keep A-Inchin' Along,'* pp. 23, 26.

45. Quoted by Helen Armstead-Johnson, "Some Late Information on Some Early People," *Encore: American and Worldwide News* 4 (June 23–July 4, 1975): 52.

46. Quoted in Henry T. Sampson, *Blacks in Blackface: A Source Book on Early Black Musical Shows* (Metuchen, N.J.: Scarecrow, 1980), p. 134.

47. *Pittsburgh Leader*, May 11, 1906.

48. Doggett, "Late Aida Overton Walker," p. 17.

49. Roger Lane, *William Dorsey's Philadelphia and Ours: On the Past and Future of the Black City in America* (New York: Oxford University Press, 1991), p. 332.

# Florence Mills

Florence Mills, the leading black American musical comedy singer and dancer of the Jazz Age and the Harlem Renaissance, was born January 25, 1896, in Washington, D.C., to John Winfree and Nellie (Simons) Winfree. She died from paralytic ileus and peritonitis in New York City on November 1, 1927.

Born in slavery in Amherst County, Virginia, the Winfrees migrated to Washington from Lynchburg because of economic depression in the tobacco industry where both were employed. They settled first in a middle-class neighborhood on K Street, where Florence was born, but were soon forced to move to Goat Alley, one of the capital's most poverty-stricken, unhealthy, and crime-ridden black slums. John Winfree worked sporadically as a day laborer and Nellie Winfree took in laundry to keep their family together. Both were illiterate, and even in a city with unusual opportunities for people of color, their prospects and futures were limited.

"Baby Florence," however, demonstrated early her extraordinary gifts for singing and dancing, and as young as age three appeared at local theater amateur hours, where she won prizes. She was even invited to entertain the British ambassador, Lord Poncefote, and his guests. The child received public recognition that no doubt contributed to her developing sense of self-worth, and she became an important source of her family's income, which imbued her with a profound sense of responsibility for those around her.

The high point of Mills's childhood occurred in 1903 when she appeared as an extra attraction in the road company production of Bert Williams and George Walker's *Sons of Ham*, where she sang "Miss Hannah from Savannah." She was taught the song by Aida Overton Walker, the great cakewalk dancer and ragtime singer who had sung it in the original show. Walker was a beautiful, sophisticated, and highly talented star who took time with a ghetto child, thereby becoming Mills's mentor and role model. Walker demonstrated that blacks with ability and determination could find a successful vocation in entertainment.

As a result of her abilities, Mills was hired at about age eight by the traveling white vaudeville team of Bonita and Hearn, entertainers who used her as a singing and dancing "pickaninny" in their routine. Mills may well have felt both gratitude for the opportunity to work on the stage and support her family as well as resentment at the crude exploitation.

At age fourteen, Mills and her sisters Maude and Olivia organized their own traveling song-and-dance act as the Mills Sisters. They played the East Coast colored vaudeville houses and received good notices in the black press for their lively performances. Sometimes dressed in male attire, Florence Mills specialized in traditional ballads and the popular tunes of the day. In 1912 she contracted a brief marriage with James Randolph.

Just before World War 1, Mills found herself in Chicago weary of long hours, low pay, and the difficult traveling conditions all blacks faced. She decided to move from vaudeville to cabaret and through Ada "Bricktop" Smith obtained a job at the notorious Panama Cafe on State Street. In the heart of the South Side's honky-tonk and red-light district, the Panama was a black and tan club well known for sexual liaisons across the color line.

With Bricktop, Cora Green, and occasionally others, Mills formed the Panama Trio, a singing group with the legendary Tony Jackson on piano. This was an exciting time in Chicago: the city was the center of black migration from the rural South, and the white gangsters who controlled the cabarets in the black community fostered the new jazz music and an open social environment. Respectable people, both black and white, however, perceived the Panama as a center of vice, and it was finally closed down.

Mills returned to vaudeville and joined the Tennessee Ten, a traveling black show then on the Keith circuit. A member of the troupe was Ulysses "Slow Kid" Thompson, an acrobatic, tap, and "rubber legs" dancer of considerable skill. Born in Arkansas in 1888, Thompson had spent his life in various circuses, carnivals, medicine, and minstrel shows. He and Mills became romantically involved, were married and established a devoted relationship that lasted until her death.

The connection with Thompson and the success of the Tennessee Ten brought Mills closer to the center of show business than she had been in cabaret and vaudeville. She was singing at Barron's Club in Harlem when she received an offer that moved her into public notice and the front rank of black entertainers. It was the opportunity to replace Gertrude Saunders as the lead in *Shuffle Along*.

*Shuffle Along* opened off-Broadway in New York in the Spring of 1921. Music and lyrics were by Noble Sissle and Eubie Blake and the book by Flournoy E. Miller and Aubrey Lyles. It was an instantaneous and total hit. Actually, there was nothing new about *Shuffle Along*: similar shows had existed in the black entertainment world for years. What was new was the discovery by white America of the zesty abandon of jazzy music and fast, high-stepping black dancing. Langston Hughes believed *Shuffle Along* even initiated the Harlem Renaissance and inaugurated the decade when "the Negro was in vogue."

## Mills Presented to National Audience as Singer and Dancer

Besides reintroducing blacks into mainstream musical theater and setting the rhythmic beat for the Roaring Twenties, *Shuffle Along* presented Mills to a national audience. Now twenty-six years old, she was a dainty woman, five-feet-four, never weighing much more than one hundred pounds, bronze colored with beautiful skin texture. She moved deftly and in her strange high voice sang "I'm Simply Full of Jazz" and "I'm Craving for That Kind of Love."

The critics could never quite describe Mills's voice with its curious breaks, soft accents, sudden molten notes, and haunting undertones. Bird-like and flute-like were among the reviewers' frequently-used adjectives. It was Mills's dancing, however, and the dancing in all the black shows spawned by *Shuffle Along* during the 1920s that completely stunned audiences. The jazz rhythms, accelerated pace, skilled precision, intricate steps, and uninhibited movement brought dance rooted in African-American folk culture to white audiences eager to break loose from restrained and respectable convention.

Mills's performances were memorable, too, for her charismatic effectiveness in presentation. Demure and modest personally and in her private life, on stage she was assured, vivacious, and as capable of intimate mutual interaction with her audiences as a black preacher. With her fey and fragile appearance she could be intense as well as melancholy, impudent as well as communicating pathos, risqué without being vulgar. Mills's popularity, however, did not mean race and racism were no longer realities; Irving Berlin said if he could find a white woman who could put over a song like Mills, he would be inspired to write a hit a week.

Anticipating the fad for black entertainment and entertainers, Lew Leslie, a white promoter, hired Mills and Kid Thompson to appear nightly after *Shuffle Along* at the Plantation Club, a remodeled night spot over the Winter Garden Theatre. The Plantation's decor included an imitation log cabin, a chandelier in the form of a watermelon slice, and a black mammy cooking waffles. Featuring Mills, the revue itself was a constellation of black talent: Will Vodery's orchestra, Johnny Dunn's cornet, Edith Wilson's double-entendre songs, and visiting performers like Paul Robeson.

The Plantation, as Thompson pointed out, was "the first high-class colored cabaret on Broadway" (Thompson, 320). It drew fashionable white clientele and helped create an accepting atmosphere for things Negro, though old stereotypical images died hard. Florence Mills left *Shuffle Along* to work full-time for Leslie, a mutually beneficial relationship that lasted throughout her career. Also, the Plantation established the format for Mills's and Leslie's future shows: unconnected singing and dancing and musical acts in the vaudeville style with a touch of minstrelsy, and with all black performers.

Leslie soon realized his nightclub production could be turned into a Broadway show. The *Plantation Review* opened at the Forty-eighth Street Theatre on July 22, 1922. Sheldon Brooks presided as master of ceremonies and did a comedy routine; otherwise the bill was the same as the club's. Audiences and reviewers were impressed with the cast's genuineness and enthusiasm and the show's buoyant spontaneity, especially the breathtaking dancing. It was all "strutting and stepping and syncopating," said the *Tribune* on July 18.

The *Plantation Review* was important for Mills, for it was here she was first seen by the New York critics. They liked her energy and vitality, her sinuous dancing, her lack of self-consciousness. She sang Irving Berlin's "Some Sunny Day" and led the Six Dixie Vamps in a "Hawaiian Night in Dixie Land" dance number. There was some criticism of her song "I've Got What It Takes But It Breaks My Heart to Give It Away," not quite the sweet, crooning number that was her specialty. But there was real appreciation for the authenticity of black song and dance, and the realization that Negro portrayals by blackface performers like Al Jolson and Eddie Cantor were only imitations of the real thing

With *Shuffle Along* and the *Plantation Revue* behind her, Mills emerged as a preeminent black female performer with the potential of breaking into the racially restricted preserves of establishment show business. America was not ready for such a bold move, but the British impresario Sir Charles B. Cochran was looking for ready-made attractions for the London stage. He made arrangements to take the Plantation company to the Pavilion in the spring of 1923. There were immediate problems. British entertainers strenuously objected, citing the competition for jobs but reinforcing that fear with color prejudice. "Nigger Problem Brought to London" ran the headline of one of Hannen Swaffer's articles in the *Daily Graphic*.

The show Cochran devised was a hybrid called *Dover Street to Dixie*. A mild comedy with an all-English cast, "Dover Street" constituted the first half and was totally unrelated to "Dixie," the second half, which was Mills and the Plantation cast in a variation of their standard routines. Prejudice against the visiting black Americans had escalated, and demonstrations were expected in the theater on opening night. Tension intensified because "Dover Street" was a disaster and the audience was restless and bored.

"Dixie" began with a fast number by Vodery's orchestra, a troupe of frantic dancers, and Edith Wilson belting out a song. Then Mills quietly made her entrance and in a small plaintive voice sang "The Sleeping Hills of Tennessee." She electrified the audience. Any threat of opposition vanished, and for the rest of that night and the remainder of the show's run, she received a fervent ovation *before* every song she sang. This was a tribute, Cochran said, he had never known London to give to any other performer.

Perhaps the most significant consequence of *Dover Street to Dixie* was the serious attention it was paid by British intellectuals. The essence of their response was that Mills's performance and that of her fellow black Americans was art, even high art, and not mere entertainment. One reviewer made the astonishing statement that Mills was "by far the most artistic person London has ever had the good fortune to see" (Johnson, 198). Constant Lambert, musical director of Sadler's Wells Ballet, was deeply inspired by Mills and "Dixie" and began adapting jazz rhythms and techniques to his work, narrowing the separation between popular and "serious" music and infusing the latter with new vitality.

Upon her return to New York, Mills received an unusual invitation—to appear as an added attraction in the *Greenwich Village Follies* annual production opening that autumn at the Winter Garden. With Bert Williams's death the previous year there were now no blacks in mainstream shows. This was the first time a black woman was offered a part in a major white production. The *Follies* cast responded by threatening to walk out. Even after management smoothed their feelings, the white cast continued to resent Mills's participation.

### All-Black Musical Comedy Opens

Mills's talent and popularity brought an even more extraordinary opportunity. Florenz Ziegfeld offered her a contract to join the *Ziegfeld Follies*, the country's leading musical revue and the apex of show business success. But Mills turned Ziegfeld down. She decided to stay with Lew Leslie and create a rival show—but with an all-black cast. Bert Williams had broken the color barrier as an individual, she said, but she could best serve the race not by merely following him herself but by providing a venue for an entire company.

Mills wanted to break through Broadway's racial restrictions *and* to create an opportunity for black American entertainers to demonstrate the uniqueness of their culture. Her decision, and what she meant by it, was not lost on the black community. The *Amsterdam News* said:

> Loyalty of Florence Mills to the race as against temptation to become a renowned star of an Anglo-Saxon musical extrava-

ganza has saved for the stage and the race what promises to be one of the most distinctive forms of American entertainment ever created—an All-Colored revue. (Undated news clipping)

The first step toward Mills's goal was *From Dixie to Broadway*, which opened at the Broadhurst Theatre in October 1924. A black musical comedy in the heart of Broadway had been the dream of black entertainers since the turn of the century, and it was now realized. The price for this acceptance was a certain modification of the show's black elements by the whites who controlled the production, but the cast's superactive energy and expressive power broke through and the show was a critical and popular hit.

The cooperative effort between blacks and whites set a pattern for "crossovers" from the black entertainment milieu to the larger, more lucrative, and more influential white world. This resulted in a minimum of traditional "darky" stage imagery. This was an absence some critics missed, but the reviewers could only applaud the vital black American style and exuberant tempo now more free from racist stereotypes.

In *From Dixie to Broadway* Mills sang "Dixie Dreams," "Mandy, Make Up Your Mind," and the song that became her theme and trademark, "I'm a Little Blackbird Looking for a Bluebird"; behind the song's sentimentality Mills saw a subliminal message: "the struggle of a race" seeking satisfaction. Most critics thought the show's high point was its satirical jazz treatment of Balieffe's "March of the Wooden Soldiers," in which Mills led the male dancers.

Mills clearly dominated *From Dixie to Broadway* and the reviewers lauded her as "a slender streak of genius" and "an artist in jazz." Writing in the *New York Telegram and Evening Mail* on October 30, 1924, Gilbert W. Gabriel gives a fuller picture of the Florence Mills who captured Broadway, as well as revealing his inability to comprehend the distinctive black American elements in her art:

> This sensational little personality, slim, jaunty, strung on fine and tremulous wires, continues to tease the public's sense of the beautiful and odd. There is an impudent fragility about her, a grace of grotesqueness, a humor of wrists, ankles, pitching hips and perky shoulders that are not to be resisted. Her voice continues to be sometimes sweet and sometimes

further from the pitch than Dixie is from Broadway. She is an exotic done in brass.

After the show's road tour, Mills broke another racial barrier. On June 27, 1924, she was the first black woman to headline at "The Taj Mahal of Vaudeville," the Palace Theatre. On Broadway at Forty-seventh Street, the Palace was the country's premier variety theatre, and it was every entertainer's dream to play there. Other blacks had been in Palace programs, but as a headliner Mills received money, billing, the best dressing room, and courtesy from management—real and symbolic achievements for a black American woman.

Mills achieved her great goal of creating a major all-black revue, but she was destined never to return to Broadway. The new show was *Blackbirds*, and it opened at the Alhambra Theatre in Harlem after having been constructed at Plantation Club performances. After successful runs in Harlem and Paris, *Blackbirds of 1926* moved to London's Pavilion Theatre, opening September 26 and lasting for an impressive 276 performances, after which it toured the British provinces.

*Blackbirds* was an extraordinary hit. Mills sang "Silver Rose" and repeated "I'm a Little Blackbird." She was so popular she became to London what Josephine Baker was to Paris. The Prince of Wales saw *Blackbirds* more than twenty times and Mills played to him when he was in the theater. She and the cast were taken up by England's ultra-sophisticated "Bright Young People" and joined their outrageous parties in London, Oxford, and Cambridge.

Mills is mentioned in all the diaries of the period and even turns up as a character in Evelyn Waugh's *Brideshead Revisited*. It is likely she had an affair with the King's youngest son, the handsome, wild, and charming Prince George, who later became Duke of Kent. It was not only royalty and decadent aristocrats who were impressed, however; artists and intellectuals caught the infectious freedom and style of the black performers and the energizing tempo of their music and dance. "For the first time," exclaimed critic Arnold Haskell, "I was *seeing* true jazz."

Perhaps because she felt more secure in a less racially-prejudiced country or perhaps because the British public and press treated her more seriously than the American public and press did, Mills expressed her race consciousness more strongly in England than at home. At an exclusive dinner party where she was lauded by Sir Charles Cochran as a great artist, she ignored his personal tributes in her response and instead made a moving plea for black freedom. "I am coal black and proud of it," she announced at a fashionable soiree where there was some question about black and white seating arrangements *(Variety,* undated clipping).

Mills saw her work as a crusade on behalf of racial justice and understanding. She literally believed that every white person pleased by her performance was a friend won for the race. Her passion led her to drive herself without respite, and it broke her health. She left *Blackbirds* and after an unsuccessful attempt at a rest cure in Germany, sailed for New York. Her condition did not improve, however, and she entered the Hospital for Joint Diseases, where she died following an operation. She was thirty-one years old.

Mills was one of the most popular people in Harlem during the 1920s. Blacks understood that she had never forgotten her roots, that she never put on airs, that she affirmed over and over again the heritage—and the struggle—they shared together. In appreciation for everything she meant to them, the people of Harlem gave her the grandest funeral within their considerable power, an outpouring of affection and recognition, music and flowers, tears and drama.

On a cold November day in 1927 a congregation of five thousand, a choir of six hundred, and an orchestra of two hundred jammed Mother African Methodist Episcopal Zion Church on 137th Street. More than 150,000 people crowded the Harlem streets to glimpse the famous mourners and participate in a bit of history, but mostly to pay their own silent tributes and say good-bye to a sister they knew was their own. It is reported that a flock of blackbirds flew over the funeral cortege as it slowly made its way up Seventh Avenue toward Woodlawn Cemetery in the Bronx.

The public tributes were lavish. In an unprecedented editorial, *The New York Times* praised "the slim dancer who blazed the way" for others to follow (4 November 1927). George Jean Nathan called her "America's foremost feminine player" *(New York Telegram,* 16 April 1927). Theophilus Lewis said Mills "always regarded herself as our envoy to the world at large and she was probably the best one we ever had" ("Florence Mills, An Appreciation"). One London newspaper commented that if Mills had been a white woman she would have been acknowledged as one of the greatest artists of her time.

Except among the cognoscenti and in black folk legend, Mills did not achieve permanent fame. Plans for a memorial fizzled in disputes over money. There were no films or recordings to perpetuate her memory. The Great Depression of 1929 abruptly rang down the curtain on the vim and verve of the Jazz Age. Lew Leslie tried to continue the *Blackbirds* series, which was her dream for celebrating authentic black American performing art, but the effort faded without Mills's vibrant and vivacious presence.

Mills made her mark in several ways. *Shuffle Along* introduced jazz song and dance to Broadway musical theater. In *From Dixie to Broadway* she starred in a black revue built around female singing and dancing rather than traditional male blackface comedy. In *Blackbirds* she created a major show composed of vital black American music and movement. She helped minimize the "darky" element in show business while bringing special black qualities to her crossover numbers. Through it all Florence Mills was first and foremost a "race woman" proud of her heritage, uncompromising in her identity, and always using her artistry to build bridges to the white world in the hope of securing greater justice for her people.

## References

*Amsterdam News.* Undated clipping.

"Florence Mills. An Appreciation." *Inter-State Tattler*, 27 November 1927.

Johnson, James Weldon. *Black Manhattan.* New York: Knopf, 1930. 188–89, 196–201, 209–10, 217, 224. Photographs, pp. 198 and 199.

Logan, Rayford W. "Florence Mills." *Dictionary of American Negro Biography.* Edited by Rayford W. Logan and Michael R. Winston. New York: Norton, 1982. 440.

*New York Telegram and Evening Mail*, 30 October 1924, 16 April 1927.

*New York Times*, 4 November 1927.

New York *Tribune.*

*Variety.* Undated clipping.

*Florence Mills*

Reid, Anne Cooke. "Florence Mills." *Notable American Women, 1607–1950*. Vol. 3. Cambridge: Harvard University Press, 1971. 545–46.

Thompson, U.S. "Florence Mills." *Negro: Anthology by Nancy Cunard, 1931–1933*. London: Nancy Cunard and Wishard and Co., 1934. 320.

**Collections**

Reviews, programs, clippings, photographs, and other materials on Florence Mills are in the libraries of Columbia University. the Hatch-Billops Collection, Harvard University, Howard University, Yale University, the Museum of the City of New York, and the New York Public Library, including the Theatre Collection and the Performing Arts Research Center at the Schomburg Center for Research in Black Culture.

# "East of Broadway": Florence Mills at Aeolian Hall

Florence Mills (1896–1927),[1] the foremost African American woman musical comedy star of the Jazz Age, made one appearance as a serious concert singer. After a lifetime of obscurity in vaudeville and cabaret followed by sensational success on Broadway and in London musical theater, the "Harlem heroine went artistic," according to an article in the January 25, 1926, *New York World*. The occasion was a recital on Sunday evening, January 24, 1926, at Aeolian Hall on West 43rd Street in New York, (where Gershwin's "Rhapsody in Blue" premiered), part of a program of the International Composers Guild. Mills had made a name for herself in revues and nightclubs, but this was the first, and only, time she ventured "east of Broadway," as the *New York Evening Journal* of January 27, 1926, called it, to perform "among the highbrows."

Mills sang *Levee Land* at Aeolian Hall, a group of four songs written expressly for her in 1925 by William Grant Still (1895–1978). Mills and Still were acquainted at least from 1921, when he played the oboe in the pit orchestra of *Shuffle Along*, Noble Sissle and Eubie Blake's dazzling revue in which Mills came to stardom and which Verna Arvey, Still's wife, correctly called "a preparatory school for colored artists."[2] Born the year before Mills, Still was thirty-one years old in 1926. He played banjo in the *Dixie to Broadway* orchestra in 1924, where Mills had the lead and his friendship had deepened with Mills and her husband, Ulysses S. "Slow Kid" Thompson, the acrobatic dancer.

*Levee Land* was Still's first attempt to use African American culture as a basis for his music, as well as one of the very first efforts toward a symphonic treatment of jazz themes, "to lift jazz to the symphonic level," as Fannie Howard Douglass phrased it,[3] assuming that that needed to be done. In composing, Still had to overcome the ultramodern training he had received from Edgar Varese, Director of the International Composers Guild. The result was a suite for chamber orchestra with soprano solo and scored for two violins, woodwinds, tenor banjo, and percussion. It has never been published. This *Levee Land* of 1926 should not be confused with a composition of the same title Stili wrote in Los Angeles in 1957 as part of five suites called *The American Scene*.

Still taught Mills the *Levee Land* songs by rote, tapping them out repeatedly with one finger on the piano until she memorized them. Arvey says Mills did not, in fact, hear the basic harmonies until the first rehearsal with the orchestra.[4] She was a willing pupil, however, totally without conceit and unspoiled by her extraordinary commercial success. She elected with the concurrence of Lew Leslie, her manager, to appear at Aeolian Hall without payment. Eugene Goossens conducted the concert orchestra, and Mills, wearing a blue silk dress, sang the four Negro dialect songs "Levee Song," "Hey-Hey," "Croon," and "The Backslider." For the first time in her long career she was nervous, but she performed "in true and proper Broadway manner," the *Musical Courier* reported.[5]

The *New York World*'s reviewer wrote, "Curious and elemental were these songs by the brilliant young Negro composer, plaintive in part, blue, crooning and sparkling with humor, and Miss Mills gave them perfect interpretation. She sang them sensuously and lovingly, but she did more, she rolled her eyes here and she shrugged her shoulders there, and the audience squirmed excitedly."[6] It was a distinguished audience that observed and participated in these lapses in decorum. Arturo Toscanini was there along with George Gershwin, Carl Van Vechten, James Weldon Johnson, Walter White,[7] and Mrs. Otto H. Kahn.[8] There was standing room only. Mills was recalled several times by applause, and the enthusiastic audience made her repeat three of the four songs.

Paul Rosenfeld who wrote for *The Dial* was probably the most knowledgeable and sophisticated music critic who ever heard Florence Mills sing. He recalled her and the concert a year after her death in 1927, and his review needs to be quoted at length:

> There she stands, with her fragile pigeon-egg skull, swaying gently, and crooning, warbling, speaking in a voice whose like has not been heard. Larger, stronger, richer, mellower

voices have sounded off this platform and off the world's other stages. This one is tiny and delicate. But it has an infinitely relaxed, impersonal, bird-like quality: one knows there has been no other voice exquisite [sic] exactly like it. In Noah's ark, they said such and such a one sang like a bird, one remembers; remembering that the simile has also been revived from time to time in the course of the world. Still, it is probable that at no time has the application been neater. Here is the very thing, the bird sitting up on a little branch in springtime, caroling; with something of smothered anguish in its tone.[9]

Still agreed with the critics' praise. According to Arvey, "he felt as if he had found a co-creator, and as if the piece had been composed for chamber orchestra and Florence Mills, rather than for soprano and orchestra."[10] Mills died the next year. There is no indication she might again have considered singing serious music, but that the most popular black music comedy singer and dance of the day was capable of concert performance of high quality, as she demonstrated at Aeolian Hall, speaks for itself. *Levee Land* was never performed again. When it was once suggested, William Grant Still asked, "Where can we find another Florence Mills?"

## Notes

1. For a short biography see Richard Newman, "Florence Mills," in *Notable Black American Women*, ed. Jessie Carney Smith (Detroit: Gale Research, 1992): 752–56.

2. Verna Arvey, *In One Lifetime* (Fayetteville: University of Arkansas Press, 1984): 60.

3. Fannie Howard Douglass, "A Tribute to William Grant Still," *The Black Perspective in Music* 2, no. 1 (Spring 1974): 52.

4. Arvey, *In One Lifetime*, 69.

5. Quoted by Leon E. Thompson, "A Historical and Stylistic Analysis of the Music of William Grant Still and a Thematic Catalogue of His Works" (D.M.A. thesis, University of Southern California, 1966): 19.

6. Quoted by Robert B. Hans, ed., *William Grant Still and the Fusion of Cultures in American Music* (Los Angeles: Black Sparrow Press, 1975): 155.

7. The NAACP, of which Johnson and White were officers, thought the Mills concert important enough to issue a press release on January 26, 1926. There is a copy in the Gumby Papers at Columbia University.

8. There is an unsubstantiated rumor that Florence Mills and Otto Kahn were lovers.

9. Paul Rosenfeld, *By Way of Art: Criticisms of Music, Literature, Painting, Sculpture, and the Dance* (New York: Coward-McCann, 1928): 95–96.

10. Arvey, *In One Lifetime*, 69.

# The Lincoln Theatre: Once a Carnival of Merrymaking

The Metropolitan African Methodist Episcopal Church on Harlem's 135th Street is a low-slung building where colorfully robed choirs sing anthems on Sunday mornings. Few members of the congregation are aware, however, that for 20 years—shortly after the turn of the century through the Jazz Age of the 1920s—their church was the Lincoln Theatre, the center of black folk entertainment in New York City, a carnival of song, dance, drama and humor that perhaps has never been equaled. In fact, the choir's platform is the only stage in New York where the great Ma Rainey ever sang.

The Lincoln gloried in down-home entertainment, from bawdy humor to urban blues. Its predecessor, the Nickelette, was a gloomy, 167-seat, storefront nickelodeon presenting fifteen-minute segments of live entertainment on a makeshift stage. One early performer, around 1903, was "Baby Florence," the child singer and dancer who grew up to be Florence Mills, the electrifying star of Sissle and Blake's *Shuffle Along* and the first black woman to break into modern Broadway musical theater. Another early performer was Andrew Tribble, the best of the black female impersonators, who created the classic stage roles of Ophelia Snow and Lilly White.

The Nickelette was purchased in 1902 by Maria C. Downs, a Puerto Rican who enlarged the seating capacity to 300 and changed the name of the theater to the Lincoln, after Abraham Lincoln, whose face graced the building's facade. Harlem was then becoming an increasingly black community, but most Harlem theaters and movie houses continued to segregate blacks into upper balcony seats, if they were admitted at all. Under Downs' proprietorship, the Lincoln became a welcome center for both black entertainers and black audiences.

Her racially open policy was so successful that she had a larger building—the present one—constructed in 1915 with a seating capacity of 850. She offered a new film every day, six vaudeville acts that changed semiweekly, and a new four-act play by a resident black stock company every week. Top prices were 25 cents at matinees and 35 cents in the evenings.

While there was competition for performers and audiences among the Lincoln, the rival Lafayette on Seventh Avenue and Harlem's other theaters, those establishments aspired to higher forms of art. The Anita Bush Stock Company, which was based at the Lincoln before moving to the Lafayette and becoming the Lafayette Players, presented pioneering dramatic sketches like Billie Burke's *The Girl at the Fort* with cast members Charles Gilpin, who later played the lead in the Provincetown Players' *The Emperor Jones*, and Arthur "Dooley" Wilson, better known as Sam the piano player in *Casablanca*. But the Lincoln's claim to fame was the raucous and rowdy floor shows that people loved.

During its heyday, all the big names of black vaudeville appeared on its stage: Bessie Smith, Bert Williams, Alberta Hunter, Ethel Waters, Butterbeans and Susie. And names that are not so familiar but that conjure up images of a golden age of African-American entertainers: Florence Parham and the 7 Ginger Snaps, the Sheiks of Harlem, Bowman's Cotton Pickers, as well as shows with names like *Shake Your Feet*, *Creole Follies* and *Miss Dinah of 1923*.

The Lincoln was the New York City showcase of the black vaudeville circuit TOBA, the Theatre Owners' and Booking Association, an organization of black theaters that regularly carried black acts. Despite exploitation of long-suffering performers, who called the organization Tough on Black Asses, TOBA provided opportunities for employment when jobs were scarce and when travel for blacks in segregated America was perilous.

The fabled Ma Rainey, "Mother of the Blues," sang at the Lincoln in 1925 and 1926. Her traveling revue in '26 consisted of a five-piece band called the Georgia Jazz Hounds, a women's chorus of "swift, snappy, soothing songsters," and her adopted son Danny, who was billed as the "World's Greatest Juvenile Stepper." Ma herself, resplendent with gold teeth, ostrich plume fan, sequined black dress and necklace of gold coins, belted out the blues. But by the late 1920s, Harlem audiences, even at the Lincoln, were becoming too urbane for her earthy songs and countrified style.

That may not have been true for a particular group of patrons for whom the Lincoln was notorious. These were the "Sharpshooters," who occupied the balcony every day, passed gin bottles back and forth, joined in the songs, and made ribald overtures to the chorus girls. They commented freely and loudly on what was happening on stage, and their spontaneous remarks were often more clever than the comedians' jokes. No one interfered with the Sharpshooters, partly because they were astute critics whose faculties were refined to the point of excellence, and partly because it would have been physically dangerous to do so.

Langston Hughes, in his autobiography *The Big Sea*, tells of actor Jules Bledsoe's "sincere but unfortunate" attempt to bring art to the Lincoln. Bledsoe starred in a revival of Eugene O'Neill's *The Emperor Jones* in front of an audience more attuned to Ethel Waters singing "Shake That Thing." When the crazed emperor, hearing the Little Frightened Fears, started running half-naked through the forest, the Lincoln audience howled with laughter. "Them ain't no ghosts, fool!" the Sharpshooters shouted. "Why don't you come on out o' that jungle—back to Harlem where you belong?"

Bledsoe, "in the manner of Stokowski hearing a cough at the Academy of Music," stopped dead in his tracks, marched to the footlights, and proceeded to lecture his audience on manners in the theater. But the Sharpshooters—always more sophisticated than their detractors realized—were happy in their role of razzing the actors and involving themselves in their performances. The emperor continued his flight, the Sharpshooters continued their laughter, and, Hughes reported, "That was the end of *The Emperor Jones* on 135th Street."

The Lincoln should be remembered for more than its contribution to the dramatic arts. It also played a role in the popularization and preservation of the blues. In 1919 Mamie Smith, a "light-complexioned, heavy-hipped, heavy-voiced" singer, was at the Lincoln in a show called *Maid of Harlem*, in which she sang composer Perry Bradford's "Harlem Blues." Bradford had been trying without success for months to interest record companies in blues songs. He finally convinced a faltering company called Okeh to record "Harlem Blues" under the title "Crazy Blues."

Only because the white singing star Sophie Tucker couldn't make the date was Smith allowed to substitute and record her Lincoln Theatre hit. "Crazy Blues" was the first commercial recording of vocal blues by a black singer backed by a black band. It sold an incredible 75,000 copies in its first month and signaled the beginning of "race records," African-American popular music recorded for the African-American market.

By housing a live orchestra, the Lincoln also made a contribution to jazz. Don Redman, the alto sax player who made major contributions to jazz, first came to New York in 1923 for a two-week stint at the Lincoln with Billy Paige's Broadway Syncopators. Duke Ellington performed at the Lincoln with a group called the Everglades Orchestra in March 1925. He returned with the Washingtonians in May. Lucille Hegamin and her Sunny Land Cotton Pickers featured a young Russell Procope on clarinet in 1926. Fletcher Henderson, whose bands included some of the best-known musicians of all time, played at the Lincoln with his Roseland Orchestra in 1926. And one of the backers of Ma Rainey was a young Oran "Hot Lips" Page on cornet.

But if any one name is identified with the Lincoln, it is Thomas "Fats" Waller. He grew up in Harlem around the corner from the theater, which was strictly off-limits die to the strictures of his religious parents. That made the Lincoln all the more attractive, and after his first surreptitious visit, Waller was hooked. What entranced him was not the flickering images of the silent pictures, but the skills of Mazie Mullins, the house pianist, in creating atmosphere and background accompaniment for the changing moods of the films. Waller bought a ticket every day, sat near the pit, watched and listened, and ran home to imitate Mullins on the Waller family piano.

Mullins could hardly miss her regular young visitor in short pants since he already weighed over 200 pounds. She eventually invited him to sit with her at the keyboard, and he slyly suggested that if she wanted to take an occasional break, he would be willing to fill in. Downs allowed the substitution because the audience loved Waller's playing. When Mullins left the job in 1919, Waller was hired at $23 a week as her replacement. He was 15 years old.

Waller became even more interested in the Lincoln's organ, an instrument installed to accompany stage acts. During one Saturday matinee, the school kids started yelling, "Make it rock, Fats!" That was all the encouragement he needed. His reputation soon spread through the community, and the great Harlem stride pianist James P. Johnson went to the Lincoln to hear Waller play. Johnson was so impressed he took Waller on as a pupil, and Waller had the great fortune of learning from one of the all-time masters of jazz piano.

During the teens and 1920s, a steady stream of white show business writers, composers and band leaders joined the black audiences at the Lincoln, not to be entertained but to find new ideas and new tunes. George Gershwin and Irving Berlin, who spent many hours in Harlem theaters, were among them. More than one melody or dance step or comedy routine that originated with a black vaudeville act wound up in a white Broadway musical or as a hit song of the day without attribution or acknowledgments, and of course without royalties.

Unfortunately, the Lincoln was not fated to survive the economic consequences of the Great Depression of the 1930s. Though its faithful patrons resisted the new commercialized Tin Pan Alley songs and wanted only the old familiar material—so much so that more sophisticated black musicians referred to the Lincoln as the "Temple of Ignorance"—Downs sold the theater in 1929 to Frank Shiffman. He turned the theater into a movie house, and when that fell on hard times, he sold the building to a church.

Today the Lincoln is the only old building on the block. The busts of Abraham Lincoln are gone. On weekends the ladies of the church serve delicious meals of chicken, fish and ribs in what might have been the backstage dressing rooms where Bessie Smith and Florence Mills and Bert Williams waited to go on stage. There is no plaque to commemorate the history that was made here, and few remember that it is the only place in New York where Ma Rainey ever sang.

# Part III
# *Religion*

"The images, symbols, and attitudes of Christianity were the highest crystalizations of the Negro's will to live he has made in this country."

—Richard Wright

# The Paradox of Lemuel Haynes

Lemuel Haynes, as Professor James Melvin Washington has pointed out, defies easy classification. Haynes was the illegitimate child of a black father and white mother. He was a plowboy who composed poetry. He was a foot soldier in a freedom revolution that denied liberty to those most in need of it. He was an intellectual and wit on a rude frontier. He was a Calvinist in the deist and rationalist environment of Vermont. He was a Federalist when the country was turning to Jeffersonian Republicanism. He lived all his life in the white world, but his detractors did not hesitate to call him "nigger."

Professor Washington suggests Haynes' "very duality allowed him to see and experience the double-meanings of 'America.'" While Washington is referring specifically to the ambiguities of Haynes and race, paradox is a concept that goes some distance as a means for understanding much of Haynes' long and unusual life.

The facts of Lemuel Haynes' birth remain obscure. His mother was probably a Scottish servant in West Hartford, Connecticut named Alice Fitch. But she may have been a woman from a prominent Hartford family named Goodwin. His father was probably a local slave of "unmingled African extraction." But he may have been a black waiter in a Hartford hotel. What is clear is that neither parent wanted anything to do with the unwelcome result of their liaison across racial and class lines.

Brought up as an indentured servant in a pious, loving and supportive foster home, Haynes learned to be a farmer, but his intellectual curiosity led him to borrow books to read after work by the fireside. "By improving his evenings," as he put it, he became his own teacher of the larger world beyond rural eighteenth-century New England. We cannot know what he thought about what he read, but we do know his imaginative mind needed to express itself as well as to absorb. We have the result in early poems and writings which are remarkable not so much for their brilliance as for the fact they were created at all.

Haynes' indenture came to an end as the American Revolution was beginning. He enlisted as a Minuteman, marched out with the local militia at the Lexington alarm, and served with the Continental army at Roxbury and Ticonderoga. By itself this is hardly unusual; his neighbors did the same. What is unusual is that beyond the local patriotism Haynes saw a larger issue. Beyond the provincial impulse for independence he perceived a greater, more philosophically based, a logically and justly expanded idea of freedom.

Haynes painstakingly articulated his thoughts in an essay he called "Liberty Further Extended" in which, essentially, he used a theory of natural rights to argue for an enlargement of the spirit of the Revolution to encompass the millions of black slaves held in bondage. By their very nature revolutionary ideas once released often find their way to places they are not supposed to go. Haynes was neither the first nor the last African American to seize on the notion of natural rights. Only a few years later it would inform part of the thinking of Gabriel in his momentous but unsuccessful slave insurrection aimed at capturing Richmond and setting off a mighty movement of black self-liberation.

It would take nearly a century for enough of the rest of the country to catch up with Haynes' vision and actualize his dream. Writing of the Civil War, Bruce Catton said this concept of human freedom "is dangerous; it takes fire, like phosphorus, whenever it is exposed to the air, and the war was exposing it to the winds of heaven." The Revolutionary War may have exposed a freedom "further extended" to Haynes, but the new nation's incapacity to see what he saw led to a second, bloodier conflict.

Haynes was not an insurrectionist, but his treatise (unpublished until 1983), if not unique in its intellectual content, remains extraordinary given the limitations of its author, the circumstances of its composition, and the fact that the Abolitionist Movement, at least as generally perceived, was years away. Objectively, it may be necessary to re-think the history of anti-slavery protest and understand it was not only a white New England phenomenon but the daily struggle of unnumbered people of color.

Subjectively, there is the question of what was going on in the twenty-three-year-old mind of Lemuel Haynes. He grew up from

## The Paradox of Lemuel Haynes

infancy in a white family whose mother favored him over her own children. He lived all his life to date in a community, a church, and an army where, as far as we know, he was fully accepted. Yet as the author of a deeply-felt poem about the Battle of Lexington he called himself "a young Mollato," and his first sustained intellectual essay had as its central proposition: "That an *African*, or, in other terms, *that a Negro may Justly Chalenge, and has an undeniable right to his Liberty.*"

Lemuel Haynes, who had his liberty, was not questioning the accepted system of indentured servitude which, in fact, saved his life. He was himself a free man in a community of free men in a New England which knew about freedom. He had never seen the cruel chattel slavery system of the South where men and women and children of color were not people but livestock. But Haynes' essay is clearly more than the mental exercise of a developing mind.

He had certainly seen and known black slaves in New England. What did they mean to him? Despite his immediate milieu Haynes defined himself as a person of color, he identified with oppressed African Americans in permanent bondage, and the young soldier imaginatively envisioned the Revolution expanding to include more than his Connecticut friends and neighbors.

Haynes' duality or "twoness," to use DuBois's familiar term, gave him the ambivalent stance of the participant observer: his involvement, at least psychologically, was restricted by his "otherness" but at the same time his perspective was enhanced. "The double-meanings of 'America'" were clear to him. Haynes lived out his life within the confines of his culture, in the white world which was the only world he knew. But he never forgot, or was allowed to forget, that what he was determined who he was. This is his paradox.

Perhaps Haynes chose the isolation of Vermont for his ministry because on that frontier what restrained New Englanders politely and obliquely called "the peculiarity of his history" made less difference. Perhaps his adulation for George Washington owed as much to the fact that Washington freed his slaves as to the molding of Haynes' life as a soldier in Washington's army. Perhaps the best he could do was to speak out on occasion on behalf of "the poor Africans among us," his father's people, and blame slavery for their abject situation rather than "any distinction that the God of nature hath made in their formation."

At any rate Haynes' intellect and energy and life went at last into his ministry rather than into any involvement with or on behalf of people of African descent. But even that was no escape from American realities. When he was eased out after his long ministry to the Rutland church he tartly commented that "he lived with the people in Rutland thirty years and they were so sagatious that at the end of that time they found out that he was a nigger, and so turned him away."

Haynes was a faithful pastor and popular preacher and speaker and writer who could turn a memorable phrase. "Lord, we are so selfish we spoil everything we do," he prayed on one occasion. "Zion trembled when he fell," he said at Job Swift's funeral. "To be for him and not for another" sounds like Karl Barth. His ability to create good prose spilled over into his political discourses: "There is counterfeit gold, and counterfeit silver, counterfeit bills, and counterfeit men." There are indeed, but Haynes is not among them.

Haynes wrote in a variety of literary forms. After his youthful attempts at poetry, largely unsuccessful one must say, he seems to have abandoned it. His ministerial career required the constant preparation of sermons—5,500 at Rutland, including 400 funeral sermons. His patriotic political addresses were influenced by the homiletical style. An exception is *Mystery Developed*, his account of the Boorn case. While essentially a piece of reportage it has all the characteristics, as William Robinson points out, of a short story.

Haynes was finally a preacher, however, and his sermons both in form and content are characteristic of his day. We might note his prodigious memorization of Scripture (often slightly misquoted) and the problem of all Calvinist preachers: why call the elect to repentance? *Universal Salvation* preached in 1805, Haynes' most famous sermon, is remarkable for its satire, its brevity, and the fact that it was reprinted throughout the Northeast in over seventy editions until as late as 1865.

Some contemporary Universalist rebuttals to *Universal Salvation* charged that Haynes' sermon devastating to their cause was not the spontaneous reply Ballou Haynes claimed it to be, but a carefully and craftily premeditated attack. In either case it is a clever piece. The Haynes sermons we do have are written and

# The Paradox of Lemuel Haynes

formal; unfortunately they reveal little of the extemporaneous gifts of the great preacher Haynes was uniformly held to be. Perhaps, then, *Universal Salvation* is important not only as a successful Calvinist rejoinder to Universalism but as a clue to Haynes' fluency, wit, and power in the pulpit.

Haynes was respected for his learning and piety, for being a good shepherd, and for his preaching and writing, but he was remembered for his wit. The house of his fellow minister Ashbel Parmlee was destroyed by fire. Haynes asked Parmlee if he had lost his sermon manuscripts, and hearing that he had, commented, "Well, don't you think they gave more light than they ever had done before?" Haynes felt his children were indolent except for his eldest son and namesake. Lemuel, Junior, Haynes explained, was an Arminian believing in the efficacy of works, while his other children were true Calvinists, sure that their faith alone would support them.

Perhaps Haynes' best line came when he inadvertently wandered into a hotel dining room where a group of local supporters were celebrating Andrew Jackson's election to the presidency. At their friendly insistence Haynes joined them in a glass of wine, proposed a toast—"Andrew Jackson, Psalm 109, verse eight"—and went on his way. Only later did someone look up the passage and discover that it read: "Let his days be few and let another take his office."

Except as a black soldier in the American Revolution Haynes' place in history has never been sure, though over the years he appears from time to time in books and articles. The reason is probably his own decision—if decision it was—to remain in the white world he never made but was the only one he knew. A number of historic "firsts" can be and have been ascribed to him: M.A. from Middlebury, minister to white congregations, etc. It should be said that while Haynes was probably the first African American ordained by a mainstream Protestant church in this country, the slaves had their own religious leaders, George Lisle was preaching to black Baptists in Georgia during Haynes' lifetime, and the Roman Catholic church in Latin America had ordained blacks and men of mixed blood to the priesthood for years.

In some ways Haynes is typically American and his story incorporates elements of American mythology: the Horatio Alger rise from obscurity, the frontier. And there are hints of larger mythic themes: the abandoned child, the permanent exile. But it is Haynes' double-consciousness, as DuBois calls it, the permanent condition of black Americans, that defines him and provides whatever understanding of this anomalous man we are likely to have. Plural identity is less a contradiction than a paradox, a truth within opposites.

The child deserted by both his black father and white mother was named Lemuel, "Belonging to God." In the Bible that meant so much to him, Lemuel is an unknown king. So Lemuel Haynes remains. In the bringing together of all his known writings he speaks again after a long silence for himself.

# Black Bishops:
# Some African-American Old Catholics and Their Churches

> "I know all about bishops.
> They move diagonally."
>
> —A Sunday School Child
> Emmanuel Church (Episcopal)
> Boston, Mass., 1989

### I. The African Orthodox Church

In his 1934 valedictory address relinquishing the primacy of the African Orthodox Church (but retaining the position of Patriarch-Archbishop of New York), George Alexander McGuire briefly recounted his autobiography, including his religious labors from 1889 to 1919 among what he called "other groups."[1] But then came 1919, a momentous year in several respects.

On July 27, a date between violent race riots in Washington and Chicago, Marcus Garvey established the Universal Negro Improvement Association's (UNIA) Liberty Hall in the old Metropolitan Baptist Church at 120 West 138th Street in Harlem and called a mass meeting to dedicate the new building. The day before, W.A. Domingo had written in Garvey's newspaper the *Negro World*: "To say that because Negroes are the victims of organized race first sentiment on the part of white people they should not organize along lines of race first to defend themselves is to inferentially condone their present oppression and counsel meek submission to its perpetuation."[2]

Reflecting on this 1919 turning point, McGuire recalled, "Down into the Valley of Decision I went with my race." McGuire, of course, was not the first black person to establish a church free from white domination. In the United States beginning with unknown root doctors and slave preachers through Richard Allen and Absalom Jones and beyond; in Africa with its 6,000 independent churches; and indeed wherever psychological and cultural and institutional colonialism has oppressed people of color, rebels and resisters have said, "Down into the Valley of Decision I went with my race." Reuben Spartas, the Ugandan nationalist and African Orthodox Church (AOC) bishop vowed two things: "to go to hell, jail or die for the redemption of Africa" and to found a church where Africans could be, in his telling phrase, "free in their own house."[3]

In their struggles for independence, however, not many African-American religious bodies or leaders have held an episcopal view of the church. That is, few have sought or claimed legitimacy by having their clergy ordained and their bishops consecrated in the historic apostolic succession as that tradition is understood, preserved, and practiced (albeit with real differences) in the Roman Catholic, Eastern Orthodox, Oriental Orthodox, Anglican, Swedish Lutheran, and Old Catholic (Utrecht) Churches.

To say it most simply, for these churches apostolic succession refers to the divinely established system of setting apart a sacerdotal priesthood which derives its authority and legitimacy from an unbroken line of bishops which, it is believed, can be traced back to the apostles themselves. By virtue of being the very successors to the apostles these bishops inherit from them the mandate to rule the church. Adherents to this system, perhaps it is unnecessary to say, consider priests and bishops legitimate in office and function only if they had been ordained in a proper line of succession.[4]

There are some black individuals and groups, however, for whom the authenticity of orders thus defined has been a vital issue. It is generally not a matter of much interest in Methodism, where the office of bishop is administrative and pastoral rather than historically validating, but in the African Methodist Episcopal (AME) General Conference of 1884, Bishop John Mifflin Brown preached the Quadrennial Sermon on "The Priesthood" in which he stated that episcopacy is "an order and not merely an office.... Our church theoretically and practically maintains the apostolic succession through our Bishops."[5]

The Conference reacted immediately, overwhelmingly, and, one is tempted to say, almost violently, with a resolution repudiating apostolic succession as a dogma totally "foreign and repugnant" to African Methodism, and literally threatening anybody who expressed contrary views with a breach of discipline.[6] The matter was not entirely laid to rest, though. In 1885 Bishop Henry McNeal Turner stated that "Episcopacy furnished the assurance of an unbroken unity, from Jesus Christ through the apostles by a line of authentic Bishops," but added with political pragmatism if not total conviction, "the Bishopric is an office and not a divine order." In 1903 James A. Davis surveyed the entire history of episcopacy to argue the case for the legitimacy of Richard Allen's consecration.[7]

George Freeman Bragg, that stalwart defender of the Episcopal Church, once preached a sermon against the AMEs, claiming that Methodists do not have real bishops, but the white Episcopalians who, he believed, did have real bishops, repeatedly failed to make him one even though he defended their exclusive right to do so.[8] He once even proposed the consecration of a colored bishop for Episcopalians in Boley and the other all-Negro communities in Oklahoma.[9]

To speak of the Episcopal Church brings up the stormy history of that denomination's conflict between wanting to evangelize freedmen without permitting either the substance or symbol of equality. A variety of schemes was proposed over the years to provide for African-American parishes, priests, and bishops—all separate from and subordinate to the white church. There was the Maryland Plan, which Bragg supported, introduced in the General Convention of 1874 by Bishop William Rollinson Wittingham.[10] It called for separate missionary districts for "races and tongues," which meant it would be conveniently possible to segregate foreign immigrants as well as Negroes.

Opponents of a plan for missionary districts did not propose racial integration, but, rather, a system of black suffragan bishops to minister to black folks within white diocesan jurisdictions. And there was the Arkansas Plan of Bishop William Montgomery Brown, which called for a separate black episcopal church—an idea, I am convinced, which influenced George Alexander McGuire who was Brown's Archdeacon for Colored Work at the time.

There needs to be a comprehensive study of the controversy over the racial episcopate in the Episcopal Church, the resources for which exist in local and national denominational records. There needs, too, to be a biography of "Bad" Bishop Brown, the last bishop tried for heresy in the Episcopal Church, who went on to become a Marxist as well as an Old Catholic and who repudiated his earlier racism.[11] Brown's personal library went to Kenyon College, but I believe his personal papers remain in his Galion, Ohio, home—unoccupied since Brown died in 1937.[12]

Unlike Bragg, McGuire left the Episcopal Church and in 1921 presided over the formation of the African Orthodox Church. He believed it important that he become a bishop, he said, so that "the Negro race, for so long a time without it, may at length have the blessing of its own autonomous Orthodox Faith with a ministry possessed of Apostolic Descent."[13] McGuire was Titular Bishop of Ethiopia in the UNIA where Garvey, in imitation of the practice of the British Empire, bestowed titles on high officials. However much a Garveyite McGuire may have been at the time, though, he knew the episcopate was not Garvey's to grant.

McGuire therefore sought consecration from ecclesiastical bodies which maintained the succession. The Episcopalians and Roman Catholics rebuffed him, but the Russian Orthodox were promising and turned him over to their so-called English Department in New York, a group of former Episcopalians. Two of these became associated with McGuire for a time: Fr. Antony and Archimandrite Patrick.

Fr. Antony, or Robert Hill, was released by the Russians to work with McGuire and the fledgling AOC, which he did, but he soon decamped to form his own schismatic group.[14] Patrick, whose name in the world was James G. Mythen, had had an extraordinary career as secretary of a men's league for women's suffrage as well as secretary of a group called the Protestant Friends of Irish Freedom.

It is unfortunate that McGuire and the Russians could not work out a satisfactory arrangement. It they had, McGuire and his followers would have become affiliated with a great historic church that might well have provided a secure home. Also, it is fascinating to conjecture how Russian Orthodoxy might have developed differently in this country with a black component. But the Russians undoubtedly required oversight by their bishops—too high a price for McGuire since the whole point of his black church was autocephalous freedom and self-determination.[15]

McGuire turned at last, as do we, to the Old Catholics. Several definitions are necessary at the outset. The first is the distinction between the historic Old Catholic Churches of Europe, centered in Utrecht, Holland, and those churches in the United States and elsewhere called Old Catholic. The European churches were formed by Roman Catholics who left that communion following what they believed to be the non-historical and un-Biblical pronouncements of the Vatican Council of 1869–1870. These separatists received the episcopate from Jansenist sympathizers in Holland who had preserved the apostolic succession outside of Rome. There is no doubt about the authenticity of the orders of these Old Catholic churches which united in the Union of Utrecht in 1889.

Many of the American churches labelled Old Catholic derive their orders, or claim they do, in some fashion, from Utrecht. Utrecht, however, does not recognize any of these bodies. The only canonically recognized Old Catholic body in the United States is the Polish National Catholic Church. Also, a number of American Old Catholic bodies derive their orders, or believe they do, from various other, primarily Eastern, churches. While these claims must be examined on a case-by-case basis, most of these churches are not acknowledged by their ecclesiastical parents as legitimate children.

The term "Old Catholic" for these bodies is thus inappropriate if not incorrect. But Old Catholic is the generic term in common usage, and, for convenience, I perpetuate the error by using it here.

Apostolic succession depends upon an uninterrupted line of bishops. In this department American Old Catholics excel: there are bishops wherever one looks and everybody seems to be one. They are, in fact, *episcopi vagantes*, "wandering bishops," "bishops at large," bishops without any particular jurisdiction or authority or recognition. *Episcopi vagantes* are a historic phenomenon, men fully consecrated but without a diocese for some reason: expulsion during religious controversies, displacement by war, the inhospitality of Muslims. The modern phenomenon is quite different, however, in that their consecrators are well aware from the beginning that these supposed overseers often have no more than paper churches, imaginary jurisdictions, and mental prelacy.

In addition to their prolific production of shepherds without sheep, *episcopi vagantes* have a pathetic history of pretentious titles, overlapping jurisdictions, and grossly inflated statistics; jealousies, disputes, defections, anathemas, and schisms; false names and mail-order degrees. Beyond the harmless delusions of playing church, however, there are, too often, more serious cases of alcoholism, pornography, and misappropriated money. George Alexander McGuire was a person of undisputed integrity and probity, but it was to this nether world of wildcat churches and disaffected churchmen he descended to obtain the apostolic succession he believed was necessary to legitimize a church and its priesthood for his race.

McGuire was consecrated on September 28, 1921, in the Church of Our Lady of Good Death, Chicago, by the notorious *episcopus vagans* Joseph René Vilatte, a man, it must be said, who personified ecclesiastical irresponsibility. Vilatte was assisted by the Rev. Carl A. Nybladh, a deposed Episcopal priest who had been consecrated earlier by Vilatte as head of the Swedish American Church, a virtually non-existent body.[16]

Vilatte's own episcopacy as Exarch and Metropolitan of the American Catholic Church (essentially a one-man sect) came from the hands of Mar Julius I (Antonio F.X. Alvarez) of the Independent Catholic Church of Ceylon, Goa, and India, a small breakaway Roman Catholic group with orders from the West Syrian Jacobite Church of Antioch, a church of undisputed historicity and authority whose apostolic succession probably antedates Rome's.

Vilatte's consecration was reportedly authorized by a special mandate of the patriarch, Peter Ignatius III. In McGuire's words, "Thus the African Orthodox Church derived its apostolic succession and became episcopal in government and polity; and while it is autonomous and independent, it aspires to be recognized as an integral portion of the Holy Catholic and Apostolic Church."[17] Unfortunately, the Syrian Orthodox Church does not recognize Vilatte, and one must assume the authenticity of McGuire's consecration either by a mechanistic view of apostolic succession or by an appeal to the obvious sincerity of his intentions and the fact that he headed a real as opposed to an imaginary church.

What work needs to be done on this, the most significant African-American Old Catholic Church and its founding patriarch? Most importantly, we need a full-scale biography of McGuire and a comprehensive history of the denomination. There are lacunae in our knowledge of McGuire's life. His early ministry in three important black Episcopal parishes in this country—Richmond, Cincinnati, and Philadelphia—has never been examined, for example. Are there sources? We all know by now that with persistence, informed conjecture, and luck a great amount of supposedly lost history can be recovered.

Roger Lane's brilliant social and intellectual history, *William Dorsey's Philadelphia and Ours: On the Past and Future of the Black City in America*, indicates that among Dorsey's hundreds of scrapbooks and biographical files preserved at Cheyney State University are clippings from the turn of the century on the young McGuire when he was rector of St. Thomas's Episcopal Church, perhaps the most elite black congregation in Philadelphia. Of two clippings Lane quotes, one reports McGuire's defense of lynching by blaming black "brutes" for the crime of alleged rape. Another singles out McGuire as an early and prominent advocate of African colonization.[18]

The later McGuire needs to be recognized as one of the major actors on the stage of black nationalism in the 1920s. He was apparently the first in this century, for example, to use the term "Uncle Tom" as a symbol of Negro subservience and servility.[19] This period is now well documented by Robert A. Hill's *The Marcus Garvey and Universal Negro Improvement Association Papers*. The first four volumes deal with the formative years to 1922 and describe in detail McGuire's intense and complex involvement with Garvey and the Garvey movement. Volume Five, covering September 1922 to August 1924, lists nearly 100 citations to McGuire in the index.[20]

To turn to the AOC itself, there are studies by Arthur Terry Thompson, Gavin White, Randall K. Burkett, and Richard Newman, but these all need to be brought up to date. The early schism led by Bishop Reginald Grant Barrow (father of the first prime minister of Barbados), a second schism in 1937, and the unprecedented reunion and reconciliation in 1965 under Bishops Gladstone St. Clair Nurse and Richard Robinson need to be researched and written in detail. The AOC's consecrations need documenting, including Bishop Nurse's elevation in 1962 of Francis Arthur Vogt, a white man, for mission work among whites on Long Island.[21]

The work of updating has begun in an excellent article by the Rev. Dr. Warren C. Platt in *Church History* (1989) entitled "The

African Orthodox Church: An Analysis of Its First Decade," an essay which draws upon the reprint edition of *The Negro Churchman* published by Kraus-Thompson in 1977 to document the church's first years. Platt is currently preparing a detailed account of a visit to services at the AOC's Holy Cross Pro-Cathedral for the "Church Review" section of *Anglican and Episcopal History*. Again, the sources for this work exist. Randall Burkett discovered in M.S. Stuart's *An Economic Detour: A History of Insurance in the Lives of Negroes* a biography of Bishop Robert Arthur Valentine (of the Barrow schism) since he happened also to be vice president of the Victory Mutual Life Insurance Company.[22]

Platt's extensive utilization of *The Negro Churchman* demonstrates the imperative need to locate and preserve and make available the AOC's scarce and ephemeral publications. A complete run of *The Negro Churchman* was unknown, for instance, until the late Bishop Nurse mentioned to me many years ago that he had a personal set. There are other titles. Volume one, number one, of *The Voice of the Patriarch* was issued in March 1934; were there others? *The African Orthodox Churchman* was a bimonthly published in New York in 1940; where are there copies? The Schomburg Center holds copies of several issues from 1941 and 1942 of *The Orthodox Messenger; The Voice of Washington Heights*, "Official Organ of the Southern Jurisdiction of the African Orthodox Church"; are there other issues in other institutions? I understand the Rev. Harold Furblur of Boston currently edits a serial called *The Trumpet*; who has seen it? The AOC in California publishes *Expression* occasionally. Are copies saved by anyone? Also, is there a collection anywhere of the various periodicals issued by the African Orthodox Church in South Africa?

This is not the place to speak in detail of the AOC in Africa except to say that the extensive spread of the church there, the adherence of hundreds of thousands of members, and its unexpected acceptance by the Greek Orthodox Communion makes it one of the most important religious bodies on the continent. George Shepperson was among the first (as usual) in noting the significance of McGuire and the AOC for the emergence of independent African churches, a part of the still largely unrecognized influence of African-American race consciousness on the rise of African nationalism. Shepperson's seminal article in the *Journal of African History* in 1960 is the foundation for understanding this untold story. More sources will become available with the publication of the Africana volumes of the Garvey Papers. Also, there is much unmined (and untranslated) material in Greek Orthodox missionary reports and other publications.

Perhaps the most important resource here are the papers of Bishop Daniel William Alexander which are now in the Pitts Theology Library at Emory University in Atlanta. I will mention that I came across these papers stored in a chicken coop in Kimberley, South Africa, in 1971, and that Robert A. Hill later negotiated their sale to Emory with the purchase price returning to the South African church. A careful guide has been prepared to the 19 boxes and 235 folders at Pitts by Anita K. Delaries, the former curator. The present curator, Jackie W. Ammerman, informs me that the papers have been used by several scholars and researchers as well as consulted by current members of the AOC in this country.[23]

One person who has used Alexander's papers is Prof. Morris R. Johnson of Miami-Dade Community College who completed in 1992 at Howard University a doctoral dissertation on "Archbishop Daniel William Alexander and the Rise of the African Orthodox Church, South Africa, 1925–1970: A Study in Race, Religion and Reformist Nationalism." Another is Prof. Michael West who is interested in the AOC as a component of the Ethiopianism which played a role, he argues, in the emergence and formation of a middle class in Southern Rhodesia, now Zimbabwe, the subject of his 1990 Harvard dissertation. In November 1991 West read a paper on "The African Methodist Episcopal Church and the African Orthodox Church in Colonial Zimbabwe, 1927–1935" at the African Studies national meeting in St. Louis. This month (May 1992) he is scheduled to present "Ethiopianism and the State in Zimbabwe" at a conference in Copenhagen co-sponsored by the Institute for Church History at the University of Copenhagen and the Institute for Commonwealth Studies in London.[24]

West has not only utilized the AOC papers at Emory, he has located relevant correspondence in the national archives of Zimbabwe. In 1925 people from Southern Rhodesia and Nyasaland (now Zimbabwe and Malawi), not unlike others, read about the AOC in Garvey's *Negro World* which was illegally smuggled into the continent. They wrote McGuire, who put them in touch with Alexander in South Africa. The Zimbabwe archives contain correspondence among Alexander, those interested in forming a church, and government officials.[25] Every research project turns up previously unknown materials.

The most interesting contemporary developments in the AOC in this country are taking place in California. A politically active, racially mixed group of men and women had gathered around Alice McLeod Coltrane, widow of John Coltrane, the great jazz saxophonist. Even before his death, John Coltrane attracted a large cult following which venerated him as a saintly if not salvific figure.[26] The Alice Coltrane group added a social service program of free food for poor people which they financed by soliciting donations in the San Francisco airport.

Following a break with Alice Coltrane, the group was recruited to the AOC by the Rev. William Green, a representative of Archbishop G. Duncan Hinkson of the AOC's Jurisdiction of the West, which, until this time, consisted solely of Hinkson's own parish in Chicago. Now retired, Archbishop Hinkson was also a practicing gynecologist. The Coltrane disciples were organized into several churches, and clergy (some of them white) were ordained.[27]

The Rev. Franzo W. King was consecrated bishop on May 6, 1984, by Hinkson, assisted by a Bishop Ajari of the St. Avvakum Old Orthodox Church in San Francisco (whom Hinkson had consecrated the day before). A black man with Rastafarian interests, King is a jazz musician who had been, like his mother, a Pentecostal preacher. His mother is Phyllis Prudhomme, founding director of the Brighter Day Theological Seminary.

Under Bishop King's paternal leadership, the church combines Old Catholic orders, identification with McGuire, sympathetic consciousness of Garvey and the church's black nationalist origins and UNIA connections, a California-style communitarianism, and religious veneration of John Coltrane who has been canonized as a saint. Especially active are the Sisters of Compassion, under the Rev. Mother Marina King and their patron saint John Coltrane, who perform various charitable functions, including operation of "prayer and information" booths at both San Francisco International and Chicago's O'Hare airports.[28]

This surprising turn of events calls for full and careful reportage. The numbers, the activism, and an apparently charismatic bishop may mean that the AOC, in true American fashion, has a whole new and different life ahead of it in California. Meanwhile, on the east coast, the church seems to be in decline. Although it retains a positive identification with its racial heritage (and canonized George Alexander McGuire in 1983), it never managed to participate in or appeal to the heightened black consciousness of the past twenty years.

The AOC's founding has been set in the larger context of African-American messianism by Elias Farajajé-Jones whose 1986 thesis at the University of Bern has been published as *In Search of Zion: The Spiritual Significance of Africa in Black Religious Movements*.[29] While the formative period of the church's history is of undoubted interest because it was a manifestation of black religious and cultural nationalism, the AOC is also a continuing institution. This means it deserves study not only because it is an unusual and atypical expression of African-American religion, but also because it continues to serve the people of the black community.

## II. The African American Catholic Congregation

The most significant contemporary black Old Catholic bishop is the Rev. George Augustus Stallings, Jr., of the African American Catholic Congregation or Imani Temple based in Washington, D.C.[30] Stallings' church is the first to split from the Roman Catholic Church in this country since the Polish National Catholic Church was formally organized in 1904, a schism also based on ethnicity.[31]

Stallings was born a Roman Catholic in New Bern, N.C., on March 17, 1948. Educated at the North American College in Rome, whose rector was James Hickey, he was ordained in 1974.[32] At St. Theresa of Avila's Church in Washington, an African-American parish, he became known for flamboyant preaching, incorporating African and Afro-American influences into the liturgy, gospel music, a charismatic personality, and increasing the church's membership from 200 to 2,000 during his twelve-year pastorate.[33] Half of the 100,000 Roman Catholics in the District of Columbia are black, although most priests are white.[34]

Stallings made money preaching at revival services outside the diocese, funds he apparently used to buy and refurbish in luxurious style a house in Anacostia. He called it Augustus Manor and lived there instead of the more humble rectory.[35]

There were anonymous charges against Stallings of homosexuality, but these were unsubstantiated by the diocese.[36] He and his bishop, the same James Hickey he had known in Rome, did disagree, however, over the appropriateness of Augustus Manor. Cardinal Hickey proposed graduate study, and when Stallings chose not to pursue advanced academic work, Hickey appointed him archdiocesan evangelist. Stallings reportedly continued to spend a great deal of time outside the diocese.[37]

Hickey apparently saw Stallings as a bright and able priest, but a person with a strong ego and independent manner who needed to be kept under greater control. Stallings interpreted their conflict as racism, the insensitivity of a white bishop in a white church to a black man and the black religious tradition. The tension increased and Stallings threatened to withdraw and form a separate religious body.[38]

Hickey dismissed Stallings as archdiocesan evangelist,[39] and warned him to abandon his "ad hoc experiment in personal ministry." Stallings' response was, "Ain't nobody going to turn me around," as well as the classic statement of all schismatics, "I have no plans to leave the church but the church may leave me."[40] On June 19, 1989, he announced the proposed establishment in Washington of Imani Temple. Imani means "faith" in Swahili.[41]

On July 2, 1989, Stallings launched Imani Temple in a four-hour service in the chapel of Howard University's Law School.[42] The ceremony was marked by drums and rattles, vestments with African motifs, and libations poured over the symbolic graves of the ancestors.[43] For one Scripture reading he substituted a passage by Howard Thurman.[44] Stallings used the Rite of Zaire, an African ritual permitted by the Vatican since 1987, but not approved for use in the United States.[45] At the service Stallings introduced special guests, including Mohammed Ali. The collection was $16,000.[46]

Hickey announced he was "saddened" by the ceremony,[47] and called it "destructive" and a public act of disobedience.[48] He warned the faithful to stay away,[49] and suspended Stallings from the priesthood,[50] but left the door open for conciliation and Stallings' return.[51] Suspension meant Stallings was forbidden to preach, celebrate mass, or administer the sacraments.[52]

## Black Bishops

"We are going all the way," Stallings responded; "We must take our destiny in our own hands."[53] Stallings claimed he had no separate denomination in mind,[54] but he continued his "gospel mass," with its red, green, and black altar cloth, for the 2,000 people who attended Imani Temple's second week of services.[55] "We are open to substantive dialogue with Cardinal Hickey," Stallings said, "but it must take place on our terms—our right to religious, spiritual, liturgical and theological self-determination.[56]

The responses to Stallings' actions were mixed. Many black Catholic lay people were supportive, while members of the white hierarchy were not, though some black priests did express sympathy.[57] The general consensus was that the larger church was indeed Eurocentric and unresponsive to black cultural needs, and there was much appreciation for Stallings' African vestments, black music, and social agenda.[58] Popular sympathy, however, clearly did not extend to the possibility of schism.[59] Many black Catholics even prided themselves on remaining in the church despite instances of racism, according to Prof. Albert Raboteau.[60]

The thirteen black Roman Catholic bishops in the United States spoke critically of the church's racism, but "sharply rebuffed" Stallings' defiance of the Cardinal Archbishop.[61] The 300-member National Council of Catholic Bishops admitted institutional racism, but reassured black parishioners of their concern and stated that Stallings' independence "wounds" the church.[62]

Stallings' response to the bishops was to point to Washington's Catholic University where he said only twenty black students were due to enroll in the next entering class of 1,000. Furthermore, there were only ten black faculty members, and the university offered no courses on black literature, music, or religion. The church ignored black disappointment and discouragement, he claimed.[63]

There was still some feeling Stallings was pursuing personal recognition and power. "The Afrocentric mind says you can have *your* church and we'll have *our* church," Stallings himself announced.[64] The Rev. Richard P. McBrien of the Theology Department at Notre Dame University predicted, "Once the television lights are off, he's done."[65]

Charges against Stallings of sexual misconduct now surfaced publicly, leading to lurid headlines such as the *Atlanta Constitution*'s of September 4, 1989: "Ex-Altar Boy Alleges Sex with Breakaway Priest."[66] Stallings' response was that the charges were merely an attempt to thwart the new church, and that Jesus Christ did not respond to Pontius Pilate.[67]

Stallings was formally excommunicated early in 1990 soon after he had canonized Martin Luther King, Jr., and announced permission for abortion and birth control, the elimination of confession, and support for the ordination of women and married men to the priesthood.[68] Vicar General William Kane of the Washington Archdiocese said Stallings and those "active in his new church" had in fact brought excommunication upon themselves: "By his public declaration that he has separated himself from the church by his renunciation of church teaching, Father Stallings has excommunicated himself." Stallings retorted, "Suppression and excommunication ... are the political tactics used by the powerful ... to further enslave and oppress the oppressed.... I cannot be cut off from Jesus Christ."[69] He added that "The Roman Catholic Church cannot excommunicate me," and "Once a priest, always a priest."[70]

Services continued at Imani Temple with a weekly attendance of 1,000 and a weekly collection averaging $20,000, both encouraged by Stallings' appearances on television, including the Oprah Winfrey show.[71]

Upon Stallings' excommunication the only black Roman Catholic archbishop broke his silence on the case and urged Stallings' followers to return to the church: "Breaking from the unity of the church is no answer to the needs and challenges of our African American Catholics," said Eugene Marino. Stallings reportedly tried to recruit Marino when he resigned as Archbishop of Atlanta a few months later after his relationship with Vicki R. Long became public.[72]

Stallings' separation became complete on May 12, 1990, when he was consecrated a bishop for the African American Catholic Congregation by one Richard M. Bridges, an Old Catholic bishop from California, assisted by two other white Old Catholic bishops, Donald L. Jolly and Emile F. Rodrigues y Fairchild.[73] Bridges' denomination is variously called the American Independent Orthodox Church[74] or the American National Catholic Church[75] or the Independent Old Catholic Churches of Los Angeles.[76] Whatever its name, it was founded in 1976 and seems to consist of two parishes, three clergy, and 75 members.[77]

Bridges himself had been consecrated by Gregory Michael David Voris, head of the American Hebrew Eastern Orthodox

Greek Catholic Church, a prelate and a denomination totally lost in obscurity.[78]

Speaking for the Roman Catholic Archdiocese of Los Angeles, Fr. Gregory Coiro said the Roman Catholic Church recognizes Old Catholic (Utrecht) ordinations as being in the historic line of succession, but it considers the actions of Old Catholic clergy illegal. "They lack the apostolic mandate which can only come from the pope," he said.[79] Stallings spoke of his own elevation to the episcopate as a solemn and memorable day in which African-American Catholics "would formalize and establish their place in history as an autonomous and independent Catholic Church."[80]

As bishop, Stallings announced his intention to ordain women and married men to the priesthood.[81] On September 8, 1991, in Washington, he ordained Rose Vernell, a former nun in the Oblate Sisters of Providence, for the West Philadelphia Imani Temple of eighty members.[82] The Women's Ordination Conference, a Roman Catholic group which had been pressing the church to open the priesthood to women, called Vernell's ordination "a prophetic act in the spirit of the gospel" and "a symbol of all the women who have left the official Roman Catholic Church to follow the call of God."[83]

Stallings now became more of a spokesperson for nationalistic black interests. He denounced Washington mayor Marion Barry's arrest on drug charges as harassment.[84] Along with Louis Farrakhan he was present during Barry's trial after the ACLU won an appeal on their right to attend.[85] Stallings commented on the white people appointed by Barry's successor, Sharon Pratt Dixon,[86] and in Brooklyn addressed members of the United African Movement.[87]

In true Old Catholic fashion, however, Stallings soon had internal problems, particularly of schism, with his own priests. He chose the Rev. Trevor D. Bentley, originally ordained in the Episcopal Church, to open a church in Los Angeles, but Bentley accused Stallings of lacking "fiscal accountability" and "doctrinal responsibility." Bentley specifically disavowed what he called "voodoo rites" by which he apparently meant Stallings' invocation of the African ancestors.[88]

Bishop Bridges, Stallings' consecrator, who had recently named Stallings an honorary archbishop, repudiated Stallings over "doctrinal differences," but the real dispute seems to have been over authority. Bridges made Hugh Randolph Caines, Jr., Stallings' priest in Philadelphia, an honorary bishop in Bridges' own church without Stallings' knowledge. If this was an attempt to woo Caines, it succeeded, as he deserted Stallings and went over to Bridges, taking his congregation with him.[89] Stallings threatened to excommunicate Caines, over whom he had jurisdiction, and also Bridges, over whom he did not. Caines apparently was originally ordained in Christ Catholic Church, another Old Catholic body, and once pleaded no contest to a felony charge of accepting a bribe when he was an inspector for the Hialeah, Florida, Fire Department.[90]

The first Roman Catholic priest to join Stallings also soon split from him. The Rev. Bruce E. Greening had been on loan to the Diocese of Richmond from his order, the Society of the Divine Saviour (of which he was the only black member), to head St. Mary's Academy in Norfolk.[91] He joined Stallings and became pastor of Umoja Temple (Swahili for "unity," ironically) in Northeast Washington. At Stallings' excommunication, however, Greening said, "We have no desire to follow the course of separation," and with his congregation of 300 sought reconciliation with the Roman Catholic Archdiocese.[92]

It seems likely, however, that Greening attempted to negotiate with Cardinal Hickey for the establishment of an African-American rite within the Roman Catholic Church as an alternative to Stallings and with himself, probably, at its head. Whatever terms for reunion Greening offered, Hickey refused them and Greening split yet again, this time to form his own independent church. Umoja Temple became St. Martin de Porres Church, and Greening was consecrated a bishop on September 28, 1990, in Washington's 19th Street Baptist Church by a trio of African Orthodox bishops: Stafford James Sweeting of Miami (His Beatitude, Stafford James I, Patriarch), Jamen B. Butler of Philadelphia (His Eminence, Jamen Bernardt, Primate), and David A. Richards of New York, who is McGuire's nephew.[93] "We are all devout Catholics," reported Bishop Butler,[94] a statement that might well come as a surprise to McGuire, Vilatte, Alvarez, and the Patriarch of the Syrian Orthodox Church.

Following the initial flurry of excitement, interest in Stallings and the African American Catholic Congregation has waned, with membership stabilizing at about 4,000 people. It is now clear there will be no exodus of black Catholics into the AACC any more than there was any significant movement of black Episcopalians into the AOC. Stallings apparently seeks to model his church on the Nation of Islam with its emphasis on black self-reliance and self-determination.[95]

What shall we say of Bishop Stallings? The *Washington Post* covered him extensively and was not particularly sympathetic (it emphasized the sex charges, for example) but its analysis is that Stallings is a working-class man striving for affluence in a church which values asceticism, a gay man in a church where homosexuality is a sin, and a black man in a church which remains white and racist.[96] Albert Raboteau believes that while Stallings draws attention to long-standing complaints, he and his church are finally a diversion from what ought to be the major issue, the church's mobilization on behalf of the poor.[97]

### III. Wandering Bishops

There are a number of African-American bishops and black Old Catholic churches which conform to the general pattern and characteristics of independent churches and wandering bishops. I will mention those I know along with whatever partial information is available, though I can make no claim for the accuracy of any of this data.[98] This of course points to the real issue: here is an entire genre of black churches and clergy virtually unknown, largely unrecorded, and certainly not studied or analyzed. Because of these churches' and prelates' obscurity and very irregularity, research would be difficult, but that of course is all the more reason why it should be undertaken.

James Augustine Arrendale (d. 1985), who claimed to have a degree in dentistry, founded in 1980 the Sacred Heart American Catholic Church (Syro-Anthiochgan) (*sic*) which opened the next year on Walton Avenue in the Bronx. He was consecrated in 1981 by Donald Anthony, of an unknown succession and jurisdiction. Arrendale's denomination consisted largely of former members of James F.A. Lashley's American Catholic Church, and, at its height, probably had three churches, two priests, and fifty members. It now seems to be defunct.

Denison Quartey Arthur claimed to have been raised in Ethiopia. In New York, however, he met John A. Hickerson who consecrated him in 1947, and Arthur became head of the Coptic Orthodox Church Apostolic with the title of Mar Lukos, Bishop of Lagos. Whether there were any actual congregations or not is unknown.

No more is known of Arthur, but there is additional information of John Hickerson, a colorful character who is also a person of considerable historic significance and who particularly deserves further study. Although the facts are, again, largely uncertain, Hickerson (sometimes Hickersayon) was a tall, gaunt, ascetic-looking, light-skinned black man who wore a crown and Oriental robes and was once described as "almost the exact image of Jesus Christ."[99] Hickerson claimed to be Ethiopian, but he was probably born in Alexandria, Virginia, and worked as a cook and sailor. Reportedly, he was licensed to preach by the Alfred Baptist Church, and may have attended Howard University.

In Baltimore around 1908 Hickerson teamed up with two other black religious prophets, Samuel Morris, known as Father Jehovia, and George Baker, apparently Morris's follower, known then as The Messenger. It was probably at this time and under their influence that Hickerson, too, assumed a title and designation: The Reverend Bishop St. John the Vine. He is sometimes known by these terms, however, in a different word order, such as The Reverend St. John Divine Bishop, or St. Bishop the Vine. Probably through phonetic use, his name became St. John de Vine, then St. John Devine, then St. John Divine—not to be confused with New York's Episcopal cathedral of that name or with George Baker, the Messenger, who himself later became Major J.J. Devine, then Father Divine.

In any event, Hickerson participated with Morris and Baker in developing and advocating the New Thought notion of the indwelling God, or "God within Man" or "Every Man a God," a variation on a later slogan of Huey Long's. Hickerson claimed Father Divine in fact stole this idea, fundamental to Father's theology let alone his own divinity, from him in 1912.[100] The trio had few followers in the early days, and when Hickerson fully realized that god-ness was also his, it is probably accurate to say that "two divinities in such a small group were sufficient."[101] In 1913 Hickerson withdrew to found his own church. This was apparently the

Church of the Living God, the Pillar and Ground of Truth, established on West 44th Street in New York.

The sequence and dates are uncertain, but Hickerson was at one time associated with Elder Warren Roberson's (sometimes Robertson) Live Ever, Die Never Church in Boston. This church seems to have experienced some difficulties, however, when Roberson was convicted of transporting minor females across state lines for immoral purposes. In the 1930s Hickerson ran a tabernacle on 110th Street in Manhattan, later relocated to West 133rd Street in Harlem. He was a powerful and dramatic preacher, famous for perpendicular leaps into the air during his delivery. He continued to preach the doctrine of "Every Man a God," and recruited various followers, each known as "A Temple of God." These included Joe World, Elijah the Firey Chariot, and Steamboat Bill and his wife Nannie Smith. Several of Steamboat Bill's sermons were recorded by the Columbia Phonograph Co., most notably "The Black Diamond Express Making 13 Stops and Arriving in Hell Ahead of Time."

Hickerson's real importance, however, is that he was an early advocate and spokesperson for Ethiopianism or religious black nationalism. He claimed to have learned Hebrew from his Abyssinian mother and to have taught it to Rabbi Arnold J. Ford who in turn taught it to Rabbi Wentworth A. Matthew. He maintained that God was not white, Jesus was African, Ethiopia was the cradle of civilization, and Africans were the true Jews, God's chosen people, who will be redeemed from exile and restored to their promised homeland. These are all ideas of great power, influence, and durability in vernacular black nationalism. They can be heard on the street today, and Hickerson was a vital link in their development and history.

In 1938 Hickerson was consecrated a bishop by Edwin Macmillan Jack, known as Bishop Yakob, of the Episcopal Orthodox Church (Greek Communion), a small group incorporated in Cuba in 1921 and in New York State in 1939. Jack was a West Indian, consecrated in 1923 by the AOC's Reginald Grant Barrow, and seems to have functioned largely in Barbados and Trinidad. In 1942 Hickerson incorporated in Manhattan the Coptic Orthodox Church Apostolic. He corresponded with His Holiness Abuna Basilios, both before and during the time Basilios was Patriarch of the Ethiopian Church. That ancient church's Archbishop Yeschaq claims it was actually Hickerson, "a man of vision ... not officially ordained but ... pro-African," who was responsible for the Ethiopians establishing in North America a church whose historicity, Orthodoxy, Africanness, and validity are all beyond question.[102]

Another black *episcopus vagans* was George S.A. Brookes of St. Paul's Church, New Haven, who had been elected vice-president of the African Orthodox Church's first General Synod in 1921. He split from the AOC with Barrow who consecrated him, and then he seceded from Barrow in 1938 to form the apparently short-lived Afro-American Catholic Church. James Amos LaFord LaPoint (b. 1932) seems to have been associated with the Episcopal Church in Haiti. In 1984 he was consecrated by Archbishop Hinkson of the AOC for the Orthodox Apostolic Church of America, of which little is known.

James Francis Augustus Lashley was consecrated (in 1928 or perhaps 1932) by William A. Tyarks, a white man consecrated by McGuire. Lashley headed the Archdiocese of New York (the denomination's only diocese, it seems) of the American Catholic Church founded in 1927 and with headquarters on West 144th Street in New York. In 1975 the American Catholic Church reported seven churches, seven clergy, and 700 members (numbers too precise—and mythic—to be taken too seriously), some in the West Indies. Lashley is now deceased, and it is reported that the body has been renamed the Orthodox Catholic Church in America, and that Lashley has been succeeded by one Michael E. Verra.

Richard Arthur Marchenna (March 17, 1911–September 2, 1982) was a long-time actor on the American Old Catholic scene. He was consecrated by Carmel Henry Carfora, a white man, one of the more notorious *episcopi vagantes*, for Carfora's own North American Old Roman Catholic Church. Marchenna consecrated over the years a dozen men (none of them black, so far as I know) including Robert Clement, founder of the Eucharistic Catholic Church, a largely homosexual group.

Ernest Leopold Petersen (d. 1959) was an AOC priest in Miami who split from the denomination and was consecrated by F.E.J. Lloyd in 1927 for the American Catholic Church (Syro-Antiochean). In 1978 the church claimed three parishes, eight clergy, and 501 members. Petersen may have had connections with Arrendale, since their churches have essentially the same name. Petersen reportedly once rejected the position of bishop coadjutor of the Diocese of Oregon in the Episcopal Church. It was said his own theological position was strongly influenced by Theosophy. Petersen was succeeded in the American Catholic Church by Herbert F. Wilkie, and the head of the church is now Archbishop Ramer Lanfers who gives a Lenox Avenue, New York City, address.

James Pickford Roberts of St. Thomas Liberal Catholic Church on 144th Street in Harlem was consecrated in 1955 by Edward Murray Matthews as the first bishop in New York of the Liberal Catholic Church, a church which combines high-church liturgy with Theosophical doctrine. In 1964 Roberts broke with Matthews to form the International Liberal Catholic Church and two years later consecrated his son as a fellow bishop.[103]

Hubert Augustus Rogers (1887?–1976), born in the West Indies, was consecrated in 1937 by William E.J Robertson of the AOC to be AOC Auxiliary Bishop of New York. He resigned in 1943, however, and became part of the North American Old Roman Catholic Church where he was successor to Carmel Henry Carfora.[104] According to one report, Rogers later resigned to become a Methodist missionary in the Dutch West Indies.

James Hubert Rogers (b. 1920), Hubert Augustus Rogers' son, was consecrated by his father in 1948 and succeeded him as primate of the North American Old Roman Catholic Church. He presides at St. Augustine's Cathedral on Wyona Avenue in Brooklyn, and in 1980 the denomination reported six churches, fifteen clergy, and 5,600 members. Another black bishop, Cyrus A. Starkey, was coadjutor to Carfora, but left the North American Old Roman Catholic Church in 1960 after Hubert Augustus Rogers took over. His subsequent history is unknown.

There are other black Old Catholic bishops of whom little is known other than their names. Abed-Negro Barbara was a bishop of the African Negro Mission in Haiti, an unknown church. Christopher M. Cragg, consecrated in 1965 by Christopher Stanley, was Patriarchal Exarch of the Turkish Orthodox Church, another unknown group, until the 1980s when he changed his name to Civet Chakwal Kristof and opened a health clinic in Chicago. Donald M. Foster was consecrated in 1961 by Hubert A. Rogers as the first bishop of the Afro-American Orthodox Church, which no longer seems to exist. Samuel T. Garner was consecrated by J.F.A. Lashley in 1976 as head of the Coptic Orthodox Church (Western

Hemisphere), a Brooklyn group. Philip Lewis is bishop of the Ethiopian Orthodox Catholic Church of North and South America, and may be connected to the Spiritual Baptists in Trinidad and Tobago.

It is easy to make light of the irregularity of Old Catholic orders and the vagaries of Old Catholic churches and their clergy, but there are serious issues beyond the superficial picture of men playing church. Many of the founders of these black Old Catholic churches were and are people denied full participation in the more mainstream and conventional institutions, a denial usually not unrelated to race. As a result, many of these men sought to establish churches whose identity and leadership were self-determined, to use a political term, autocephalous, to use a religious one, free and independent in any terminology.

At the same time, however, they wanted to claim the authority of history and the legitimacy of tradition, particularly the status of divine approval suggested by apostolic succession. Very much present is the notion that people of color as well as whites have a right to possess this powerful religious sanction. This brand of legitimacy has an additional appeal in its mystique: based in an ancient European city or an exotic Eastern see, it antedates this racist country and transcends this society. Old Catholicism is a way to affirm blackness and it is a way not be American.

There is also the issue of the historic churches' own exclusivity. Some of these churches' own early founders, it must be said, claimed charismatic rather than institutional authority at their own beginnings, and it is ironic to see their descendants deny space to newcomers. Bishops in the early church were probably pastors of local churches rather than administrators of bureaucracies, so it becomes difficult to argue against a contemporary proliferation of bishops when they are essentially parish priests. Finally, the claims to unique status and divine singularity on the part of traditional churches are perceived by many as only further evidence of the boundlessness of human pretension.

So the black Old Catholic churches serve their people, link to Christian history, and connect with the world-wide struggle of people of color for freedom and autonomy. They may not trace to the Afro-Protestant folk church that emerged from slavery, but there is no reason for black institutions to be uniform, and, it can be argued, black Old Catholicism has stronger ties to ancient, precolonial African Christianity. In their own way, then, they are indigenous churches of the African-American "nation within a nation." With their own freedom they can celebrate the heritage of the past, the vision of the future, and freedom itself.

## Notes

1. George Alexander McGuire. "Valedictory Address of Archbishop McGuire as Primate of the African Orthodox Church." *The Voice of the Patriarch* 1:1 (March 1934), 1.

2. Robert A. Hill, ed. *The Marcus Garvey and Universal Negro Improvement Association Papers. Volume I, 1826–August 1919.* Berkeley: University of California Press, 1983, p. 469.

3. Fred B. Welbourn. *East African Rebels: A Study of Some Independent Churches.* London: SCM Press, 1961, p. 81.

4. I am indebted to the Rev. Dr. Warren C. Platt for his help in formulating a succinct definition here.

5. *Journal of the 18th Session and 17th Quadrennial Session of the General Conference of the African Methodist Episcopal Church in the World. Held in Bethel Church, Baltimore, Md., May 5th to 26th 1884.* Edited by Rev. Benjamin W. Arnett, D.D. and Rev. M.E. Bryant, Secretary. Philadelphia: Rev. James C. Embry, General Business Manager, n.d. (1884?), p. 152.

6. *Journal*, pp. 167, 235. I am grateful to Prof. David W. Wills of Amherst College for drawing the 1884 AME convention to my attention. The Episcopal Committee of the church reported (*Journal*, p. 166) that some AME ministers were considering reordination by an Episcopal bishop, which may have been the occasion for raising the issue; I have no information on why they may have thought their orders were in doubt—though this is a phenomenon that surfaces in various churches from time to time.

The strong resolution condemning apostolic succession (as well as "heavy" ritualism and the wearing of robes) was adopted 127 to 11. Six bishops voted for the resolution, but two others, Brown and T.M.D. Ward, were absent (conveniently for Brown) and Henry McNeal Turner who agreed with Brown abstained. High-church ritualism continued, it seems, to insinuate itself, and the General Conference of 1900 meeting in Columbus granted permission to bishops and ministers to wear robes, probably because some were already doing so. The high-church Turner once announced that Jesus, Luther, Wesley, and Whitefield had all worn robes.

John Mifflin Brown's famous sermon was mostly a lengthy defense of the historic independence from Rome of the English church, the ultimate source of AME orders as well as any claim it might have to apostolic succession. The rationale for the Conference's condemnation was essentially theological: while there are two true orders of ordained ministry, there can be no separate priesthood since, by Reformation doctrine, every Christian is a priest. Reordination would be unthinkable as it would effectively deny AME history, invalidate marriages, stigmatize dead AME bishops, and evoke "the scorn of the Reformed churches." (*Journal*, p. 167.)

George Freeman Bragg was well aware of Bishop Brown's sermon and said, "It was one of the ablest, and scholarly, discourses, ever delivered in this country and created a great sensation." This is in *Heroes of the Eastern Shore*, Baltimore: Author, 1939, p. 15.

Henry McNeal Turner once argued that AMEs ought to have a presiding archbishop, not only to bring more order to the denomination, but "to represent our connectional interest with his escort of Bishops before the President of the United States and the Congress of the United States with an authority and power that would strike awe into the nation's heart." This is in the *Christian Recorder* of March 25, 1880, as quoted by Stephen Ward Angell, *Bishop Henry McNeal Turner and African-American Religion in the South*, Knoxville: University of Tennessee Press, 1992, p. 149.

The question of episcopacy became an issue for the AME Zion Church in the 1860s when it considered union with the AMEs so that the two major black Methodist denominations would not compete in evangelizing freed slaves eager to join black-led denominations. The Zion church was, of course, not attracted to any traditional theory of apostolic succession, but in their conversations the question did arise as to how a bishop was made. The Zion Church held that any three regularly ordained elders (i.e., ministers) could ordain a bishop if they needed to, a position Daniel Alexander Payne himself publicly agreed with since that was, in fact, how he had become a bishop himself.

There were practical discussions, too, about whether overseers should be called by the more democratic title of superintendent and subject to election every four years, as they were in the Zion Church. The Zionists were willing to adopt the title of bishop and elect them for life in order to conform to AME usage, as long as they could select their own men. The proposed union, of course, did not take place. The Zion Church was also willing to discuss joining with the nearly all-white Methodist Episcopal Church, but a majority in the ME General Conference of 1868 would not tolerate a black bishop, and so these conversations ended, also. I am indebted to Prof. William Gravely for clarifying this for me.

7. Henry McNeal Turner. *The Genius and Theory of Methodist Polity Practically Illustrated Through a Series of Questions and Answers*. Philadelphia: Publication Department, AME Church, 1885, pp. 119, 126. James A. Davis. *The History of Episcopacy: Prelatic and Moderate, with an Introduction by the Rt. Rev. B.T. Tanner*. Nashville: AME Church Sunday School Union, 1902.

8. This manuscript sermon of Bragg's is held by the Schomburg Center where its classmark is MG 244.

9. George F. Bragg. "Churches." *Crisis* 5:8 (August 1913), 166.

10. George F. Bragg. *"The Whittingham Canon." The Birth and History of the Missionary District Plan*. Baltimore: Author, n.d. X

The Roman Catholic Church debated the same issue. At the Second Plenary Council in Baltimore in 1866, called in part to consider the Church's obligation to the freed slaves, Rome proposed that a bishop with national jurisdiction be responsible for all African Americans. The idea was probably that of Martin J. Spaulding, the Archbishop of Baltimore. The bishops rejected the scheme for several reasons, not least of which was their unhappiness over "an ecclesiastical man" with whom they would have to share authority. See Cyprian Davis, *The History of the Black Catholics in the United States*. New York: Crossroad, 1992, pp. 116–22.

The AME Church also faced the question of suffragan bishops. Bishop Henry McNeal Turner on his visit to South Africa in 1898 was implored by the Africans to set apart James M. Dwane as a suffragan or missionary bishop to care for the fast-growing South African Church. Although he had reservations, Turner did consecrate Dwane as a "vicar bishop," subject to the approval of the AME Council of Bishops at home and the next General Conference, which would be in 1900. Turner received some criticism in the States, and enemies of the AME Church in South Africa claimed Dwane's consecration was not legitimate and so convinced the government to deny AME ministers the right to perform marriages. In 1899 Dwane left the AME for the Anglican Church, taking 17 ministers with him. See Stephen Ward Angell, *Bishop Henry McNeal Turner and African-American Religion in the South*. Knoxville: University of Tennessee Press, 1992, pp. 233

11. Speaking in 1926, Brown said, "The black man is the great white hope" and Harlem is "the most likely place" for "the new order to begin." He urged black people to march into white churches "not to listen to the dead formulas of an age which has past, but to bring with you the gospel of life and liberation." Speaking of the white churches, Brown admonished his black audience, "I want to see them liberated. I want you to go into them and set them free." See *The New York Times*, February 23, 1926, 17.

12. Letter to Richard Newman from Keith Flory, William M. Brown Memorial Library, Galion, Ohio, April 10, 1977.

13. A.C. Terry-Thompson. *The History of the African Orthodox Church*. New York: Author, 1956, p. 39.

14. Fr. Antony participated actively in the AOC's first General Synod and served as Dean of Endich Theological Seminary. When he left the AOC he founded an independent church in Harlem and was excommunicated by the Russians. This story needs to be told.

15. The Greek Church was another route McGuire might have taken. Robert Morgan, a Jamaican and former Methodist, was an Episcopal deacon who was deposed for "abandonment" of his ministry. Morgan apparently claimed Greek ordination by the Patriarch of Constantinople and allegedly tried to organize an African-American Greek Orthodox Church in Philadelphia. McGuire knew Morgan, who is a promising subject for research.

16. George Freeman Bragg noticed the appearance of Vilatte in 1898 and wondered if a bishop with Eastern orders could play any role with those African Americans who found episcopacy important.

17. "African Orthodox Church: Statistics, Denominational History, Doctrine, and Organization." *Census of Religious Bodies 1926*. Washington: Department of Commerce, Bureau of the Census, 1928, pp. 6–7. McGuire's use of "aspires" is a curious reservation.

18. Published in New York by Oxford University Press in 1991.

19. Thomas F. Gossett. *Uncle Tom's Cabin and American Culture*. Dallas: Southern Methodist University Press, 1985, p. 365. McGuire's famous statement, "The Uncle Tom nigger has got to go," was reported in the *New York World*, August 17, 1920, 10.

20. Robert A. Hill, ed. *The Marcus Garvey and Universal Negro Improvement Association Papers, Volume 5. September 1922–August 1924*. Berkeley: University of California Press, 1986.

21. McGuire consecrated at least two white bishops. One was William F. Tyarks, a defector from F.E.J. Lloyd's American Catholic Church whom McGuire, assisted by Daniel William Alexander, set apart in 1928 as head of the American Catholic Orthodox Church. McGuire later deposed Tyarks (who went to prison for organizing fraudulent charities). Another was Cyril John Clement Sherwood, consecrated in 1932 for the American Holy Orthodox Catholic Apostolic Eastern Church, which, despite its inclusive title, apparently existed exclusively in the mind of Bishop Sherwood. He became a member of the AOC conclave and his white face stands out in photographs of the AOC hierarchy.

## Black Bishops

As a matter of historical interest, it may be that the first black bishop to consecrate whites was Silverio Gomes Pimenta (1840–1922), the Roman Catholic Archbishop of Mariana, who consecrated four white men in Brazil. DuBois says Pimenta was the first black Catholic bishop in Latin America. There needs to be a biography of Pimenta in English; there are several in Portuguese. The first African–American Roman Catholic bishop in this country was James A. Healy. With the recent death of his biographer, Albert S. Foley, someone needs to see if there is unpublished material among Fr. Foley's papers, given the difficulties he faced in publishing the full account of the Healy family.

The first black Episcopal bishop was James Theodore Holly, and we have David Dean's biography. Although consecrated by the Episcopal Church, Holly was actually consecrated for the L'Eglise Orthodoxe Apostolique Hatienne, an independent national church which had fraternal relations with the Episcopal Church until Holly's death when it became a missionary district. Technically, the first black bishop in the Episcopal Church was Samuel David Ferguson, consecrated in 1885 as fourth Missionary Bishop of Cape Palmas, later Liberia.

22. Stuart's book was published by Wendell Malliet and Co. in New York in 1940. Bishop Valentine's biography is on pp. 106–8.

23. Jackie W. Ammerman letter to Richard Newman, April 15, 1992. Also, telephone interview, April 13, 1992.

24. West is currently a post-doctoral fellow at Northwestern. In September 1992 he joins the History and Afro-American Studies Departments at the University of Illinois-Champaign.

25. Telephone interview with Michael West, April 24, 1992.

Prof. Robert Edgar of Howard University tells me he has seen similar materials in the State Archives in Pretoria as well as the Cape Provincial archives.

26. James Lincoln Collier. "John Coltrane: A Jazz Messiah." *The Making of Jazz: A Comprehensive History*. New York: Dell, 1978, pp. 478–93.

27. Telephone interview with the Rev. William Green, April 2, 1992.

28. *Expression* (Summer 1991), passim.

29. Published in Bern and New York by Peter Lang in 1990.

30. "Years of Defiance: Roots of Stallings' Rebellion," *Washington Post*, April 29, 1990, p. 41; "Concern about Stallings' Lifestyle Fueled Conflict," *Washington Post*, April 30, 1990, p.1; "Stallings Builds a Black Church Far From Rome," *Washington Post*, May 1, 1990, p. 1.

31. "Black Priest Defies Church, Forming Own Congregation," *New York Times*, July 3, 1989, p. 8.

32. "An Act of Faith and Defiance," *Washington Post*, July 2, 1989, p. B3.

33. "Stallings, A Stylish Catholic Priest, Ignites a Controversy with His New Church," *Washington Times*, July 3, 1989.

34. "Cardinal Forbids Mass by Black Priest," *New York Times*, June 25, 1989, p. 18.

35. "Years of Defiance: Roots of Stallings' Rebellion," *Washington Post*, April 29, 1989, p. 41.

36. "Concern about Stallings' Lifestyle Fueled Conflict," *Washington Post*, April 30, 1990, p. 1.

37. "Years of Defiance: Roots of Stallings' Rebellion," *Washington Post*, April 29, 1990, p. 41.

38. "Black D.C. Priest Plans Separate Catholic Church," *Washington Post*, June 20, 1989.

39. "Cardinal Bars Priest from Saying Mass; Stallings Is Worried about Black Parish," *Washington Post*, June 25, 1989.

40. "Cardinal Forbids Mass by Black Priest," *New York Times*, June 25, 1989, p. 18.

41. "Maverick Priest Girds for Another Fight with Authority," *Washington Post*, July 1, 1989.

42. "Priest Founds Separatist Black Congregation," *Los Angeles Times*, July 3, 1989. "Blacks Launch Breakaway Catholic Church," *Atlanta Constitution*, July 3, 1989.

43. "Black Priest's Defiance Wins Support," *Washington Post*, July 3, 1989.

44. "Black Priest Defies Church, Forming Own Congregation," *New York Times*, July 3, 1989, p. 8.

45. "Black Priest Defies Church, Forming Own Congregation," *New York Times*, July 3, 1989, p. 8.

46. "Black Priest's Defiance Wins Support," *Washington Post*, July 3, 1989.

47. "Black Priest's Defiance Wins Support," *Washington Post*, July 3, 1989.

48. "Cardinal Suspends Washington Priest Who Defied Orders," *New York Times*, July 5, 1989, p. 1. "Catholic Priest Suspended for Defying Orders. Afro-American Temple Labelled 'Destructive,'" *Atlanta Constitution*, July 5, 1989.

49. "Hickey Criticizes Plan to Create Black Church," *Washington Post*, June 21, 1989.

50. "Cardinal Suspends Washington Priest Who Defied Orders," *New York Times*, July 5, 1989, p. 1.

51. "Stallings' Dissent Throws Church into Confrontation: Dispute Attracting National Attention," *Washington Post*, July 7, 1989.

52. "Black Priest Suspended in D.C."

53. "Black Priest's Defiance Wins Support," *Washington Post*, July 3, 1989.

54. "Maverick Priest Says He Is No Luther But a Man of Ethnic and Religious Soul," *New York Times*, July 9, 1989, p. 22.

55. "'Ain't No Stopping Us Now,' Stallings Exults: More Than 2,000 Spirited Worshippers Crowd Imani Temple's Second Week of Services," *Washington Post*, July 10, 1989.

56. "Stallings Sets Forth Terms for Agreement with Hickey," *Washington Post*, July 11, 1989: "Priest, Holding Masses in Defiance of Church, Seeks Reconciliation," *New York Times*, July 10, 1989.

57. "Black Catholic Clergy to Mull Afro-American Rite," *Atlanta Journal*, July 28, 1989.

58. "For Blacks, Worship Calls for Commotion Along with the Devotion," *Los Angeles Times*, July 20, 1989.

59. "Few Blacks Back Maverick Priest: Catholics Debate His Methods," *Newsday*, July 23, 1989, p. 15. "Breakaway Priest Wins Few Followers," *New York Times*, August 6, 1989; "Catholic Church Should Practice What It Preaches," *Washington Post*, July 20, 1989.

60. "In Brooklyn, Support for a Maverick Priest," *New York Times*, July 10, 1989.

61. "Black U.S. Bishops Critical of Priest; Creation of African American Congregation Rejected as Selfish and Ill-Advised," *New York Times*, July 13, 1989.

62. "Black Priest Is Termed Threat to Catholic Unity," *New York Times*, July 15, 1989: "Bishops Admit Legacy of Racism, Ask Priest Back," *Atlanta Constitution*, July 15, 1989.

63. "Dissident Priest Says Catholic University Shows Bias Against Blacks," *New York Times*, July 23, 1989.

64. "Breakaway Black Priest: New Schism?" *Los Angeles Times*, July 25, 1989.

65. "Black Catholic Priest Leads a Revolt in D.C.," *Atlanta Constitution*, July 13, 1989.

66. "Ex-Altar Boy Says He Had Sex with Stallings," *Washington Post*, September 4, 1989.

67. "Rebel Priest Says Sex Charge Is Effort to Thwart Black Church," *Atlanta Constitution*, September 5, 1989. "Renegade Black Priest Looking at Atlanta as a Site for Church," *Atlanta Constitution*, October 30, 1989: "Stallings Talks to Media But Not About Sex Allegation," *Washington Post*, September 8, 1989, p. C6: "Stallings Declines to Comment on New Allegations," *Washington Post*, May 4, 1990.

68. "Black Catholics in Splinter Sect Ordain Woman. Ex-Nun Becomes Priest in Breakaway Church," *New York Times*, September 9, 1991, p. A10. "Breakaway Priest Is Excommunicated, Archdiocese Reports," *New York Times*, February 6, 1990: "Stallings Builds a Black Church Far From Rome," *Washington Post*, May 1, 1990, p. 1. "Stallings' Followers Grapple with Excommunication," *Washington Post*, February 10, 1990, p. G14: "Church in Capitol Sets Its Own Rules. Group That Broke with Rome Will Permit Abortion and Ordination of Women," *New York Times*, February 5, 1990.

69. "Maverick Black Catholic Priest Won't Accept Excommunication."

70. "Stallings and His Followers Excommunicated, Church Says," *Washington Post*.

71. "Stallings Builds a Black Church Far From Rome," *Washington Post*, May 1, 1990. p. 1.

72. "Breakaway Church Seeks to Recruit Ex-Archbishop," *Los Angeles Times*, August 4, 1990, p. A4. "Nation's Only Black Archbishop Breaks His Silence on Stallings. Followers Urged to Return to the Church," *Washington Post*, February 26, 1990.

73. *Afro-American*, February 10, 1990, p. 7; *Los Angeles Sentinel*, May 3, 1990, p. 1.

74. Gary L. Ward, Bertil Persson, and Alan Bain, *Independent Bishops: An International Directory*, Detroit: Apogee Books, 1990, pp. 58, 383.

75. "Rift in Stallings' Ranks," *The Christian Century*, November 6, 1991, p. 1023; "Maverick Catholic Schism Develops," *Los Angeles Times*, October 21, 1991.

76. "Breakaway Black Catholic Priest Becomes Bishop of D.C. Church," *Atlanta Constitution*.

77. Karl Pruter, and J. Gordon Melton, *The Old Catholic Sourcebook*, N.Y.: Garland Publishing, Inc., 1983, p. 83.

78. Gary L. Ward, Bertil Persson, and Alan Bain, *Independent Bishops: An International Directory*. Detroit: Apogee Books, 1990, p. 58.

79. "Dissident Church Leader Preaches in Los Angeles," *Los Angeles Times*.

80. "Breakaway Black Catholic Priest Becomes Bishop of D.C. Church," *Atlanta Constitution*.

# Black Bishops

81. "Stallings to Ordain Married Men. Woman to be Deacon in Baltimore Rite," *Washington Post*, December 8, 1990.

82. "Black Catholics in Splinter Sect Ordain Woman. Ex-Nun Becomes Priest in Breakaway Church," *New York Times*, September 9, 1991, p. A10.

83. "Stallings to Ordain First Woman Priest," *Washington Post*, September 7, 1991, p. G10.

84. "Stallings Denounces Barry's Drug Arrest," *Washington Post*, April 8, 1990.

85. *Afro-American*, June 30, 1990, p. 4.

86. *Afro-American*, February 23, 1991, p. 1.

87. *New York Amsterdam News*, June 22, 1991, p. 9.

88. "Rift in Stallings' Ranks," *The Christian Century*, November 6, 1991, p. 1023.

89. "Maverick Catholic Schism Develops," *Los Angeles Times*, October 21, 1991.

90. "Stallings Builds a Black Church Far From Rome," *Washington Post*, May 1, 1990, p. 1.

91. "Norfolk Priest Joins Stallings' Revolt," *Washington Post*, August 3, 1989; "Black Priest Disciplined After Backing Stallings in Breakaway Church," *Atlanta Constitution*, August 3, 1989.

92. "Priest, 300 Parishioners Quit Stallings, Group Seeks to Stay with Roman Church," *Washington Post*.

93. "Ex-Associate of Stallings Forms New Rite. Archdiocese Says Greening, Followers Are Excommunicated," *Washington Post*, October 6, 1990.

94. "Catholic Rite Observes Birthday. Year-Old Congregation Combines Faith, African Cultural Heritage," *Washington Post*, September 30, 1991.

95. Paul Elie, "Hangin' With the Romeboys: Black Catholics in a White Church," *The New Republic*, 206 (May 11, 1992), 22.

96. "Years of Defiance: Roots of Stallings' Rebellion," *Washington Post*, April 29, 1990.

97. Thomas J. Stahel, "Albert J. Raboteau," *America* 166:4 (April 25, 1992), 340.

98. Information on these Old Catholic churches is scattered through the following sources: Peter Anson, *Bishops at Large: Some Autocephalous Churches of the Past Hundred Years and Their Founders*, London: Faber and Faber, 1964; Elmer T. Clark, *The Small Sects in America: An Authentic Study of Almost 300 Little Known Religious Groups*, N.Y.: Abingdon Press, 1949; J.

Gordon Melton, *The Encyclopedia of American Religions*, Wilmington: McGrath Publishing Co, 1978; Wardell J. Payne, ed., *Directory of African American Religious Bodies: A Compendium by the Howard University School of Divinity*, Washington: Howard University Press, 1991; Arthur C. Piepkorn, *Profiles in Belief: The Religious Bodies of the United States and Canada, Volume I. Roman Catholic, Old Catholic and Eastern Orthodox*, N.Y.: Harper and Row, 1977; Karl Pruter and J. Gordon Melton, *The Old Catholic Sourcebook*, N.Y.: Garland Publishing, Inc., 1983; Gary L. Ward, Bertil Persson, and Alan Bain, *Independent Bishops: An International Directory*, Detroit: Apogee Books, 1990.

99. John Hoshor, *God in a Rolls Royce, the Rise of Father Divine: Madman Menace or Messiah*. N.Y.: Hillman-Curl, Inc.,1936, p. 34.

100. T.R. Poston, "'I Taught Father Divine' Says St. Bishop the Vine," *New York Amsterdam News*, November 23, 1932, p. 1.

101. Fred Lamar Pearson, Jr., and Joseph Aaron Tomberlin, "John Doe, Alias God: A Note on Father Divine's Georgia Career," *The Georgia Historical Quarterly* 60:1 (Spring 1976), 44.

102. Archbishop Yeschaq, *The Ethiopian Tewahedo Church: An Integrally African Church*, N.Y.: Vantage Press, 1989, p. 191. There are bits of information on Hickerson in the following: St. Clair McKelway, with A.J. Liebling, "Who Is This King of Glory?" *True Tales from the Annals of Crime and Rascality*, N.Y.: Random House, 1951; Robert A. Parker, *The Incredible Messiah: The Deification of Father Divine*, Boston: Little Brown and Co., 1937; Theodore Schroeder, "A 'Living God' Incarnate," *The Psychoanalytic Review: An American Journal of Psychoanalysis* 9:1 (Jan. 1932), 36–45; Theodore Schroeder,"Living Gods," *Azoth: The Occult Magazine of America* 3:4 (Oct. 1918), 202–5; Jill M. Watts, *God. Harlem U.S.A.: The Father Divine Story*, Berkeley: University of California Press, 1992.

103. "Consecration of a Bishop: Ordination Ceremony Is Led by Negro Liberal Catholic Bishop," *Sepia* 9:3 (March 1961), 58–60; Leslie Rumble, "Are Liberal Catholic Orders Valid?" *The Homiletic and Pastoral Review* 58:6 (March 1958), 559–71; *New York Age* (November 19, 1955), 6; *Pittsburgh Courier* (October 15, 1956), 1.

104. Jonathan E. Trela, *A History of the North American Old Roman Catholic Church*, Scranton: Polish National Catholic Church, 1979.

*Interviews*

Jackie W. Ammerman, telephone, April 13, 1992
James Bramble, March 29, 1992

# Black Bishops

William Green, telephone, April 2, 1992
Robert Hood, telephone, March 31, 1992
Channing R. Jeschke, telephone, April 13, 1992
Warren C. Platt, March 29, 1992
David A. Richards, telephone, April 14, 1992
Michael West, telephone, April 24, 1992
Jill M. Watts, telephone, May 19, 1992

*Note*
The citations to newspaper stories on George A. Stallings and the AACC are primarily from clippings in the "George A. Stallings" vertical file at the Schomburg Center for Research in Black Culture. Not every clipping includes full bibliographical information.

## IV. A Bibliography on Black Bishops

"African Orthodox Church: Statistics, Denominational History, Doctrine and Organization." *Census of Religious Bodies 1926*. Washington: Department of Commerce, Bureau of the Census, 1928.

Andrews, Theodore. *The Polish National Catholic Church in America and Poland*. London: SPCK, 1953.

Angell, Stephen Ward. *Bishop Henry McNeal Turner and African-American Religion in the South*. Knoxville: University of Tennessee Press, 1992.

Anson, Peter F. *Bishops at Large: Some Autocephalous Churches of the Past Hundred Years and Their Founders*. London: Faber and Faber, 1964.

"Apostolic Succession in the African Orthodox Church." *The Negro Churchman* 3:1 (January 1925), 1–2.

Atiah, Aziz. *A History of Eastern Christianity*. London: Methuen & Co., 1968.

Bain, Alan. *Bishops Irregular: An International Directory of Independent Bishops*. Bristol: Author, 1985.

Bethell, Tom. "Heretic As Hero." *The American Spectator* 22:9 (September 1989), 11–13. [On George A. Stallings].

"Black Priest in Schism?" *The Christian Century* 106–21 (July 5–12, 1989), 649. [On George A. Stallings].

Bowen, J.W.E. *An Appeal For Negro Bishops But No Separation*. N.Y.: Eaton & Mains, 1912.

Bradley, David H., Sr. "The Development of the Episcopacy." *A History of the A.M.E. Zion Church, Part II. 1872–1968*. Nashville: The Parthenon Press, 1970, pp. 120–48.

Bragg, George Freeman. "Churches." *Crisis* 5:8 (August 1913), 166.

———. *Heroes of the Eastern Shore*. Baltimore: Author, 1939.

———. *History of the Afro-American Group of the Episcopal Church*. Baltimore: Church Advocate Press, 1922.

———. "Negro Bishops." *The Negro Churchman* 7:4 (May 1929), 2–3. [Reprinted from *The Living Church*].

———. "The Whittingham Canon." *The Birth and History of the Missionary District Plan*. Baltimore: Author, n.d.

Brandreth, Henry R.T. *Episcopi Vagantes and the Anglican Church*. London: SPCK, 1947.

Brown, John M. "The Quadrennial Sermon." *Journal of the 18th Session of the General Conference of the African Methodist Episcopal Church in the World. Held in Bethel Church, Baltimore, Md, May 5th to 26th 1884*. Edited by Rev. Benjamin W. Arnett, D.D. and Rev. M.E. Bryant, Secretary. Philadelphia: Rev. James C. Embry, General Business Manager, n.d.

Brown, William Montgomery. *The American Race Problem*. Galion: The Bradford-Brown Educational Co., n. d.

———. *The Crucial Race Question. or, Where and How Shall the Color Line Be Drawn?* Little Rock: The Arkansas Churchman's Publishing Co., 1908.

———. *My Heresy: The Autobiography of an Idea*. N.Y.: John Day and Co., 1926.

Burkett, Randall K. *Black Redemption: Churchmen Speak for the Garvey Movement*. Philadelphia: Temple University Press, 1978.

———. *Garveyism as a Religious Movement: The Institutionalization of a Black Civil Religion*. Metuchen: Scarecrow Press, 1978.

———, and Richard Newman, eds. *Black Apostles: Afro-American Clergy Confront the Twentieth Century*. Boston: G.K. Hall & Co., 1978.

Castro, Fernando Pedreira de. *Dom Silverio Gomes Pimenta*. Petropolis: R.J. Vozes, 1954.

*Catholic Bishops and Archbishops of America*. Providence: John W. Kirwin, 1899. [On James A. Healy].

Clark, Elmer T. *The Small Sects in America: An Authentic Study of About 300 Little-Known Religious Groups*. Rev. ed. N.Y.: Abingdon, Press, 1949.

Collier, James. *The Making of Jazz: A Comprehensive History*. N.Y.: Dell, 1978. [On John Coltrane].

*Consecration Ceremony of Bruce Edward Greening BMdeP to the Office of Bishop The Independent African-American Catholic Rite.* N.P. [Washington, D.C.?]: n.p., n.d. [1990?].

"Consecration of a Bishop: Ordination Ceremony Is Led by Negro Liberal Catholic Bishop." *Sepia* 9:3 (March 1961), 58–60.

"Convincing Letter from Chief Consecrator of Archbishop Vilatte." *The Negro Churchman* 1:8 (August 1923), 5–6.

Davis, Cyprian. *The History of Black Catholics in the United States.* N.Y.: Crossroad Publishing Co., 1992.

Davis, James A. *The History of Episcopacy: Prelatic and Moderate; With an Introduction by the Rt. Rev. B.T. Tanner.* Nashville: AME Church Sunday School Union, 1902.

Dean, David M. *Defender of the Race: James Theodore Holly. Black Nationalist Bishop.* Boston: Lambeth Press, 1979.

DeMille, D. "Medical Minister," *Sepia* 7 (July 1959), 58–62. [On AOC Archbishop G. Duncan Hinkson].

Elie, Paul. "Hangin' With the Romeboys: Black Catholics in a White Church." *The New Republic* 206:19 (May 11, 1992), 18–26. [On George A. Stallings].

Farajaje-Jones, Elias. *In Search of Zion: The Spiritual Significance of Africa in Black Religious Movements.* Bern: Peter Lang, 1990.

"Father Stallings' Choices." *America* 161:4 (August 12–19, 1989), 75.

Foley, Albert S. *Bishop Healy: Beloved Outcaste: The Story of a Great Priest Whose Life Has Become a Legend.* N.Y.: Farrar, Straus and Young, 1954.

Gailor, Thomas F. "Problems of the Racial Episcopate." *The East and the West* 12 (January 1914), 67–72.

Giles, Etienne Victor. "James Theodore Holly, First Bishop of Haiti." *Living Church* 71 (Feb. 28, 1925), 598.

Githieya, Francis. "The New People of God: The Christian Community in the African Orthodox Church (Karing'A) and the Arathi (Agikuyu Spirit Churches)." Ph.D. dissertation, Emory University, 1992.

Gossett, Thomas F. *Uncle Tom's Cabin and American Culture.* Dallas: Southern Methodist University Press, 1985.

Hartshorn, W.N. *An Era of Progress and Promise. 1863–1910.* Boston: The Priscilla Publishing Co., 1910. [On George A.McGuire].

Harzmichali, Nectaire. "L'Eglise Orthodoxe Grecque et la messianisme en Afrique." *Social Compass* 22:1 (1975), 85–95.

Hadyn, J. Carleton. "James Theodore Holly (1829–1911): First Afro-American Episcopal Bishop: His Legacy to Us Today." *Journal of Religious Thought* 33:1 (Spring–Summer 1970), 50–62.

Hill, Charles Leander. "The Episcopacy—Its Functions, Its Authority, Its Limitations." *The A.M.E. Church Review* 78:208 (April–June 1961), 3–6.

Hill, Robert A., ed. *The Marcus Garvey and Universal Negro Improvement Association Papers.* Vol. I. 1826–August 1919. Berkeley: University of California Press, 1983. Vol. II. 27 August 1919–31 August 1920. Berkeley: University of California Press, 1983. Vol. III. September 1920–August 1921. Berkeley: University of California Press, 1984. Vol. IV. 1 September 1921–2 September 1922. Berkeley: University of California Press, 1986. Vol. V. September 1922–August 1924. Berkeley: University of California Press, 1986. Vol. VI. September 1924–December 1927. Berkeley: University of California Press, 1989. Vol. VII, November 1927–August 1940. Berkeley: University of California Press, 1990.

Hogue, William M. "The Episcopal Church and Archbishop Vilatte," *The Historical Magazine of the Protestant Episcopal Church* 34:1 (March 1965), 35–55.

Hood, J[ames] W[alker]. *Sketches of the Early History of the African Methodist Episcopal Zion Church with Jubilee Souvenir and an Appendix.* N.Y.: Author [?], 1914.

———. *One Hundred Years of the African Methodist Episcopal Zion Church, or, The Centennial of African Methodism.* N.Y.: A.M.E. Zion Book Concern, 1895.

Horner, Norman A. "An East African Orthodox Church," *Journal of Ecumenical Studies* 12:2 (Spring 1975), 221–33.

Hoshor, John. *God in a Rolls Royce, The Rise of Father Divine: Madman, Menace, or Messiah.* N.Y.: Hillman-Curl, Inc., 1936. [On John A. Hickerson].

Huelin, Gordon, ed. *Old Catholics and Anglicans, 1931–1981.* Oxford: Oxford University Press, 1983.

Johnson, James H.A. *The Episcopacy of the A.M.E. Church or the Necessity for an Ample Force of Bishops.* Baltimore: Hoffman and Co., 1888.

Johnson, Morris. "Archbishop Daniel William Alexander and the Rise of the African Orthodox Church in South Africa, 1925–1970: A Study in Race, Religion and Reformist Nationalism." Ph.D. dissertation, Howard University, 1992.

Kanyiles, Daniel James (Mar James II). "The History of the African Orthodox Church in the Republic of South Africa, 1924 to 1988." Unpublished paper, University of California at Santa Barbara.

Keizer, Lewis S. *The Wandering Bishops: Heralds of a New Christianity*. Seaside: Academy of Arts and Humanities Monograph Series, Number 2, 1976.

Kelly, Josephine. *Dark Shepherd*. Patterson: St. Anthony's Guild Press, 1967. [On James A. Healy].

Klukowski, Constantin. *History of St. Mary's of the Angels in Green Bay (Wis.) 1898–1954*. Pulaski: Franciscan Fathers, 1954. [On Joseph René Vilatte].

Kramer, Edward C. "Director General's Page," *Our Colored Missions* 19:4 (April 1933), 55; M.P. Harris, "Correspondence," *Our Colored Missions* 19:5 (May 1933), 78; Sarah Dean, and A Member of St. James Parish, "Correspondence: The Healy Family," *Our Colored Missions* 19:6 (June 1933), 93.

Lane, Roger. *William Dorsey's Philadelphia and Ours: On the Past and Future of the Black City in America*. N.Y.: Oxford University Press, 1991.

Lee, R.L. *Racial Episcopacy—Reasons*. Greenville: M. Kanaga, 1915.

Lewis, Carlos. *Catholic Negro Bishops: A Brief Survey of the Present and the Past*. Bay St. Louis: Divine Word Publications, 1958.

Lewis, Carol A. "An Error Corrected by Historical Investigation: In re Archbishop Francisco Xavier de Luna Victoria." *Journal of Negro History* 33:4 (October 1948), 418–25.

Lucey, William L. *The Catholic Church in Maine*. Francestown: Marshall Jones Co., 1957. [On James A. Healy].

McCarriar, Herbert G., Jr. "A History of the Missionary Jurisdiction of the South of the Reformed Episcopal Church." *Historical Magazine of the Protestant Episcopal Church* 41:2 (June 1972), 197–202; 41:3 (Sept. 1972), 287–323.

Macdonald, A.J. *Episcopi Vagantes in Church History*. London: SPCK, 1945.

McGough, Michael. "Equal Rites." *The New Republic* 201 (August 28, 1989), 11–12. [On George A. Stallings].

McGuire, George Alexander. "The Episcopalians and Archbishop Vilatte." *The Negro Churchman* 1:8 (August 1923), 3–5.

———. "Our Episcopal Succession." *The Negro Churchman* 1:1 (January 1923), 2.

———. "Our Interview with the Patriarch of Constantinople." *The Negro Churchman* 1:4 (April 1923), 1–2.

McKelway, St. Clair, with A.J. Liebling. "Who Is This King of Glory?" *True Tales from the Annuals of Crime and Rascality*. N.Y.: Random House, 1951, pp. 147–97. [On John A. Hickerson].

Melton, J. Gordon. *The Encyclopedia of American Religions*. Volume I. Wilmington: McGrath Publishing Co., 1978.

"Methodist Episcopal Negro Bishops." *Voice of the Negro* 1:7 (July 1904), 207+.

Moede, Gerald F. *The Office of Bishop in Methodism*. Zurich: Publishing House of the Methodist Church, 1964.

Moss, C.B. *The Old Catholic Movement, Its Origins and History*. London: SPCK, 1948.

Natsoulas, Theodore. "Patriarch McGuire and the Spread of the African Orthodox Church to Africa." *Journal of Religion in Africa* 12:2 (1981), 81–104.

Newman, Richard. "Archbishop Daniel William Alexander and the African Orthodox Church," *International Journal of African Historical Studies* 16:4 (1983), 615–30. Reprinted in Richard Newman, *Black Power and Black Religion: Essays and Reviews*. West Cornwall: Locust Hill Press, 1987, pp. 109–30.

———. "Bishop James A. Healy: A Bibliography of Secondary Sources." *Newsletter of the Afro-American Religious History Group of the American Academy of Religion* 4:2 (Spring 1980), 3–4.

———. "The Origins of the African Orthodox Church," *The Negro Churchman*, Millwood: Kraus Reprint Co., 1977, pp. iii–xxiv. Reprinted in Richard Newman, *Black Power and Black Religion: Essays and Reviews*. West Cornwall: Locust Hill Press, 1987, pp. 83–107.

Norris, John William. *The AME Episcopacy: A Paper Read Before the Baltimore AME Preachers' Meeting*. Baltimore: The Afro-American Co., 1916.

Oliveria, Alipio Odier de. *Tracos Biographicos de D. Silverio Gomes Pimenta*. São Paulo: Escolas Profissionaes Salesianas, 1940.

Ortiz, Bendito. *O Arcebispo Negro*. Petropolis: Editoria Vozes, Ltd., 1942.

Ostling, Richard N. "Black Catholics vs. the Church." *Time* 134 (July 10, 1989), 57. [On George A. Starlings].

———. "Catholicism's Black Maverick." *Time* 135 (May 14, 1990), 67. [On George A. Stallings].

"Our Colored Catholics." United States Catholic Historical Society, *Historical Records and Studies* 28 (1937), 259–61. [On Francis Xavier de Luna Victoria y Castro].

Parker, Robert A. *The Incredible Messiah: The Deification of Father Divine*. Boston: Little, Brown and Co., 1937. [On John A. Hickerson].

"Patriarchal Bull Permitting Consecration of Pere Vilatte." *The Negro Churchman* 1:8 (August 1923), 1–2.

Payne, Wardell J., ed. *Directory of African American Religious Bodies: A Compendium by the Howard University School of Divinity*. Washington: Howard University Press, 1991.

Pearson, Fred Lamar, Jr., and Joseph Aaron Tomberlin. "John Doe, Alias God: A Note on Father Divine's Georgia Career." *The Georgia Historical Quarterly* 60:1 (Spring 1976). 43–48. [On John A. Hickerson].

Persson, Bertil. *A Collection of Documentation on the Apostolic Succession of Joseph René Vilatte*. Solna, Sweden: St. Ephrem's Institute, 1974.

Philip. E.M. *The Indian Church of St. Thomas*. Nagercoil: London Mission Press, 1954.

Piepkorn, Arthur C. *Profiles in Belief: The Religious Bodies of the United States and Canada Vol. I Roman Catholics, Old Catholic, Eastern Orthodox*. N.Y.: Harper & Row, 1977.

Pitts, David. "Is a Separate Church the Answer to Blacks' Prayers?" *Black Enterprise* 20 (October 1989), 28. [On George A. Stallings].

Platt, Warren C. "The African Orthodox Church: An Analysis of Its First Decade." *Church History* 58:4 (December 1989), 474–88.

———. "Holy Cross Pro-Cathedral of the African Orthodox Church." *Anglican and Episcopal History* 46:4 (December 1977), 474–89.

———. "Intercommunion Between the Episcopal Church and the Polish National Catholic Church: A Survey of Its Development." *Internationale Kirchliche Zeitschrift* (July–September 1992), 142–65.

———. "The Polish National Catholic Church: An Inquiry into Its Origins." *Church History*, forthcoming.

Poston, T.R. "'I Taught Father Divine' Says St. Bishop the Vine." *New York Amsterdam News* (Nov. 23, 1932), 1. [On John A. Hickerson].

Pruter, Karl. *Bishops Extraordinary*. San Bernardino: The Borgo Press, 1986.

———. *A History of the Old Catholic Church*. Scottsdale: St. Willibrord Press, 1973.

———. *The Strange Partnership of George Alexander McGuire and Marcus Garvey*. Highlandville: St. Willibrord Press, 1986.

———, and J. Gordon Melton. *The Old Catholic Sourcebook*. N.Y.: Garland Publishing, Inc., 1983.

Randolph, Laura B. "What's Behind the Black Rebellion in the Catholic Church?" *Ebony* 45 (November 1989), pp. 160+. [On George A. Stallings].

Reimers, David M. "Negro Bishops and Diocesan Segregation in the Protestant Episcopal Church, 1870–1954." *Historical Magazine of the Protestant Episcopal Church* 31:3 (September 1962), 231–42.

Rumble, Leslie. "Are Liberal Catholic Orders Valid?" *The Homiletic and Pastoral Review* 58:6 (March 1958), 559–71.

Rushing, Byron. "A Note on the Origins of the African Orthodox Church." *Journal of Negro History* 57:1 (January 1972), 37–39.

Schomburg, Arthur A. "Archbishop Victoria—A Negro: First Native Archbishop in the Americas." *Interracial Review* 10:8 (August 1937), 120–22.

Schroeder, Theodore. "A 'Living God' Incarnate." *The Psycho-analytic Review: An American Journal of Psychoanalysis* 19:1 (Jan. 1932), 36–45. [On John A. Hickerson].

———. "Living Gods." *Azoth: The Occult Magazine of America* 3:4 (Oct. 1918), 202–5. [On John A. Hickerson].

Schultz, Paul G.W. *The Background of the Episcopate of Archbishop René Joseph [sic] Vilatte*. Glendale: Guardian Angel Press, 1976.

Shepperson, George. "Notes on Negro American Influence on the Emergence of African Nationalism." *Journal of African History* 1:2 (1960), 299–312. [On George A. McGuire].

Souza, Joaquim Silverio de. *Vida de D. Silverio Gomes Pimenta*. São Paulo: Escolas Profissionaes do Lyceu Coracao de Jesus, 1927.

Stahel, Thomas H. "Albert J. Raboteau." *America* 166:14 (April 25, 1992). [On George A. Stallings].

———. "The Case of Father Stallings: Bishop Emerson J. Moore." *America* 168:8 (March 3, 1992), 187–88.

Stuart, M.S. *An Economic Detour: A History of Insurance in the Lives of American Negroes*. N.Y.: Wendell Malliet and Co., 1940. [On AOC Bishop Grant Barrow].

Tavard, George. *A Review of Anglican Orders: The Problem and the Solution*. Collegeville: Liturgical Press, 1990.

Terry-Thomas, Arthur C. *The History of the African Orthodox Church*. N.Y.: Author, 1956.

Tillett, Gregory. *Joseph René Vilatte: A Bibliography*. Sydney: The Vilatte Guild, 1980.

Toote, Fred A. "Bishop Robertson's Consecration." *The Negro Churchman* 1:12 (December 1923), 1–2.

Trela, Jonathan E. *A History of the North American Old Roman Catholic Church*. Scranton: Polish National Catholic Church, 1979.

Trindade, Ramundo Octavio da. *Biographie de Dom Silverio Gomes Pimenta i Arcebispo de Mariauna*. P Ste Nova, 1939.

Trotman, Arthur S. "That 'House of Bishops!'" *The Negro Churchman* 2:4 (April 1924), 3–4.

Turner, Henry McNeal. *The Genius and Theory of Methodist Polity, or the Machinery of Methodism Practically Illustrated Through a Series of Questions and Answers.* Philadelphia: Publication Department, A.M.E. Church, 1885.

*Twenty-Fifth Anniversary Souvenir Journal of the African Orthodox Church.* N.p. [N.Y.?]: n.p., n.d [1946?].

Ward, Gary L., Bertil Persson, and Alan Bain. *Independent Bishops: An International Directory.* Detroit: Apogee Books, 1990.

Watts, Jill M. *God, Harlem U.S.A.: The Father Divine Story.* Berkeley: University of California Press, 1992. [On John A. Hickerson].

Welborn, F.B. *East African Rebels: A Study of Some Independent Churches.* London: SPCK, 1961.

Wentinck, D.E. "The Orthodox Church of East Africa." *Ecumenical Review* 20:1 (1968), 33–43.

West, Michael O. *African Middle-Class Formation in Colonial Zimbabwe. 1890–1965.* Ph.D. dissertation, Harvard University, 1990.

———. "Ethiopianism and Colonialism: The Establishment of the African Orthodox Church in Zimbabwe, 1929–1934." Prepared for Conference on Christian Missionaries and the State in the Third World Sponsored by Institute of Church History, University of Copenhagen and Institute of Commonwealth Studies, University of London. Lyngby Landbrugsskole, Denmark, May 28–31, 1992.

Whalen, William J. *Separated Brethren: A Survey of Protestant, Anglican, Orthodox, Old Catholic, and Other Denominations in the United States.* Huntington: Our Sunday Visitor, 1972.

White, Gavin. "Patriarch McGuire and the Episcopal Church." *Historical Magazine of the Protestant Episcopal Church* 38:2 (June 1969), 109–41. Reprinted in Randall K. Burkett and Richard Newman, eds., *Black Apostles: Afro-American Clergy Confront the Twentieth Century.* Boston: G.K. Hall & Co., 1978, pp. 151–80.

Wielewinski, Bernard, comp. *Polish National Catholic Church, Independent Movements, Old Catholic Church and Related Items: An Annotated Bibliography.* Scranton: Polish National Catholic Church Commission on History and Archives, 1990.

Wilson, A.N. *Unguarded Hours.* London: Hamlyn, 1978. [A novel in which the central character becomes an *episcopus vagans*].

Wipfler, William. "The Establishment and Development of the L'Eglise Orthodoxe Apostolique Haitienne." M.A. thesis, General Theological Seminary, 1955.

Woodward, Joseph H. *The Negro Bishop Movement in the Episcopal Diocese of South Carolina: A Psychological Study*. McPhersonville: Herbert Woodward, 1915.

Yesehaq, Archbishop [Mandefro, L.M.]. *The Ethiopian Tewahedo Church: An Integrally African Church*. N.Y.: Vantage Press, 1989.

# An Interview with
# Sherry Sherrod DuPree

The DuPree African American Pentecostal Collection, now open to researchers at the Schomburg Center for Research in Black Culture, is one of the first attempts to document the history of black Holiness and Pentecostalism. Richard Newman recently conducted the following interview with Sherry Sherrod DuPree, founder of the collection.

***

**RN:** When did you first start collecting black Pentecostal materials?

**SD:** It was over ten years ago, 1981.

**RN:** And what inspired you to start?

**SD:** I was a librarian at the University of Florida at the time and I became very aware of the lack of resources—both primary and secondary—for African American religion in general, but especially for any study of the black Holiness and Pentecostal movements.

**RN:** Why do you think that's been the case? Why didn't those resources exist?

**SD:** Well, there are several reasons. These churches are relatively new denominations, after all, and I think they've been more concerned internally with practicing their religion rather than studying it. Also, it has to be said that these groups have been pretty much outside the mainstream and so they've been ignored by the establishment.

**RN:** Do you mean that as black churches they've been ignored by the whites who write textbooks and hold conferences and all that?

**SD:** Yes, that's certainly part of it, but they've also been ignored because they're outside the Protestant religious mainstream and have never been considered quite respectable. And of course it's also true that Pentecostal people have traditionally been working class folks, and that means they're often invisible, and when they are seen, they're not taken very seriously.

**RN:** What about gender bias?

**SD:** It's true that women often play a large role in these churches, and we know there's prejudice against women.

**RN:** That's a formidable catalogue. But isn't the situation changing? I mean in all the categories you've just spelled out?

**SD:** Yes, it's true. They are all changing.

**RN:** Say something about that.

**SD:** First of all, the Pentecostal movement itself is mature enough now to be interested in its own history. Young Pentecostal students are exploring their roots and writing about their own distinctive religious background. The older generation, which only had an oral tradition, is encouraging the younger generation to preserve their heritage.

**RN:** Wait a minute. Does the fact that Pentecostals are now exploring their own history mean that the movement is losing some of its immediacy and becoming more established? Is Pentecostalism in transition, in other words, "from sect to church," a process every other denomination has gone through?

**SD:** Yes, it surely is. Churches that used to be storefronts are now temples and cathedrals. What began as a religion of the poor now has many middle class members. Ministers are now often Bible-school or even seminary trained.

**RN:** So, inside the movement itself, you're saying, historical consciousness is part of that transition, that inevitable transition?

**SD:** I believe it is. Women's dress standards in the churches are changing, for example. Also, prayer meetings are not as anointed as they used to be. But the Bible doesn't change and people's needs don't change. We're only seeing changes in the ways people are being reached.

RN: So, despite the transition, Holiness and Pentecostal churches still maintain their uniqueness and their vitality?

SD: Oh, yes. The mainstream churches are losing members to the Pentecostals every day. The Church of God in Christ, for instance, is the fastest growing major denomination in the country. It adds about 200,000 people and 600 churches annually, and it's now the fifth largest American church.

RN: That brings us back to another of the reasons Pentecostal materials weren't collected and why that's changing. That is, people outside are only now becoming aware of the movement because of the size and new visibility of the churches. Is that true?

SD: Indeed, it is. And one result, of course, is a greater interest in documentation. Scholars are now asking: who are these people and where did they come from? I believe it was you who wrote somewhere that Azusa Street and 1906 would eventually take their place in the literature along with 1517 and the Diet of Worms. And wasn't there even a course on Pentecostalism at Harvard last year for the first time?

RN: Yes, it was taught by Harvey Cox who recently wrote about it in the *Christian Century*. I guess that makes it an official trend. Let's come back, though, to the DuPree Collection. How did you go about finding material?

SD: Holiness and Pentecostal materials tend to be largely ephemeral: pamphlets, programs, self-published sermons and biographies, clippings from religious papers, that sort of thing. No one was preserving it, certainly no libraries, so I just traveled wherever and whenever I could, tracking it down from ministers, ministers' widows, long-time church members, any place I thought I might find anything.

RN: How much traveling did you actually do?

SD: I've been over 200,000 miles in 38 states.

RN: That's astonishing! Tell me some of the treasures you found.

SD: From Robert and Florence McGoings of Baltimore, I located some copies of *Contender for the Faith*; that's the publication of the Church of Our Lord Jesus Christ of the Apostolic Faith, a Oneness group founded by Robert C. Lawson in 1919. And some cassette tapes of Lawson's sermons and his communication with Haile Selassie.

**RN:** Anything from Azusa Street itself?

**SD:** Yes, I found a copy of the manual of doctrine and some issues of the *Apostolic Faith* newspaper put out by the Azusa Street Mission. There's information of the daily activities of the revival, and news of Lucy Farrow and Julia Hutchins who were missionaries to Africa, and ship passenger records. There are William J. Seymour's sermon texts, and healing testimonies, and names of people who received the baptism of the Holy Ghost.

**RN:** That's all very valuable—and very elusive—information. We know that newspapers are one of the best sources of black history and one of the least accessible sources at the same time. Did you locate others?

**SD:** Yes, at the Center for Research Libraries in Chicago I went through a great many unindexed African American newspapers looking for information and copying relevant material.

**RN:** What papers?

**SD:** Oh, *The Florida Star* from Jacksonville, the *Tri-State Defender* that covers Arkansas, Tennessee and Mississippi, the *Louisiana Weekly*, papers like that.

**RN:** And what did you find?

**SD:** Well, there's a wealth of information here. Obituaries, schedules of church services, news of convocations, missionary travels. There are frequent stories on the personalities of leader-centered groups like Father Divine and Daddy Grace and Prophet Jones.

**RN:** What about women leaders?

**SD:** Yes, I found articles on Mother Horn in New York, Mother Waddles in Detroit, and Mother Mattie Poole and Elder Lucy Smith, both of Chicago.

**RN:** You mentioned cassette tapes a few minutes ago. What are some of those in the Collection?

*An Interview with Sherry Sherrod DuPree* 153

SD: I have tapes of interviews and gospel music. There are convention tapes from the Bible Way Church of Our Lord Jesus Christ, Washington, DC. There are tapes of Elder Richard "Mr. Clean" White, preaching and singing. And I taped Sunday services at Williams Temple Church of God in Christ in Gainesville, Florida, from 1982 to 1987.

RN: What about videos?

SD: Yes, there's film of Bishop James McKnight, leader of the Florida-based Church of God By Faith. COGIC Bishop F.D. Washington's funeral was filmed in Brooklyn in 1988. There's footage of Elder Detroit Williams and many others.

RN: Music is certainly important in this tradition. How is that represented in the Collection?

SD: Oh, yes, it's there. I located a rare copy of C.P. Jones' booklet *The History of My Songs*, published in 1908. There's sheet music like Robert E. Roberts' "Thirsty After Thee, O Lord." There are copies of the *Middle Atlantic Regional Gospel Festival Newsletters*.

RN: Photographs and pictures?

SD: There are images of the early pioneers: William J. Seymour, C.H. Mason, C.P. Jones. And rare photographs of Lelia W. Mason, C.H. Mason's second wife, and Mary Magdalena Tate who founded the Church of the Living God the Pillar and Ground of Truth Without Controversy. As far as I know, she was the first black woman to found a Pentecostal denomination.

RN: We agreed that ephemera have been crucial to the movement. You must have collected a great deal.

SD: It is important. I have pamphlets from Aenon College, women's convention badges, theses from Bible colleges, gospel sheet music, souvenir journals, Sunday School literature, youth meeting programs.

RN: Well, this is all an extraordinary collection and one that required an extraordinary commitment and energy to bring together.

SD: I just hope it's used for a better understanding of the Holiness and Pentecostal traditions.

**RN:** You've certainly used it that way yourself. I speak of your *Biographical Dictionary of African American Holiness Pentecostals, 1880–1990*, which is an extremely useful book. And you have a new one coming, do you not?

**SD:** Yes, Garland brought out in 1995 my 700-page bibliography. It's entitled *The African-American Pentecostal Movement: An Annotated Bibliography*.

**RN:** That's certainly going to be a very useful resource. I assume you used information you gathered there in your recent *Yearbook of American Churches* article?

**SD:** That's right. Kenneth Bedell of the National Council of Churches edits the *Yearbook*, which is of American and Canadian churches, by the way. The article is called "The Explosive Growth of the African American Pentecostal Church."

**RN:** I saw it, and I noticed your husband provided the demographic maps.

**SD:** Yes, Herb is a geographer, as you know. Should I mention the finding aid to the DuPree Collection at Schomburg?

**RN:** Of course. That's Chris McKay's inventory?

**SD:** She did a wonderful job listing the contents of the collection and I believe copies are available from Schomburg.

**RN:** Sherry, I want to thank you not only for all you've done to advance Pentecostal scholarship, but for being gracious enough to take time for this interview.

**SD:** Thank you. I enjoyed it.

## Part IV
## *Reading*

"Every assembledge of negroes for the purpose of instructing in reading or writing ... shall be unlawful assembledge. Any justice may issue his warrant to any officer or other person, requiring him to enter any place where such assembledges may be, and sieze any negro therein; and he, or any other justice, may order such negro to be punished with stripes."

—*The Code of Virginia*, 1860

# Vindicating the Race: Collectors of African-American Books

Collectors of old and rare African-American books have always had a motivation different from the imperatives that drive other bibliophiles. Historically, those collectors, both black and white, have not been particularly interested in the book as object: first editions, signed copies, fine printing and binding, condition, or even the hope of financial appreciation. They have been committed, rather, to gathering these books simply to demonstrate that they exist.

In the face of pseudoscientific and popular views of black inferiority, books by and about people of African descent stood as evidence that black people had their own history and literature and culture and were capable of thinking and creating and writing. Indeed, black collectors in particular saw themselves as vindicators of the race, "race men" as they used to be called, part of a movement devoted to racial consciousness, uplift, and defense.

Some collectors of Afro-Americana have been non-traditional bibliophiles in other respects as well. One was Oliver Jones, a black Civil War veteran and a coal miner in Fayette County, West Virginia, in the 1890's. Working in the mine with him was the young Carter G. Woodson, who later earned a Ph.D. in history from Harvard and founded both the Association for the Study of Negro Life and History and Negro History Week, now Black History Month. Woodson told Jones' story.[1]

The mine owners forced the workers to buy in company stores, but Oliver Jones turned his modest home into a kind of tea shop where fellow miners could gather after work. Woodson recalled that Jones's house was a veritable reading room with its substantial library and the dozen black and white daily newspapers to which he subscribed.

Jones was a well-educated man, Woodson remembered, but even more remarkable than his being a coal miner who collected books was the fact that Oliver Jones could neither read nor write. He hired Woodson to read to him and his co-workers, who were also illiterate, because he knew the power and pleasure of books and loved them.

Jones was especially interested in black military history and owned copies of George Washington Williams' *A History of the Negro Troops in the War of the Rebellion* and Joseph T. Wilson's *The Black Phalanx*, as well as William J. Simmons' *Men of Mark: Eminent, Progressive and Rising* and other books portraying black achievement. "My interest in penetrating the past of my people was deepened and intensified," Woodson wrote of his time with Jones.

Another unlikely black bibliophile was Bert Williams, the vaudeville and Ziegfeld Follies star, arguably the greatest comedian ever to appear on the American stage. Underneath the burnt-cork make-up he was forced to wear, Williams was a deeply serious, even tragic man, fully aware that despite his talent he was consigned forever to playing "darky" roles.

Williams owned a wide-ranging and well-read library, but black history was a special interest. One of his treasures was a copy of John Ogilby's *Africa* published in London in 1670 which provides a historical description of many African tribes. Williams used to say, "I think with this volume I could prove that every Pullman porter is the descendant of a king."[2]

As far as was known, the first person intentionally to gather a library of books written by black people was a white man, Johann Friedrich Blumenbach (1752–1840). He was an anatomist who taught medicine at the University of Göttingen for sixty years and is generally considered the father of modern physical anthropology. Because he attempted to classify humankind into racial groups, Blumenbach would today probably be considered something of a racist, particularly since it was he who coined the term Caucasian.

In fact, though, Blumenbach was an advanced, even radical thinker for his day. He demonstrated that black people were human beings rather than animals (which most Europeans believed), that dark skin color was caused by environment rather than a

Biblical curse, and that despite their varieties, people of all races constitute only one species—thus eliminating any inherent biological basis for either racial inferiority or superiority. As a scientist gathering data Blumenbach collected everything that proved the Negro's full humanity, including books written by Africans and people of African descent.[3]

Blumenbach had a copy of Phillis Wheatley's *Poems on Various Subjects, Religious and Moral*, the first book published by an African American and the second book of poetry by an American woman. A small, sickly child when she was bought from "a parcel of small negroes" on a Boston wharf, Wheatley was cosseted by her owners and encouraged to write. She produced poems in a classical style, and her book was first issued in London in 1773. It has remained in print ever since.

Blumenbach also owned several almanacs calculated in the 1790's by Benjamin Banneker, the Maryland free black who was a self-taught astronomer. Something of a mathematical genius, Banneker helped survey the District of Columbia, constructed a striking clock without ever having seen one, and came to the attention of Thomas Jefferson. His almanacs, sponsored by local antislavery societies, were authoritative throughout the region.

Works by at least two African authors were in Blumenbach's library. Anthony William Amo, a native of Guinea, received a doctorate from Wittenburg in 1734 and taught there as well as at Halle and Jena. Blumenbach possessed two treatises of Amo's in philosophical psychology, *Diss. inaug. Philosophica de humanae mentis απαφεςα seu sensionis ac facultatis sentiendi in mente humana absentia, et earum in corpore nostro organico ac vivo proesentia....* and *Disp. philosophica continens ideam distinctam eorum quae competunt vel menti vel corpori nostro vivo vel organico.*

J.E.L. Capitein was a captured African slave who studied theology at Leyden. Blumenbach owned published sermons and poems of Capitein as well as his 1742 Latin dissertation, the title of which indicates the extent of Capitein's Europeanization: *Dissertatio politico-theologica de servitute libertati Christianae non contrana.* Capitein preached for a while in Amsterdam but then disappeared; one story is that he returned to Africa, perhaps disillusioned with his own thesis.

Collectors of Afro-Americana have never had an easy task. The few books of history or social science running against the grain of

American racism, as well as creative works of fiction and poetry by writers of color have all had trouble being taken seriously and finding publishers. As a result, many were printed privately, distributed locally, and never found their way into libraries, let alone bookstores. For the dedicated collector, of course, the very elusiveness of black material made the hunt all the more exciting and discovery all the more gratifying.

The largest and best known collection in this country was assembled by Arthur Alphonso Schomburg (1874–1938).[4] Born in San Juan, he was the illegitimate child of a black Puerto Rican laundress and a German merchant. Schomburg's life-long passion for collecting reportedly sprang from a childhood experience when a grammar school teacher responded to his question about black history by informing him that black people had no history.

Schomburg became the leader of a network of zealous book lovers who hunted obscure volumes, swapped fishermen's stories about the ones they landed and the ones that got away, and devoutly believed they were reclaiming a lost heritage. For them, books were not a hobby or diversion: "The American Negro must remake his past in order to make his future," Schomburg wrote. "When we consider the facts, certain chapters of American history will have to be reopened."[5]

Possessed of and by an international vision, Schomburg saw the interrelatedness of Africa and the worldwide Diaspora of African peoples in Europe, the Caribbean, and North and South America. Too poor to travel extensively himself, Schomburg prevailed upon his friends to seek out rarities on their trips. He gave Albert Smith a list of items relating to black artist Henry O. Tanner to look for in France. Langston Hughes dutifully sent home from Russia material on Pushkin and Ira Aldridge, the expatriate Shakespearean actor.

Among Schomburg's treasures were Juan Latino's *Ad Catholicum*, Latin verse and epigrams published in Grenada in 1573. A full-blooded African, Latino held the chair of poetry at the University of Grenada. Schomburg located a copy of Jupiter Hammon's 1787 broadside *Address to the Negroes in the State of New York*, the first published African-American poet, as well as a first edition of William Wells Brown's novel *The President's Daughter: A Narrative of Slave Life in the United States*. Issued in London in 1853, *The President's Daughter* was based on Thomas Jefferson's relationship with his slave Sally Hemings. It had to be significantly revised before it could be published in this country.

Schomburg amassed some 5,000 books, 3,000 manuscripts, and 2,000 prints. At the urging of the Urban League, the Carnegie Corporation purchased the entire collection for $10,000 and presented it to the 135th Street Branch of the New York Public Library in 1926. Today it forms the basis of the holdings of the renamed Schomburg Center for Research in Black Culture. The Schomburg Center now houses in Harlem over five million items in all media. It documents the black experience throughout the world and serves an international community of scholars.

With their overriding goal of preserving these scarce books and the history and culture they represent, it is not surprising that both black and white bibliophiles were eager to have institutions take over their collections so they could be saved and made available for study and research. Jesse Moorland, a Colored Y.M.C.A. official and Congregational minister, donated his large library to Howard University in 1914 thus creating the first research collection of black material in an American university.

Among other significant black collectors, the 3,000 books of Charles D. Martin, a Moravian minister in Harlem, were purchased by North Carolina Central University in 1950. Daniel A.P. Murray was a librarian at the Library of Congress for 50 years and his own books are preserved there. In 1946 Atlanta University bought the books, manuscripts, and ephemera of Henry Proctor Slaughter, a lawyer and journalist.

White collectors shared the same conviction about vindicating African American history, and many of their collections, too, found their way to institutions. The anti-slavery books and pamphlets of Samuel J. May, the abolitionist Unitarian minister, went to Cornell. Arthur B. Spingarn, a New York attorney and N.A.A.C.P. official, collected books by black authors, and his library is now at Howard University's Moorland-Spingarn Research Center. Carl Van Vechten, critic, writer, arbiter of fashion, and the most prominent white person involved in the Harlem Renaissance, collected indefatigably and named his collection which he donated to Yale for his friend James Weldon Johnson.

What specifically was the lost history these bibliophiles wanted to regain, and the false history they wanted to correct? What was the testimony of the books they lovingly and sacrificially rescued from literal and figurative dustbins? Schomburg said there were three major facts for which his library provided evidence: blacks have been pioneers in the struggle for their own freedom, distinguished blacks have been wrongly disassociated from the race as "exceptions," and Africa was an ancient center of culture and civilization.

The political and psychological implications of these facts are clear. Vindication of the race was perceived, however, not only as a message to the oppressive world. It was also seen as a redemptive power within the black community itself. As the Philadelphia book collector Robert W. Adger wrote a century ago: "We want the newspapers, the churches and the parents to tell their children what our past condition was, and about those dear people who are dead and gone, of the sacrifices they made in our behalf and the grand opportunities [we] are now afforded."[6]

## Notes

1. Carter G. Woodson, "My Recollections of Veterans of the Civil War," *The Negro History Bulletin* 7:5 (Feb. 1944), 115–16.

2. Mabel Rowland, ed. *Bert Williams, Son of Laughter*, New York: The English Crafters, 1923, p. 183.

3. *Johann Friedrich Blumenbach on the Natural Varieties of Mankind, De Generis Humani Varietate Nativa, The Anthropological Treatises of Johann Friedrich Blumenbach, with Memoirs of Him by Marx and Flourens, an Account of the Anthropological Museum in Göttingen, by R. Wagner and a Dissertation of John Hunter, Translated and Edited from the Latin, German and French Originals, by Thomas Bendyshe*. New York: Bergman Publishers, 1969, p. 311.

4. Elinor DesVerney Sinette, *Arthur Alfonso Schomburg: Black Bibliophile and Collector*. Detroit: The New York Public Library and Wayne State University Press, 1989.

5. Arthur A. Schomburg, "The Negro Digs Up His Past," *Survey Graphic* 6:6 (March 1925), 670–72.

6. Quoted by Tony Martin, "Race Men, Bibliophiles, and Historians: The World of Robert M. Adger and the Negro Historical Society of Philadelphia," in Wendy Ball and Tony Martin, *Rare Afro-Americana: A Reconstruction of the Adger Library*. Boston: G.K. Hall & Co., 1981, p. 31.

# The First Printed Protest Against Slavery: George Keith's *Exhortation* of 1693

The first in the long catalogue of anti-slavery literature published in British North America was George Keith's pamphlet *An Exhortation and Caution to Friends Concerning Buying or Keeping of Negroes* printed in New York by William Bradford in 1693.[1] Keith, a contentious and squabbling Quaker schismatic, was preceded in protesting slavery by the better-known Germantown memorial of 1688, but that was a petition which did not see print until 1844.[2]

Keith's *Exortation* is an essay of six pages measuring 19 1/2 x 10 cm. It was printed by Bradford, New York's first printer, who had been forced out of Pennsylvania because he was a Keithian sympathizer in an intense internecine religious controversy which seriously split the Quaker colony. Only one complete copy of the original leaflet is known to exist. It is in Friends' Library, London, where it was found in the nineteenth century by Charles R. Hildeburn, librarian of the Philadelphia Athenaeum and a bibliographer of Pennsylvania imprints.[3]

Several American libraries do have photostatic copies of the *Exhortation*, and an imperfect original does exist in this country.[4] It was part of the Barnwell sale in Philadelphia on July 13, 1921, and is now held by the Huntington Library. Keith's tract was reprinted with an introduction by George H. Moore of the Lenox Library in 1889 in the *Pennsylvania Magazine of History and Biography*, and issued at the same time as a separate.[5] J. William Frost also reprinted it in his *The Keithian Schism Controversy in Early Pennsylvania*, but discussed it only cursorily.[6] In the main, however, Keith's pamphlet is a little-known publication despite its place in the literature of antislavery, African Americana, religious controversy, and printing history. The *Exhortation* was originally printed sometime after October 13, 1693, in the first year of William Bradford's career as Royal Printer in New York. Wilberforce Eames says the pamphlet was the 23rd product of Bradford's press in New York, which was located in Dock Square at the Sign of the Bible, since commemorated by a memorial tablet at 81 Pearl Street.[7] Bradford learned the printing trade in London and originally set up his press in Philadelphia, but he was arrested there for printing an earlier tract by Keith which criticized the Quaker establishment, and so accepted the invitation to move to New York.

Who was the author of this historic pamphlet? Born in 1638, George Keith was a Scotsman with an M.A. from Aberdeen who was converted in 1663 from his native Presbyterianism to the Society of Friends.[8] His Calvinist background and training made him particularly interested in doctrinal issues and formulations; his intelligence and zeal made him a brilliant, energetic, and prolific Quaker apologist and polemicist; and his argumentative and quarrelsome temperament made him ripe for controversy, contention, and schism.[9]

Keith rose to the highest circles in the Society of Friends. He accompanied George Fox, William Penn, and Robert Barclay on their missionary trip to Germany and Holland, and in America he became master of Penn Charter School. A surveyor by trade, Keith ran the line between East and West Jersey.[10] At George Fox's death, Keith began to criticize what he perceived to be looseness and lack of purity in Quaker belief and practice, perhaps thinking his rigor would establish him as Fox's successor.

Keith's criticisms were theological, concerning the nature of Christ, but also political as he attacked the "worldly power and greatness" of the supposedly unadorned Quaker officials who controlled Pennsylvania. Partly because of legitimate religious differences, partly because of the power issue, and partly because of Keith's offensive intemperance, he was disowned in 1692 by the Society's Yearly Meeting which found him guilty of "a mischievous and hurtful separation." Keith and numerous followers countered by organizing themselves as "Christian Quakers," combining in doctrine and organization elements of his own dual background as Presbyterian and Friend.[11]

The Keithians were not finally successful as a sect, and the Baptists and others drew off many of their members. Keith himself eventually entered the Church of England, took Anglican orders in 1702, and returned to America as the first travelling missionary of the Society for the Propagation of the Gospel. He was, not surprisingly, particularly successful in debating Quakers. Returning to England, Keith became rector at Edburton and died there in 1716.

Much sentiment in Pennsylvania in the latter part of the seventeenth century was opposed to slavery, not because of the Quaker influence, but due to the anti-slavery stance of German immigrants from Kirchheim who had settled in Germantown.[12] Although Quakers came in time to be a major anti-slavery voice, early Quakers did not oppose slavery and many, including even William Penn, actually owned slaves.[13] Penn did urge provision for slaves' education and spiritual welfare, but the strongest early anti-slavery expression came in fact from these German settlers.

It was their opposition to life-long indentured servitude for blacks which resulted, in 1688, in their presentation of an anti-slavery memorial to the Philadelphia Yearly Meeting. The Meeting found it "too weighty a matter" to consider, however, and so postponed action. Their petition remained in manuscript for over 150 years, but it may very well have influenced George Keith, who certainly knew of it at the time.

It is unclear why Keith and his Christian Friends five years later chose to address themselves to the issue of slavery at their October 1693 Monthly Meeting. Keith's own interests were mainly theological, and he was concerned about the place of Friends in government, but he was not interested, so far as we know, in social abuses or social reform. Slavery was not a significant contemporary issue among Quakers, who would wait 100 years to become definite in their disavowal and outspoken in their opposition.

Perhaps, building on the German Friends' petition was a way for Keith to challenge or embarrass the Quaker establishment from which he had become so estranged. Perhaps he and his followers simply were in fact offended by human enslavement and found it contrary to their religious convictions and an affront to a religious community. Whatever the motivation, the *Exhortation* is a striking statement.

It begins with an assumption: "Seeing our Lord Jesus Christ hast tasted death for every man, and given himself a Ransom for all...." Keith's theological presupposition is immediately linked, however, with a rather surprising anthropological one: "... and that Negroes, Blacks and Taunies are a real part of Mankind ... and are capable of Salvation, as well as White men...." The presupposition goes on to assert that all true believers are to bear the image of Christ, who came not "to bring any part of Mankind into outward Bondage, Slavery or Misery, nor yet to detain them, or hold them therein, but to ease and deliver the Oppressed and Distressed, and bring them into Liberty both inward and outward."

These assumptions led Keith to a "therefore." It follows, he argues, that faithful Friends will demonstrate "the fruits of the Spirit" and not only be kind to slaves but actually set free all who are in bondage. The only legitimate purpose in buying blacks, Keith says, is to manumit them. And there is a special imperative to liberate children who have been born into slavery. While the basic reason for this is that slavery "suits not the Mercy, Love and Clemency that is essential to Christianity, nor to the Doctrine of Christ, nor to the Liberty the Gospel calleth all men unto," one additional effect is the possibility that the ex-slaves will be so impressed by the example of their liberators they will themselves be led to "imbrace the true faith of Christ."

Keith then presents a series of five "reasons and causes" against keeping blacks for "term of life," after prudently suggesting that a "reasonable" length of service might compensate owners for their investment. His first reason is that it is contrary to the belief of Christian Quakers to buy stolen goods. Under Mosaic law, stealing a person is a more serious offense than stealing goods: stolen goods are to be restored fourfold while anyone who steals a person is to be put to death.

The second reason is the Golden Rule. Since "we and our children" would certainly not choose to be kept in perpetual bondage, so neither should Christians inflict "such intolerable punishment to their Bodies and Minds" on anyone else. Criminals may well deserve punishment, but Africans, in contrast, "have done us no harm" so it is particularly inhumane to oppress them and their innocent children.

Thirdly, God has commanded, "Thou shalt not deliver unto his master the Servant that is escaped from his master unto Thee," as reported in Deuteronomy 23:15–16. This means for Keith that freed slaves should not be reenslaved, and he suggests that if this is

God's will under the law, even more should grace and mercy be manifested under the Gospel.

The fourth cause is the divine commandment: "Thou shalt not oppress an hired Servant that is poor and needy" (Deut. 24:14–15). Keith then lists various sufferings inflicted upon blacks: they are enslaved, taken from their native countries, cruelly treated, separated from their families, starved, and dealt with, in fact, worse than the slaves of infidels like the Turks and Moors! This catalogue of cruelty led Keith prophetically to conclude, "Surely the Lord doth behold their oppression and afflications, and will further visit for the same by his righteous and just judgment."

The last reason is that slaves are the "Merchandise of Babylon by which the Merchants of the Earth are made Rich." But the money made by trafficking in human beings can only draw God's wrath, Keith says, and Christians are called to renounce Babylon and separate themselves from a wicked world.

Although buttressed with Biblical proof texts, Keith's arguments are not narrowly legalistic in nature. He appears genuinely horrified by human oppression, a theme which recurs prominently throughout the tract. Perhaps Keith felt himself the victim of the Quaker establishment. Perhaps his conscience made him unusually sensitive to the people around him. Perhaps he did have a vision of a radical religious liberty "both inward and outward." Whatever his own imperatives, Keith proclaims a just God who punishes oppressors and a merciful God who offers everyone freedom.

All in all, Keith's statement is a sensitive and humane one, moreso than his time and place would lead one to expect. What he says and how he says it is qualitatively different, for example, both in content and expression from Cotton Mather's *Rules for a Society of Negroes* published the same year. Keith's *Exhortation* has a modern flavor and tone lacking in the broadside written by Mather, who, incidentally, was one of Keith's Puritan opponents. A comparison of the two documents would be fruitful, as would a study of Keith's pamphlet in relation to other Quaker anti-slavery statements.

While Keith's interest in blacks and slavery may have been peripheral, his significance is not simply that he was the author of the first printed protest against slavery in America. George Keith clearly articulated a position, obvious and straightforward as it may now appear, that would take over 150 years to be held by sufficient numbers of his countrymen to bring at last to an end the horrors of American slavery.

## Notes

1. Sabin 37193; Evans 636; Wing (2nd ed.) K162; Hildeburn 61; McMurtrie (1928) 27. Sabin errs in calling this a Philadelphia imprint, as does Edwin Wolf 2nd in his "Black Americana: A New World of Books," *AB* (Nov. 1, 1976), 2366.

2. The manuscript of the Germantown petition was discovered by Nathan Kite who published it in *The Friend*, a Philadelphia Quaker periodical, under the title "The German Friends" in Vol. 17, no. 15, First Month [January], Seventh Day [Saturday], 1844, p. 125. There is additional and corroborative information in William Kite, "First Germantown Friends," *The Friend* [Philadelphia] 48 (1874), 51–52; and Hildegard Binder-Johnson, "The Germantown Protest of 1688 Against Negro Slavery." *Pennsylvania Magazine of History and Biography* 65 (1941), 145–56. I am indebted to Diana Peterson of the Haverford College Library for bringing these references to my attention. See also J. Herbert Fretz, "The Germantown Anti-Slavery Petition of 1688," *Mennonite Quarterly Review* 33 (1959), 42–59.

3. Actually, Hildeburn located it in the Devonshire Meeting House library, but that was moved to the Friends' House library at 173 Euston Road, London, in 1926.

4. The National Union Catalogue reports copies at the Library of Congress, The New York Public Library, the John Carter Brown Library at Brown University, and the William L. Clements Library at the University of Michigan. Peter Drummey of the Massachusetts Historical Society informs me that they also have a photostat; and Nancy Burkett of the American Antiquarian Society says the *Exhortation* is available on microform in the *Early American Imprints* series issued by Readex.

5. Vol. 13, pp. 265–70. Both are entitled "The First Protest Against Slavery in America."

6. Norwood, Pa: Norwood Editions, 1980, pp. xvii, 213–18.

7. "The First Year of Printing in New York, May, 1693–April, 1694." *Bulletin of The New York Public Library* 32 (1928), 3–24. This was also issued as a separate. See also George H. Moore, *Historical Notes on the Introduction of Printing into New York, 1693*. N.Y.: Author, 1888, p. 12.

8. There are numerous biographical sketches, but only one full-length biography of Keith: Ethyn Williams Kirby, *George Keith (1638–1716)*. N.Y.: D. Appleton-Century Co., 1942.

9. A most important and highly useful publication is William S. Reese, "Works of George Keith Printed in America: A Chronological Bibliography." *Princeton University Library Chronicle* 39 (1978), 98–124. The *Exhortation* is no. 21.

10. Pomfret, John E. *The Province of West New Jersey, 1609–1702*. Princeton: Princeton University Press, 242–58.

11. There is much material on the Keithian schism. See, for instance, Jon Butler, "'Gospel Order Improved': The Keithian Schism and the Exercise of Quaker Ministerial Authority in Pennsylvania." *William and Mary Quarterly* 31 (1974), 431–52. Horace M. Lippincott, "The Keithian Separation." *Bulletin of Friends Historical Association* 16 (1927), 49–58. The "interrelated nature of religious, economic and political positions" is emphasized by Gary B. Nash, *Quakers and Politics, Pennsylvania 1681–1721*. Princeton: Princeton University Press, 1968, p. 158.

12. Cheesman A. Herrick, *White Servitude in Pennsylvania: Indentured Labor in Colony and Commonwealth*. Philadelphia: J.J. McVey, 1926.

13. The long development of anti-slavery sentiment is discussed by Herbert Aptheker, "The Quakers and Negro Slavery." *Journal of Negro History* 25 (October 1940), 331–62.

# Books and Writers
# of the Harlem Renaissance

It was originally known as the "New Negro" movement, and the phrase "Harlem Renaissance" did not become popular until Melvin Tolson's 1940 master's thesis at Columbia. Whatever the nomenclature, there certainly was a vital and self-conscious blooming of African-American culture centered in New York through the decade of the 1920s. It resulted in some of the most significant—and collectible—black literature yet produced. Although the books themselves are now elusive, they constitute a monument to a glittering period of African-American creativity.

While books were central to this Renaissance, the revolution was not just in writing and publishing. Florence Mills was on Broadway; Josephine Baker was in *Revue Nègre* in Paris; Louis Armstrong had moved to Chicago from New Orleans; and Bessie Smith (whose voice was the most significant one of the century, Patrick O'Connor once told me while he was editor of *Opera News*) was singing the blues. Richmond Barthé sculpted and Aaron Douglas painted—when he was not designing gloriously patterned and colored dust jackets for black-authored novels. This was an age named for low-down black music, and middle-class white Americans were learning how to loosen up and move to what we now politely call vernacular black dances, with names like the Charleston and the Black Bottom.

Why did it all happen? It may simply have been because the Great Migration of blacks—from oppressive South to indifferent North, and from country to city—provided in Harlem a community large enough to sustain a full and complex cultural life. Besides Nathan Huggins' *The Harlem Renaissance* (1971), there are two broadly painted pictures of the time: David Levering Lewis' *When*

*Harlem Was in Vogue* (1981) and Jervis Anderson's *This Was Harlem: A Cultural Portrait, 1900–1950* (1982). A very useful reference book is Kellner's *The Harlem Renaissance: A Historical Dictionary for the Era* (1984).

### Renaissance Men (& Women)

Countee Cullen (1903–1946) was perceived at the time as one of the most accomplished Renaissance writers—and, because he was so young, as the one with the most promise. His childhood is mysteriously elusive, but as a boy he was adopted by the Rev. Frederick Asbury Cullen, minister of Harlem's fashionable Salem Methodist Church, and his wife. Cullen blossomed early: he edited the newspaper at DeWitt Clinton High School as well as *The Magpie*, the student literary magazine where in January 1921 his poem, "I Have a Rendezvous with Life," was published.

Cullen's poetic style was traditional, conservative, formal, romantic—what we might now call Eurocentric. It was certainly not representative of an experimental decade. Keats was Cullen's model, and he once told Langston Hughes he wanted to be a poet, not a Negro poet.

In 1925, while a graduate student at Harvard, Cullen published *Color*, his first and probably best collection of poems. It was quickly followed by *The Ballad of the Brown Girl: An Old Ballad Retold* (1927); *Copper Sun* (1927); *Caroling Dusk* (1927), an anthology of black poets; and his own third collection, *The Black Christ and Other Poems* (1932).

Cullen wrote one novel, *One Way to Heaven* (1932), which is not perfect but is better than the critics have allowed. It concerns a working-class couple—she a pious domestic and he a con artist—and their unlikely but romantic relationship. Satirical pictures of her employer and Harlem society have lost some but by no means all of their bite.

Cullen declined as a writer, producing little in the 1930s and '40s, and ultimately he failed to live up to his early youthful promise. Several of his lines have entered the language, though—

"What is Africa to me:/ Copper sun or scarlet sea ...," for example; and perhaps the best known and most poignant: "Yet do I marvel at this curious thing/ To make a poet black and bid him sing!"

Although he is no longer very well known, James Weldon Johnson (1871–1938) was one of the most talented African Americans of his day—musician, lawyer, politician, and N.A.A.C.P. activist as well as author. While serving a Republican national administration as American consul in Corinto, Nicaragua, he wrote his only novel, *The Autobiography of an Ex-Colored Man*. A sophisticated psychological story, it was published anonymously in 1912 by Sherman, French and Co., in Boston.

Something of a forerunner of the Renaissance, the book made little impact until Alfred Knopf reissued it in 1927 in Johnson's name, adding a "u" to "Colored," for the British market, and also adding an introduction by the Renaissance's chief white patron, Carl Van Vechten. It is the story of a man of mixed race who decides to pass for white because of the hopelessness of American racism. While fiction, the book was based on the life of a black friend of Johnson's, Judson D. Wetmore, who had attended the University of Michigan Law School as a white man.

Also in 1927, Viking brought out Johnson's *God's Trombones: Seven Negro Sermons in Verse*—poems which abandoned Negro dialect, but utilized the colorful language and distinctive rhythms of black preaching, a folk art Johnson deeply appreciated and feared was being lost. This was Johnson's own favorite of his books, and, at his request, he was buried holding a copy of it in his hands.

Johnson's other books are *Fifty Years and Other Poems* (1921), *Self-Determining Haiti* (1920), *The Book of American Negro Poetry* (1922), *The Book of American Negro Spirituals* (1925), *Black Manhattan* (1930), *Saint Peter Relates an Incident of the Resurrection Day* (1930), *Along This Way* (1933), and *Negro America, What Now?* (1934).

Nella Larsen (1891–1964) is only now emerging as the Renaissance's finest novelist. Little is known of her life. She said she was the child of a Danish mother and a black West Indian father. Following her father's death, her mother remarried—this time to a white man—and Larsen found herself situated marginally between the races. She became a nurse, then a librarian, working in the children's room of the 135th Street Branch, which housed Arthur Schomburg's collection of African-Americana.

Encouraged by her social friends Walter White and Carl Van Vechten, Larsen spent five months thinking about a novel and six weeks writing one. The result was *Quicksand*, published by Knopf in 1928, and praised by everyone from Alain Locke and W.E.B. DuBois, the intellectual guides of the Renaissance, to *The New York Times*.

*Quicksand*'s story of Helga Crane is a patently autobiographical account of an emotionally developing modern woman wrestling with the problems of identity. Behind the obvious "tragic mulatto" theme is the issue of class, as Crane finds herself unsatisfied by bourgeois life in Europe and America, including black America.

Behind this, however, are the questions of gender as Crane (and presumably Larsen) encounters sex, sexism, and sexuality on many levels, not least of all in her own powerful physical feelings. This pioneering feminist novel went out of print around 1930 and remained unavailable until Macmillan reissued it in 1971. It is now being mined by scholars of women's studies, as well as read as a first-rate piece of writing.

*Quicksand* was followed the next year by *Passing*, and in 1930 Larsen became the first black woman to receive a Guggenheim grant for creative writing. Perhaps because of an unproved charge of plagiarism, perhaps because of an extremely embarrassing divorce from her physicist husband Elmer Imes, Larsen never published another book. Not only that, she moved from Harlem, abandoned her friends, returned to nursing, and lived in obscurity and anonymity for more than 30 years. Those who knew of her death didn't know who she was, and those who knew who she was thought she had died years before.

### Langston Hughes

Langston Hughes (1902–1967) remains the best known writer of the New Negro movement, in part because he was one of the few who survived the 1920s and continued as a productive author in a variety of formats. Hughes is thus the most accessible to collectors of the Renaissance figures. He not only wrote more books, and more popular ones, but he made part of his precarious living reading from them and selling copies to his audiences. His flowing handwriting and green ink inscriptions are so familiar some book

## Books and Writers of the Harlem Renaissance

dealers joke that an unsigned Hughes first edition is worth more than a signed one.

Thanks to Arnold Rampersad's brilliant biography *The Life of Langston Hughes*, published in two volumes by Oxford University Press in 1986 and 1988, we also know Hughes better than we do some of his Harlem contemporaries, despite the fact that Hughes' own personal life was a cagey exercise in masks, subterfuge, and dissimulation. His life was deceptively simple, just like his poems.

Hughes' first book of verse, *The Weary Blues*, was published by Knopf early in 1926 at the recommendation of Carl Van Vechten. With an inspired bright jacket by Miguel Covarrubias, the collection contains the famous "The Negro Speaks of Rivers," as well as poems which not only have jazz and blues as their subjects but in their rhythms as well. Hughes' deep love for common black people and their vibrant language and music made him their spokesperson through his writing, where he lifted racial folk expression to high art. And the loving appreciation plain people returned to him sustained Hughes in a deceitful and unfriendly world.

More blues poems followed the next year in *Fine Clothes to the Jew*. The title, as unfortunate as Van Vechten's *Nigger Heaven*, referred to taking one's possessions to a pawnbroker. Most black reviewers were very critical, seeing the lyrics merely as reflections of the most vulgar and unedifying black lowlife. But Rampersad finds it Hughes' greatest work—comparable, he says, to *Leaves of Grass*, with its full and masterful expression of authentic blues language, emotion, culture, and beat.

Additional books of Hughes' still within the general time frame of the Renaissance are *Not Without Laughter* (1930), fiction; *Dear Lovely Death* (1931), poems; *Scottsboro Limited* (1932), poems and a play; and *The Ways of White Folks* (1934), short stories.

The most important single book to come out of the Renaissance, and the one every collector searches for at yard sales and on discount tables, is Jean Toomer's experimental *Cane* (1923). Toomer (1894–1967) was born into Washington, D.C.'s elite, blue-veined African-American aristocracy; he was the grandson of Pinckney Benton Stewart Pinchback, who was briefly a U.S. Senator from Louisiana during the Reconstruction period.

*Cane* is an avant-garde work, an impressionistic, lyrical collage of stories and poems and combinations of the two, a remarkable book that was enthusiastically reviewed and received at the time and has been frequently reissued. It has been much analyzed and it continues to be discussed and debated. Full of symbolic imagery, *Cane* explores the black experience in white America and the recurrent question of African-American identity, and is at its most powerful when looking at the lives of racially and sexually exploited black women

*Cane* is a creative masterpiece, and much of the material for it came to Toomer while he was teaching school in an isolated area of rural Georgia, where the innate beauty and dignity of the people led him to comprehend that identity comes from affirming one's history. While this insight illuminated *Cane* it has less effect on Toomer himself, who finally decided that he had no Negro blood and was in fact a member of a new "American" race. He drifted off to become a disciple of the Russian mystic Georgei Gurdjieff. Toomer continued to write, however, and many of his manuscripts remain unpublished.

Currently, the most popular writer of the Renaissance is Zora Neale Hurston (1891–1960), a bright, witty, high-spirited woman trained in anthropology who was not above playing the "darkey" to get what she needed from white people. Aided by Robert E. Hemenway's *Zora Neale Hurston: A Literary Biography* (1977) and by the interest of Alice Walker, Hurston has been rediscovered and resurrected. Her books are back in print, and there is even an annual Hurston festival in her hometown, all-black Etonville, Florida.

Most commentators would end the Renaissance early in the 1930s when the hard times of the Great Depression made the realism of Richard Wright more appropriate than the vivacious experimentalism of the Jazz Age. Hurston's books date from the '30s, but she was a very real presence among the Renaissance's "niggerati," as she and Wallace Thurman dubbed them, and her writing remained more reflective of that period.

Hurston's first book was *Jonah's Gourd Vine* (1934), a fictional account (based on her parents' marriage and life) of a black Baptist preacher who is a powerfully holy man in the pulpit but who can't stay away from the sisters during the week. This is not at all the conventional comedy, however, but a real tragedy in which the preacher tries to understand the profound conflicts within himself between spirit and flesh. One of the novel's several strengths is its expression of the eloquent poetic verbal art of the preacher, the ge-

## Books and Writers of the Harlem Renaissance

nius with words characteristic of black folk culture in general and the Afro-Protestant folk church in particular. Interestingly enough, Hurston was the only one of the major Renaissance writers who actually came from the rural southeast center of African-American life.

Hurston's other books are *Mules and Men* (1935), a collection of black folklore, including extensive information on voodoo; *Their Eyes Were Watching God* (1937), generally considered her best novel; *Tell My Horse* (1938), another folklore collection, this one with Caribbean material; *Moses, Man of the Mountain* (1939), a novel on the Africanization of Christianity; *Dust Tracks on a Road* (1942), her orchestrated biography; and *Seraph on the Suwanee* (1948), a novel about Southern whites.

One of the more unappreciated members of the Renaissance is Wallace Thurman (1902–1934), a wise, cynical, troubled, smart, critical, dark-complected bohemian from Salt Lake City. A journalist and editor, Thurman wrote and worked for both black and white publications, including *True Story*, and ghosted under the pseudonyms Patrick Casey and Ethel Belle Mandrake. A leader of the New Negro group's younger avant-garde circle (and the only one with a steady job), he edited (and paid for) *Fire!!* (1926), their anti-black-establishment aesthetic magazine/manifesto. It was an exciting publication, but, unsurprisingly, it only lasted for one issue and many of those copies were accidently destroyed—in a fire, of course.

Thurman wrote *Negro Life in New York's Harlem: A Lively Picture of a Popular and Interesting Section* (1928), an insider's view, issued from Girard, Kansas, as Haldeman-Julius Little Blue Book No. 494. The same year he married the political radical Louise Thompson, but they soon separated, presumably because of Thurman's homosexuality.

His first novel was *The Blacker the Berry* (1929) which dealt with a despairing young woman who, like Thurman, is dark-skinned and experiences, as he did, color prejudice within the race from lighter Negroes. The title is an ironic twist on the rural saying, "The blacker the berry, the sweeter the juice."

Thurman's next novel was *Infants of the Spring* (1932), a clever and insightful satirical parody of the Renaissance itself. There is an amusing and easily recognizable cast: Sweetie May Carr is Zora Neale Hurston, Tony Crews is Langston Hughes, DeWitt Clinton is

Countee Cullen, Dr. Parkes is Alain Locke, Dr. Manfred Trout is Rudolph Fisher, and Raymond Taylor is Thurman himself.

Thurman was personally unable to meet his own high artistic standards, and he believed the same was true for the other New Negro writers, with the possible exception of Toomer. He turned to nonracial themes and with Abraham L. Furman, a white man, coauthored a novel called *The Interne* (1932), a poorly received hospital exposé. In Hollywood he wrote the scenarios for *High School Girl* and *Tomorrow's Children*, both low-budget films, the latter of which is interesting because it dealt with the taboo subject of eugenic sterilization. Thurman was self-destructive: he drank too much and died unceremoniously of tuberculosis at the age of 32 in City Hospital on Welfare Island, the very institution he had used as the center and symbol of disillusionment in *The Interne*.

Another underappreciated and underrated New Negro was Rudolph "Bud" Fisher (1897–1934), a wit and intellectual, scientist and novelist who published simultaneously in the *Atlantic Monthly* and the *Journal of Infectious Diseases*. Born in Washington, D.C., Fisher graduated with a Phi Betta Kappa key from Brown University, then from Howard Medical School, and became an X-ray specialist in New York.

His first book was *The Walls of Jericho* (1928), a satirical but realistic novel of Harlem life which humanized its inhabitants by avoiding the usual stereotypes perpetrated by both black and white writers. The novel cleverly dissects black class strata (with some bias against the "dicty" bourgeoisie) in a love story about a piano mover and a Kitchen Mechanic (black slang of the day for a housemaid). The description of the General Improvement Association and its costume ball is a funny takeoff on the N.A.A.C.P.

Fisher's *The Conjure Man Dies: A Mystery Tale of Dark Harlem* (1932) is considered the first detective story by an African American. Dr. John Archer and Detective Perry Dart (archer and dart!) solve the Harlem murder of an African conjurer, and Fisher foreshadows Chester Himes.

Fisher led an active and productive life but died early of overexposure to radiation just a few days after Wallace Thurman's death during Christmas week 1934. Their deaths, along with the general grimness of the 1930s, pretty much signaled the end both of renaissance and Renaissance.

It has been a long time now since Alain Locke—Howard University philosopher, first African-American Rhodes Scholar, and godfather of the Harlem Renaissance movement—published *The New Negro* (1925), expanding an issue of *Survey Graphic* magazine into a book, and proclaiming a new day in black arts and letters. The flourishing of talent was certainly real enough, and there are a good many other writers who have a place here: Gwendolyn Bennett, Arna Bontemps, Sterling Brown, William Waring Cuney, W.E.B. DuBois, Jessie Fauset, Frank S. Horne, Charles S. Johnson, Georgia Douglas Johnson, Claude McKay, Richard Bruce Nugent, George S. Schuyler, Anne Spencer, Eric Walrond, Walter White.

We are currently experiencing another important flourishing of African-American culture. This time rap and hip-hop are the music, and Romare Bearden and Jacob Lawrence the artists, but again, books are central. In the summer of 1992 three of the novels on *The New York Times* bestseller list were by black women. Whatever the ultimate name or content or direction of the present renewal, it will at least in part be possible because of the pioneers of the Harlem Renaissance.

# Shaping the Future
## New Guide and Database Will Range Across African-American History and Culture
### (with Henry Louis Gates, Jr.)

The story of people of African descent in this country has often been ignored or distorted, and accurate literature covering their history and culture often simply did not exist. Over the past twenty-five years, however, new interest in the black experience has produced an explosion of books and articles across academic disciplines. A group of specialists is presently engaged in analyzing this material and establishing a collection of bibliographies and bibliographic essays that will constitute a single comprehensive research guide to the literature of African-American history and culture. The scholars who are creating the *Harvard Guide to African-American* History maintain they are helping to shape the future of African-American studies, and they believe the very nature of American historical research will be rethought and redefined as a result of their work.

These specialists include men and women whose work is at the forefront of African-American scholarship. The *Guide's* general editors are Evelyn Brooks Higginbotham, Harvard University; Darlene Clark Hine, Michigan State University; and Leon Litwack, University of California, Berkeley. Randall K. Burkett, Harvard University, is an associate editor, as is Lawrence Dowler of Harvard's Widener Library. The project is housed at the W.E.B. Du Bois Institute for Afro-American Research, Harvard University, the institutional sponsor. Founded in 1975, the institute is an interdisciplinary research center in African-American studies.

Drawing on a breadth of scholarship in many fields, the editors and compilers are selecting and organizing the newest, best, and most relevant material in order to make available to students at all levels a basic research tool that will provide access to the whole spectrum of African-American history. The *Guide* will also show the extent of black involvement in the larger realms of American history and American studies, and offer these disciplines an opportunity to reconsider their own shape and content.

Based on the model of the *Harvard Guide to American History*, which appeared more than forty years ago and has profoundly influenced research and researchers in American history ever since, the African-American *Guide* has the modern advantages of developments in technology. The new *Guide will* not only be published in an 800-page book by Harvard University Press, but the data will also be available in state-of-the-art electronic form as well.

The decision to produce the *Guide* as a book was made in order to reach the widest possible audience: school, public, and small college libraries, in addition to individuals, who may not have access to expensive and rapidly changing technology. The decision to produce the *Guide* as a database was made in order to be able to update the bibliographies easily, and also to explore new ways of disseminating information, perhaps through existing library network systems.

The *Harvard Guide to African-American History* will consist of two sections: bibliographic essays and bibliographies. The essays are necessary, in part, because some of the records of black history and culture are found in forms not always considered by traditional researchers and not always available in conventional handbooks or sources: music, oral history, folklore, and film, for example. In addition, essays will cover the more familiar and more widely utilized nonbook categories of manuscripts, serials, and government documents and records.

There will be a special bibliographic essay on the story of women in the black experience. Information on women was not always included in older sources, and the *Guide* essay reflects the widespread and growing interest in the history and roles of women as areas of research interest. Elsa Barkley Brown of the University of Michigan, who is writing this essay, will examine past and present methodological trends, comment on relevant works, and sketch out major issues.

Besides Brown, the authors of bibliographic essays include Thomas Cripps, Morgan State University; James Danky, State

Historical Society of Wisconsin; Deborah Newman Ham, Library of Congress; Portia K. Maultsby, Indiana University; and Elinor DesVerney Sinnette, Moorland-Spingarn Research Center, Howard University.

The bibliographies themselves are arranged chronologically, beginning in 1440. They are set in time periods that are particularly appropriate for African-American history and that reflect the uniqueness of the African-American experience within the broader outline of American history. This periodization may well call for a new look at how American history is presently organized.

The bibliographers are Richard J.M. Blackett, Indiana University; John H. Bracey, Jr., University of Massachusetts at Amherst; Clayborne Carson, Stanford University; Eric Foner, Columbia University; Nancy Grant, Washington University; Joseph Miller, University of Virginia; Gary B. Nash, University of California, Los Angeles; Stephanie J. Shaw, Ohio State University; Jeffrey Stewart, George Mason University; John K. Thornton, Millersville University; Joe Trotter, Carnegie-Mellon University; and Peter Wood, Duke University.

African-American history begins in Africa, with its own history and culture, and the momentous changes that began there with the earliest incursion of the Portuguese on the West African coast. The first *Guide* bibliography starts with this background and context, and goes on to outline the history of slavery and the slave trade and the rise of the New World. It focuses on the development of plantation slavery and the gradual codification of laws in Virginia which transformed indentured servitude into permanent and perpetual slavery based on race and color.

The interdisciplinary nature of African-American history becomes evident, then, at the very outset of this chronology. Demography, law, and political science are all elements which need to be taken into account. With the institutionalization of slavery, the rise of free black communities, slave resistance, and the poetry of Phillis Wheatley, new elements appear that require the inclusion of studies and perspectives from sociology, literature, art, and religion in order to understand them.

Documenting this story has raised many questions with which the editors of the *Guide* are still wrestling: what to include, where to place it, and in what format? Should nontraditional sources be integrated with traditional monographs? Uniformity and compatibility of entries is a constant problem. These issues are being resolved as satisfactorily as possible, and if some inconsistencies remain, it is expected they will be overcome by the creation of a complete and thorough index.

The editors realize that subject access is as crucial a need in the *Guide* as chronological organization. That is, it is just as likely for a researcher to look at, say, the black church across time lines, as it is for a researcher to examine a particular period itself, the "New Negro" era of 1915–1932, for example. To meet that need, a list of subjects was agreed upon with each chronological bibliography subdivided into subject areas such as medicine and health, science and technology, the arts, and architecture, so that specific topics and themes can be traced through chronological sections.

The great strength of the *Guide* is its selectivity, and the expertise of the contributors guarantees that entries are being chosen by leading researchers in the field. Even the sophistication of the editors, however, has not eliminated a lively and ongoing discussion: what are the criteria for inclusion? Each of the dozen chronological periods has room for only a thousand or so entries. The editors are selecting those references they believe to be the most important for surveying and understanding the historiographical literature of each particular time period.

A model bibliography was created near the outset of the project by Eric Foner of Columbia University. He had recently completed his definitive study of the Reconstruction period and had amassed for his own use in writing his book a comprehensive bibliography of the period immediately following the Civil War.

With a universe of materials at hand, he selected from them for the *Guide* citations for those published writings that represent descriptive and analytical materials of intellectual significance and of the highest value to the researcher. "To have Eric Foner as a guide through the literature of Reconstruction is a student's dream," one of the other editors commented.

The new interest in black history, both popular and academic, has had one unexpected result. Several commercial publishers and vendors have recently released a number of African-American reference books because there is now a considerable market for material.

The original idea for a comprehensive *Guide to African-American History* came from the late Nathan I. Huggins, chair of

*Shaping the Future*

Afro-American studies at Harvard and director of the W.E.B. Du Bois Institute. He met with a group of scholars in 1988 who immediately shared his enthusiasm for the concept and began to plan ways to implement it. At Huggins's death in 1989, it was felt the project should continue, not only because of its intrinsic merit, but also as a tribute to one who pioneered black studies, set the highest intellectual standards, and helped shape the field.

With an estimated total of well over 10,000 entries, the *Harvard Guide to African-American History* will be large enough to encompass a broadly defined discipline and small enough to be practical and useable. It will bring order to a mass of material, will help solidify a rapidly expanding field, and, perhaps most important, by revealing gaps in the story of African Americans, will point to work that remains to be done.

# "Remarks Called For And Otherwise":
# The Career of Charles F. Heartman, Bookseller
*(with Pamela J. Petro)*

In 1937 Clarence Brigham, the director of the American Antiquarian Society, wrote that "the history of Charles F. Heartman's auction house is the story of a personality as much as of a business." This remark falls in the category of compound understatement. Not only did Heartman's energetic personality shape his book auctions, his enthusiasm was such that it spilled over into a number of adjacent activities, including bookselling, bibliographical and scholarly research, and a variety of publishing ventures: all individual, but each a related aspect of a single career.

Not surprisingly, labels skid off Charles Heartman in all directions. He was an entrepreneur with a knack for the grand gesture, once hiring an entire Pullman car to relay friends and customers to a gala book auction held in his Metuchen, New Jersey, home; yet Heartman pursued his talent for showmanship in a field which generally attracted contemplative, rather than active, personalities. Nonetheless, the business of antiquarian bookselling profited immeasurably from Heartman's energy, which manifested itself both in the eclectic range of his interests and in the passionate conviction he brought to such diverse subjects as the first editions of Edgar Allan Poe and guidebooks to New Orleans bordellos.

While his specialty was unquestionably rare Americana, Heartman directed his painstaking methods of inquiry seemingly without discrimination into whatever subjects interested him at the moment. Thus, in addition to the 312 auction catalogues and 160 bookseller's lists dealing with Americana and related subjects he issued between 1913 and 1953, it is not surprising to discover that he also published a bibliography (and a critical essay) on

Phillis Wheatley, nor that he turned his hand to an aphrodisiac cooking manual which consisted of nearly 200 "historical recipes" and "diversified dainties" entitled *Cuisine de l'Amour* (1942).

Heartman's energy was at least as legendary as his eclecticism. He was not content, for example, simply to note his creed that "no second printing could be a first edition"—rather, Heartman's editorial partner Harry B. Weiss reported, he "shouted" this information "time and time again" in his column "Remarks Called For and Otherwise" in *American Book Collector*. Heartman was certainly aware of his own reputation and he enjoyed it—and he even occasionally quoted in print statements like the following by Weiss, analyzing his character: "combined with ideas and knowledge, [Heartman] has an unusual amount of energy. And on top of all this he is also a colorful and extremely individualistic person, impatient of opposition."

Heartman was born in 1883 in Braunschweig, Germany, where he began collecting books and prints as a child. After working for several years as a journalist and later as an editor-publisher (he edited *Der Literat*, a short-lived literary periodical when he was only seventeen), he left an increasingly unstable Germany in 1907 for the comparative security of England. In London Heartman met and married another German expatriate, Martha Esche, who financially supported his efforts to learn the book trade until the couple emigrated to the United States in 1911, with only $40 between them.

Heartman met with a decidedly inauspicious start in New York City. In 1911 alone he was fired twice, once from the *New York Herald* for having a wife (apparently a liability to a reporter for the society section) and once from a janitorial position after renting more flats in the apartment building where he worked than his boss, the superintendent. Between dismissals from paying jobs, Heartman worked voluntarily for a bookseller named Deutschberger, who had "promised to introduce him to the mysteries of the book business." During this apprenticeship, Heartman purchased a number of German pamphlets on socialism and anarchism from a pushcart bookseller on Houston Street for $5. Examining the set, Heartman found that it included the printed report of the First Social Democratic Convention ever held in Germany, previously supposed to have been unpublished. Heartman sold the lot to Dr. Eisemann of Baer and Company, Frankfurt, for

$200—so remarkable a sum that he had the check certified before Eisemann sailed for Europe, an overcautious blunder that cost him further business with Baer and Company.

Heartman's windfall enabled him to move in 1912 from his cramped bookshop-apartment on 22nd Street, which he described as being in "the worst of the New York gashouse district," to more spacious quarters on Lexington Avenue. Like many booksellers at the time, Heartman bought books at auction on credit—a policy the auction houses encouraged so as to be paid not in cash but in prime titles of their own choosing. As Heartman noted in his candid reminiscence, *Twenty-five Years in the Auction Business and What Now?* (1938), "in this manner quite a number of booksellers and print dealers were in perpetual bondage to the auction house."

Never one to tolerate serfdom for very long, especially when combined with the sixty percent commission then charged by auction houses on consignment items, Heartman leased space above his shop in order to begin holding his own book auctions. His first auction was held on June 9 and 10, 1913, with R.E. Sherwood as the auctioneer. Although the auction was a success, Heartman's most enduring memory a quarter-century later was one of embarrassment over the catalogue. Before the sale he was advised by a friend that "the most important thing in an auction ... is to have a swell name on the cover [of the catalogue]." Taking this advice to heart but having no impressive name at hand, Heartman invented the following title: "Heartman's Auctions, The First Part of the Library of G.H. Mayer of Brooklyn, New York." After the sale not only did a number of customers wish to know more of Mayer, but one gentleman actually informed Heartman that he never knew G.H. Mayer owned so many interesting books! After this episode, Heartman rarely issued a catalogue with a collector's name on the cover, legitimate or otherwise.

Heartman's auctions had an immediate and far-reaching impact on the antiquarian book trade. His original motto, "I aim to protect the seller, because the buyer can protect himself," resulted in his becoming, as he himself noted, "a great stabilizing factor ... in the auction game, bringing about the revolutionary change of a top [consignment] charge of 25 percent." Yet Heartman soon came to learn that the buyer also needed protection, most often from the seller or consignor of the material. As he recalled, "I found out quickly that one could not always buy at auction without running into the competition of the owner." Because of this, as well as the long-standing custom of "protection" then practiced by other auction houses that resulted in enormously inflated prices, Heartman also gathered a reputation for scrupulously guarding the interests of the buyer, and always prided himself on being able to supply at a moment's notice the name of the underbidder on any item.

Due to his carefully-cultivated friendships with out-of-the-way dealers and rare book scouts, as well as with librarians (who seemed somehow to reserve their duplicates especially for him), Heartman always had a great supply of unusual material for his auctions. Yet he was chiefly amused by the fact that a great many of his books came from other auction houses. "Abominable cataloguing and bunching" made way for many of these items to be "so cleverly" re-catalogued, as again Heartman himself noted, that often the underbidder of the previous sale wound up purchasing the same material at Heartman's auction for a much higher price.

It was in such cataloguing, however, that Heartman excelled, and in addition to his bookseller's lists these auction catalogues are not only valuable records of astute finds, but models of exacting bibliographical and scholarly research as well. Indeed, Clarence Brigham noted that the title "Rare Americana" found on most of these issues was more than justified, as "No dealer or collector in recent years has uncovered so many scarce and unusual items in this field as Mr. Heartman." "This field" came to assume an almost religious significance for Heartman. He wrote:

> It is not a hobby, it is a creed ... to me it seems that only the Americana collector has reached the heights of supreme Contentment.
>
> I look at my set of sixteen Presidents, lithographed in color by Currier ... and I am immediately enwrapped in a century crowded with historical events, unbelievably romantic and decisive....
>
> Within a year I had sold a number of items printed in Cambridge, Massachusetts, two of them earlier than 1660. I had eleven hitherto undescribed Indian Captives, ... I sold unique New England Primers; the manuscript of a forty-niner who went over the plains; Revolutionary Orderly books ... What would I have rather handled? A Gutenberg Bible? A Shakespeare folio? A Keats letter? A Royal binding? Not me.

One of Heartman's outstanding catalogues, the contents of which was sold almost in its entirety to the Huntington Library, was entitled *Six Hundred Pamphlets, Broadsides and a Few Books, written in the English Language and relating to America, issued prior to eighteen hundred. Bibliographically, Historically, and Sometimes Sentimentally Described* (1919). Another noteworthy catalogue, *Americana, Printed and in Manuscript* (1930), included the Stuart-Bute Papers relating to the Revolutionary War, priced at $47,500, and the manuscript of the first eight stanzas of Edgar Allan Poe's poem "For Annie," at $17,500. Heartman was particularly interested in Poe and eventually published *A Census of First Editions and Source Material by Edgar Allan Poe* in 1932.

One of Heartman's most important legacies is in the area of Afro-Americana, where his publishing, collecting, and at least one of his sales catalogues constitute a lasting contribution to a field little valued in his own day. Heartman published a half-dozen pioneering Black titles, most of them prior to the First World War. He issued the first bibliography of Phillis Wheatley and wrote a critical essay that is a striking tribute to the first Afro-American woman poet. He also published six broadsides by and about Wheatley in a limited edition of twenty-five, Arthur A. Schomburg's bibliographical checklist of American Negro poetry, and Oscar Wegelin's bibliography and selected writings of Jupiter Hammon.

In 1947 Heartman issued Catalogue 120, *Americana, Printed and in Manuscript,* with the aside, "while there is an emphasis on the subject of [the] Negro and slavery most of such Items are of interest otherwise." The catalogue listed 2,282 items, many of such rarity—and low price—as to be doubly stunning today There were ten Phillis Wheatley pieces, including two London first editions and an original 1774 pen-and-ink portrait. There was an American (1774) and an English (1747) first edition of Daniel Horsmanden's journal on the "Negro conspiracy" in colonial New York as well as a 1795 Banneker almanac for $40, a Jupiter Hammon 1806 *Address* for $47.50, and a contemporary (1831) account of Nat Turner's rebellion for $30. With title after title "Not in Sabin" or "Not in Work," the catalogue remains an extremely important bibliography, especially with Heartman's long and informative, if opinionated, descriptions.

Often the prefaces were one of the most interesting aspects of Heartman's catalogues, as they featured always lively and occasionally definitive commentaries. Clarence Brigham noted, for example, that Heartman's preface on "First Editions" in a catalogue published 30 November 1929 "was virtually an essay on this form of collecting." Heartman also took pains to make his catalogues visually interesting and often included striking color reproductions, such as that of the first state of Filson's map of Kentucky, printed in *Americana, Printed and in Manuscript* (1930). For these reasons, and of course for their unquestionable bibliographical value, complete sets of all Heartman catalogues were collected by libraries throughout the world, including the Bibliothèque Nationale in Paris, the British Library, the Bodleian, the Library of Congress, and The New York Public Library.

An unusual footnote to Heartman's catalogues is that in addition to bibliographical material, their places of publication read almost like a road map of the East Coast. All of their lives Heartman and his wife were plagued by a curious wanderlust. After leaving Lexington Avenue, Heartman moved once more in New York City before leaving for Rutland, Vermont, in 1920, in search of lower taxes and evidence that New England was badly in need of a book auction house. Discovering the former but not the latter, Heartman moved again in 1921 to Perth Amboy, New Jersey, where he stayed only one year before buying an old mansion in Metuchen, which he filled with colonial furnishings so pleasing that he couldn't persuade himself to leave for another thirteen years.

In was in Metuchen that Heartman held his most famous auction sales, in which he developed his reputation for "skillfully" combining "country dinners, pecans and books." As Heartman wrote, "Metuchen, New Jersey became a place for bookish people to gather"; not surprisingly, in light of Heartman's habit of serving an elaborate meal, often prepared by Mrs. Heartman, at each sale. He continued: "I think Mrs. Heartman's cooking has become quite famous all over the United States and because of her unbounded hospitality, often visitors arrived ... the day before the sale or stayed a day after."

Several of Heartman's auction parties have since passed into legend, such as the sale at which Wilberforce Eames, William Clements, Lathrop Harper, and Otis G. Hammond were among those who "gathered in an upstairs room and discussed collectors and collecting for most of the afternoon." Other unusual auctions included the Washington's Birthday sale of 1927, which doubled as a surprise party for the New York bookseller Gabriel Wells, who received a Heartman edition, "Gabriel Wells, the Philosopher. An Essay by Temple Scott," and the George H. Sargent sale at which Edward Newton volunteered as auctioneer to sell Sargent's collection—of Newtoniana.

After thirteen years in Metuchen, Heartman again grew restless, and in 1935 he moved to New Orleans, where he established with his associate Charles R. Knight the short-lived Pelican Galleries for antiquarian books. Heartman spent only a year in Louisiana, however, before purchasing a 400-acre tract in Hattiesburg, Mississippi, which was to become "The Book Farm." Although he at first intended to establish a "cooperative colony for intellectuals," Heartman spent most of his seven years on the farm in his traditional capacity as auctioneer-bookseller. After the experiment at Hattiesburg, Heartman was henceforth content to remain in the South, convinced he could fulfill the region's need for "an intelligent force who through writing and speaking ... can be of great educational value," and who would be willing to provide "unselfish ... advice to librarians as well as collectors." Heartman's wish to "develop an educational desire" among those who would know more of their Southern heritage—as well as a market for his books—eventually led him to Biloxi in 1943, New Braunfels, Texas, in 1947, and ultimately back to New Orleans in 1951, where he remained until his death in 1953.

Although none of these diverse locations ever became permanently associated with Americana or the antiquarian book trade, Heartman's homes are nonetheless commemorated on the title pages of his life-long project, "Heartman's Historical Series." Though perpetually a financial disaster, Heartman published the series from 1915 until his death, issuing a total of seventy-eight volumes in all. These included bibliographies, original work by contemporary authors, and historical reprints. In addition to predictable titles such as *The New-England Primer Issued Prior to 1830* (1934) and *A Checklist of Printers in the United States from Stephen Dave to the Close of the War of Independence* (1915), Heartman also published some wonderfully eccentric material, including Number 50, *The Blue Book*: "A Bibliographical Attempt to describe the

Guidebooks to the houses of *Illfame* in New Orleans as they were published there. Together with some pertinent and illuminating remarks pertaining to the *Establishments* and *Courtesans* as well as to *Harlotry* in general in New Orleans" (1936, edition limited to 15 copies). In *The Blue Book* Heartman admitted that "the writer has had many interesting bibliographical adventures, both as a research worker and as a student of the subject," despite his labelling New Orleans "a cancer on the body of the United States."

One of Heartman's most impressive offerings was Number 8 in the series, Phillis Wheatley's *Poems and Letters*, with an appreciation by Arthur Schomburg. Four hundred copies were printed, 9 on Japan vellum. The vellum copies became significant collector's items, with number 3 now at Fisk, number 4 at Howard, number 5 at the Schomburg Center, and number 9 in the Heartman Collection at Texas Southern University. In 1945 Heartman also published *North American Negro Poets* by Dorothy B. Porter, the distinguished Afro-American librarian and bibliographer.

There are two significant collections of Heartman's Afro-Americana, one at Xavier University (a black Roman Catholic school in New Orleans) and the other at Texas Southern University in Houston. The Heartman Negro Collection at Texas Southern, perhaps the largest black collection in the Southwest, consists of some 6,000 books, 5,000 pamphlets, and 4,000 newspapers, as well as broadsides and maps. The 4,000 manuscripts at Xavier form an even more valuable collection; they date from 1724 to 1897 and cover slaves and slavery in Louisiana, including deeds, municipal records, rosters, and similar material. With considerable prescience, Heartman in 1945 said "there is a deplorable lack of understanding about the importance and value of the cultural heritage among the Negroes at large, but more particularly in the South. In the desire for economic betterment and pressure for political advantages, it is too often overlooked how necessary it is to be fully conversant with past achievements and an analytical knowledge of the whole question."

In addition to the Historical Series, Heartman also found time to publish and edit two book-collecting journals. From 1925 to 1927 he edited *The American Collector*, "A Monthly Magazine for Americana—Lore and Bibliography" (later known as *The Americana Collector*), of which he published approximately 1,000 copies of each issue. After selling *The Americana Collector*, Heartman enjoyed a brief hiatus until 1932, when he became the editor and publisher of a new journal called *The American Book Collector*, "A Monthly Magazine for Book Lovers," which he co-edited with Harry Weiss. Not surprisingly, subscribers claimed that the first thing they read in either magazine was Heartman's editorial; indeed, these essays are remarkable diatribes, railing with Germanic fury against "fakes, forgeries and dishonest bibliographical statements" as well as anything else that happened to annoy Heartman while he had pen in hand. As Weiss put it, "Mr. Heartman never bothered to sugar-coat his bitter pills." Included among Heartman's many self-proclaimed "patients" were the German press in the United States (in 1918 Heartman wrote warning of "The Necessity of Prohibiting the German Press from a Different Viewpoint," which was reprinted by the American Defense Society) and The New York Public Library, whose morality Heartman called into question after an exhibition featuring Walt Whitman's scandalous *Leaves of Grass*.

As Madeleine B. Stern notes, despite his always candid "but not always palatable views," Heartman remained an exacting scholar and bibliographer to the end of his life. After twenty-five years of auctioning Americana, Heartman had the honesty to question the validity of his work, writing "there slowly arose in me, a feeling of the emptiness of my profession. I ... refer to the ... prostitution of our most nobel heritage for material gain. It was heartbreaking to witness that all the things of beauty ... and all the emotional and sentimental evidences of our past had become just a playbill for the unscrupulous to achieve gain or cheap advertising."

Despite these legitimate fears, Heartman could never bring himself to leave the field altogether. A man of many professions, Heartman ultimately had only one vocation—the discovery and identification of rare Americana as a means of preserving the history of his adopted country. Following the lead of his peers, to say that Charles Heartman pursued this vocation with skill, intelligence, tenacity, and a touch of eccentricity would again be an understatement.

# Index

Aaron, Samuel 5
Aberdeen University 164
Abolition Movement 4–14
*Abyssinia* 61, 62, 63
Academy of Music 95
Accooe, Willis 61
*Ad Catholicum* 160
Adam, R.B. 11
Adams, John Quincy 13
*Addie Pray* 45
Adger, Robert W. 162
Aenon College 153
Aeolian Hall 89, 90
*Aesthetic Papers* 10
*Africa* 158
African American Catholic Congregation 117–23
African American Greek Orthodox Church 132
*African American Women's Writings* 29
African Methodist Episcopal Church 108, 129–30 n6
African Methodist Episcopal Zion Church 130 n6
African Negro Mission 127
African Orthodox Church 107–17, 122, 123, 125, 126, 127
Afro-American Catholic Church 126
Afro-American Orthodox Church 127

Ajari, Bishop 116
Alcott, Bronson 8
Aldridge, Ira 160
Alexander, Daniel William 115, 132 n21
Alfred Baptist Church 124
Alger, Horatio 105
Alhambra Theatre 84
Ali, Muhammad 25, 118
*Alice's Adventures in Wonderland* 3
"All Coons Look Alike to Me" 69
*All God's Chillun Got Wings* 21
Allen, Horace R.B. 15
Allen, Mord 63
Allen, Richard 108, 109
*Along This Way* 173
American Antiquarian Society 168 n4, 187
*The American Anti-Slavery Almanac for 1847* 13
American Anti-Slavery Society 5, 12
American Arbitration Society 19
American Catholic Church 123, 126, 127, 132 n21
American Catholic Orthodox Church 132 n21
American Civil Liberties Union 121
American Hebrew Eastern Orthodox Greek Catholic Church 120–21

*197*

American Holy Orthodox Catholic Apostolic Eastern Church 132 n21
American Independent Orthodox Church 120
American National Catholic Church 120
American Play Company 18–19
*The American Scene* 90
American Tobacco Company 57
Ammerman, Jackie W. 115, 133 n23
Amo, Anthony William 159
Amos 'n' Andy 61
Anderson, Jervis 172
Anderson, Regina. *See* Andrews, Regina
Andrews, Regina 40
Anita Bush Stock Company 94
*Anthology of Magazine Verse for 1918* 17
Anthony, Donald 123
Antisdale, Louis Martin 15
Anti-Slavery Book Depository 13
*Anti-Slavery Bugle* 6
*Anti-Slavery Examiner* 6
*Anti-Slavery Reporter* 6
Antony, Father 110, 132 n14
*An Appeal in Favor of that Class of Americans Called Africans* 4
*L'Arbalete* 24
Armstrong, Louis 171
Arrendale, James Augustine 123
Arthur, Denison Quartey 124
Arvey, Verna 89, 90, 91
Association for the Study of Negro Life and History 157
"At Jolly 'Coon'-ey Island" 57
*Authors Take Sides on Vietnam* 25
*The Autobiography of an Ex-Colored Man* 173

*The Baby's Christmas* 14
"The Backslider" 90

Bagghley, John 25
Bagwell, Orlando 49
Baker, George 124
Baker, Josephine 26, 33, 56, 84, 171
Baldwin, James 25, 29, 33
Balieffe, Nikita 83
"The Ballad of Margie Polite" 19
*The Ballad of the Brown Girl* 172
Ballou, Hosea 104
*Balm in Gilead: Journey of a Healer* 48, 51
*Bandanna Land* 63–64, 65, 66
Bank Street College of Education 51
Banneker, Benjamin 159, 191
Baraka, Amiri 20
Barbara, Abed-Negro 127
Barclay, William 164
Barron's Club 79
Barrow, Reginald Grant 113, 125, 126
Barry, Marion 121
Barth, Karl 104
Barthé, Richmond 171
Basilios, His Holiness Abuna 125
Bearden, Romare 179
Bedell, Kenneth 154
Bell, Clive 26
Benet, Stephen Vincent 8
Bennett, Gwendolyn 179
Bentley, Trevor 121
Berg, Albert A. 3, 21
Berg, Henry W. 3
Berlin, Irving 80, 81, 97
*Beyond Bias: Perspectives on Classrooms* 51
Bible Way Church of Our Lord Jesus Christ 153
*The Big Sea* 95
"Biglow Paper" 13
Billy Paige's Broadway Syncopators 96

*Index*

*Biographical Dictionary of African American Holiness Pentecostals, 1880–1910* 154
Bishop, Hutchins C. 58, 66
Black Bottom 171
*Black Boy* 24
*The Black Christ and Other Poems* 172
Black History Month 157
*Black Manhattan* 173
Black Patti. *See* Jones, Sissieretta
*The Black Phalanx* 158
*Blackbirds of 1926* 84, 86
*Blackbirds of 1927* 85
*The Blacker the Berry* 177
Blackett, Richard J.M. 183
Blair, Nancy 22
Blake, Eubie 79, 89, 93
Bledsoe, Jules 95
Blumenbach, Johann Friedrich 158–59
"Bon Bon Buddy, the Chocolate Drop" 63, 64
Bond, Julian 26
Bone, Robert A. 16
Bonita and Hearn 78
Bontemps, Arna 37, 179
*The Book of American Negro Poetry* 18, 173
*The Book of American Negro Spirituals* 173
Boston Athenaeum 4
Bowman's Cotton Pickers 94
Boyle, Kay 26
Bracey, John H., Jr. 183
Bradford, Perry 95
Bradford, William 163–64
Bragg, George Freeman 109, 130 n6, 131 n8, 132 n16
Braithwaite, Fiona 17, 20
Braithwaite, William Stanley 17
"The Branded Hand" 6
*Brewsie and Willie* 25
"Bricktop." *See* Smith, Ada

*Brideshead Revisited* 84
Bridges, Richard M. 120, 121–22
Brigham, Clarence 187, 190, 192
Bright, John 7
Brighter Day Theological Seminary 116
Broadhurst Theatre 83
Brookes, George S.A. 126
Brooks, Mary M. 9
Brooks, Sheldon 80
Brown, Elsa Barkley 182
Brown, Joe David 45
Brown, John 7–10, 12
Brown, John Mifflin 108, 129 n6
Brown, Sterling 56, 179
Brown, William Montgomery 109–10, 131 n11
Brown, William Wells 160
Brown University 178
Browning, Elizabeth Barrett 13
Brymn, James T. 64
Buchanan, James 6
Bundles, A'lelia 32
Burgoyne, I.I.H. 26
Burke, Billie 94
Burkett, Randall K. 113, 114, 181
Bush, Anita 63
Butler, Jamen B. 122
Butterbeans and Susie 94

Caines, Hugh Randolph, Jr. 122
Cambridge University 32
Campbell, Joseph 17
*Cane* 175–76
*The Cannibal King* 61
Cannon, Katie 49–51
Cantor, Eddie 81
Capitein, J.E.L. 159
Carew, Jean V. 51
Carfora, Carmel Henry 126, 127
Carnegie Corporation 161
Carnegie-Mellon University 183
*Caroling Dusk* 127
Carson, Clayborne 183

*Casablanca* 94
Case, Lora 8
Casey, Patrick 177
Catholic University 119
Catton, Bruce 102
Chaflin, William 7
Channing, William Ellery (1780–1842) 4
Channing, William Ellery (1818–1901) 9
Chaplin, Charles 60
Chapman, Maria Weston 13
Charleston 171
Chesnutt, Charles W. 39
Child, Lydia Maria 4, 7
"The Chocolate Venus" 58
Christ Catholic Church 122
Christian Quakers 164–69
Church, Frederick S. 15
Church of God by Faith 153
Church of Our Lady of Good Death, Chicago, IL 112
Church of Our Lord Jesus Christ of the Apostolic Faith 152
Church of the Living God, the Pillar and Ground of Truth 125
Church of the Living God the Pillar and Ground of Truth Without Controversy 153
"Civil Disobedience" 9
Clare College 32
Clay, Cassius M. 12, 13
Clay, Cassius (Mohammad Ali) 25
Clement, Robert 126
Clements, William 192
*Clorindy, or The Origin of the Cake Walk* 59
*Clotel; or, The President's Daughter: A Narrative of Slave Life in the United States* 160
Cochran, Charles 81, 85
*The Code of Virginia* 155
Coiro, Gregory 121

Cole, Bob 57, 59, 61, 64, 69
Coles, Robert 48
*Color* 18, 172
*The Colored Patriots of the American Revolution* 13
*Colored People* 29–34
Colored YMCA 161
Coltrane, Alice McLeod 116
Coltrane, John 116
Colum, Padraic 17
Columbia Medical School 48
Columbia Phonograph Co. 125
Columbia University 44, 171, 183, 184
Conde, J.M. 15
*The Conjure Man Dies: A Mystery Tale of Dark Harlem* 178
Connelly, Marc 22
Conrad, Joseph 3
*Conscience and the Constitution* 13
*The Constitution A Pro Slavery Compact; or Extracts from the Madison Papers* 12
*Constitutionalist* 6
Cook, Charles Cram 21
Cook, Will Marion 59, 60, 61
Coon songs 67–73
*Copper Sun* 18, 172
Coptic Orthodox Church Apostolic 124, 125
Coptic Orthodox Church (Western Hemisphere) 127–28
*Corentyne Thunder* 44
Covarrubias, Miguel 175
Cox, Harvey 151
Cragg, Christopher M. 127
"Crazy Blues" 95–96
*Creole Follies* 94
*The Creole Show* 59
Cripps, Thomas 182
Cromwell, Gladys 17, 35
Cromwell, Oliver 9
"Croon" 90
Cruikshank, George 11

# Index

Cry, *The Beloved Country* 25
*Cuisine de l'Amour* 188
Cullen, Countee 18, 20, 35–41, 172, 177
Cullen, Frederick Asbury 37, 172
Cummings, E.E. 11
Cummings, Marion Morehouse 11
Cuney, William Waring 179
Cushman, Charlotte 11

Dabney, Ford 72
Daddy Grace 152
Dale, Allen 61
"The Dance of the Falasha Maids" 63
Danky, James P. 182
Davis, Angela 26
Davis, James A. 109
Davis, Thadious M. 39, 40
Dean, David 133 n21
Dean, Dora 57
*Dear Lovely Death* 175
*Declaration of the Anti-Slavery Convention Assembled in Philadelphia, Dec. 4, 1833* 4
Delaries, Anita K. 115
Demaray, Elyse 40
"Le depart de 'Big Boy'" 24
Devine, Major J.J. 124
Devonshire Meeting House 168 n3
DeWitt Clinton High School 172
Dickens, Charles 3
Dickinson, Emily 12
Diffenderffer, S.A. 11
Diggs, John 21
*The Dispersion of Seed* 9
"Dixie Dreams" 83
Dixon, Sharon Pratt 121
Dodson, Owen 20
Doggett, R.G. 72
Domingo, W.A. 107
Douglas, Aaron 18, 171

Douglass, Fannie Howard 90
Douglass, Frederick 13
Douglass High School, Baltimore 37
*Dover Street to Dixie* 181
Dowler, Lawrence 181
Downs, Maria C. 93–94, 96, 97
Dramatists Guild 19
Driving tacks 59
Drummey, Peter 168 n4
Du Bois, William E.B. 20, 35–41, 103, 106, 133 n21, 173–74, 179
Du Bois, Yolande, 35
Dudley, S.H. 64–65
Duhamel, Marcel 24
Duke of Kent 84
Duke University 32, 183
Dunbar, Paul Lawrence 16, 59
Duncan, Isadora 56
Dunn, Johnny 80
Du Pree, Herbert 154
Du Pree, Sherry S. 149–54
*Dust Tracks on a Road* 177
Dwane, James M. 131 n10

Eames, Wilberforce 164, 192
Earls, Tony 49
Eastman, Max 18
*Echoes of Harper's Ferry* 9
*An Economic Detour: A History of Insurance in the Lives of Negroes* 114
Edgar, Robert 133 n25
Edward VII 62
L'Eglise Orthodoxe Apostolique Hatienne 133 n21
Elijah the Fiery Chariot 125
Eliot, T.S. 3
Ellington, Duke 96
Ellison, Ralph 1, 29
Emerson, Ralph Waldo 8, 9, 13
Emory University 115
*The Emperor Jones* 21–22, 94, 95
*Encyclopedia Africana* 33

Endich Theological Seminary 132 n14
English Emancipation League 11
Episcopal Orthodox Church (Greek Communion) 125
*Episcopi vagantes* 111–12
Esche, Martha 188
"Ethiopia" 63
Ethiopian Orthodox Catholic Church of North and South America 128
Ethiopian Orthodox Church 125
Eucharistic Catholic Church 126
Europe, James Reece 65
*Exercises Marking the Opening of the James Weldon Johnson Memorial Collection of Negro Arts and Letters Founded by Carl Van Vechten* 20
*An Exhortation and Caution to Friends Concerning Buying or Keeping of Negroes* 163

*A Fable for Critics* 12
Farajajé-Jones, Elias 117
Farrakhan, Louis 121
Farrow, Lucy 152
Father Divine 124, 152
Father Jehovia 124
Fauset, Jessie 179
Ferguson, Samuel David 133 n21
Fields, James T. 13
*Fifty Years and Other Poems* 173
*Figures in Black* 29
*Fine Clothes to the Jew* 175
*Fire!!* 177
Fisher, Dorothy Canfield 24
Fisher, Fred 67
Fisher, Rudolph 177, 178
Fisk University 35
Fitch, Alice 101
Fletcher, Tom 56
Flory, Keith 132 n12
Foley, Albert S. 133 n21

*Folks from Dixie* 16
Foner, Eric 183, 184
*For Fremont and Freedom! Campaign of Fifty-Six* 6
"For Me and My Gal" 68
Ford, Arnold J. 125
Foster, Jeanette 58
4-11-44 59
*Four Saints in Three Acts* 20–21
Fox, George 164
*Free Joe and Other Georgia Sketches* 15
Fremont, John C. 6
Friends' Library, London 163, 168 n3
*From Dixie to Broadway* 83, 86
Frost, A.B. 15
Frost, J. William 163
*A Full Statement of the Reasons ... Respecting Abolitionists as Anti-Slavery Societies* 14
Furblur, Harold 114
Furman, Abraham L. 178
*The Future of the American Negro* 16

Gabriel, Gilbert W. 83
Gandhi, Mohandas K. 9
Garner, Samuel T. 127
Garrison, William Lloyd 4, 9, 12–13, 14
Garvey, Marcus 107, 110, 115
Gates, Henry Louis, Jr. 26, 29–34, 61, 181–85
Gee, Lottie 63
George Mason University 183
Georgia Jazz Hounds 94
Gershwin, George 89, 90, 97
Gilpin, Charles 21, 94
*The Girl at the Fort* 94
*God's Trombones: Seven Negro Sermons in Verse* 18, 173
*Going to Meet the Man* 25
"Golly, Ain't I Wicked" 65

# Index

*The Good High School: Portraits of Character and Culture* 51
Goossens, Eugene 90
Gordan, John D. 20
Grant, J. Lackey 66
Grant, Nancy 183
Graziano, John 74 n16
Great Migration 171
Greek Orthodox Church 132 n15
Green, Ashbel 32
Greeń, Beriah 4
Green, Cora 78
Green, William 116
*The Green Pastures* 22–23
Greene, J. Lee 43
Greening, Bruce E. 122
*Greenwich Village Follies* 82
Grossner, Maurice 21
Gubert, Betty K. 39
Gumby Papers 92
Gurdjieff, Georgei 176

Halliday, Grace 59
Ham, Deborah Newman 183
Hammerstein, William 65
Hammon, Jupiter 160, 191
Hammond, Otis G. 192
Hampton Institute 7
Hanaford, Edwin 64
Hansberry, Lorraine 19
Hargous, Robert L. 62
*The Harlem Renaissance* 171
*The Harlem Renaissance: A Historical Dictionary for the Era* 172
*Harlem Shadows* 18
Harney, Ben 57
Harper, Lathrop 192
*Harper's Weekly* 16
Harris, George 11
Harris, Joel Chandler 14–16
Harrison, Richard B. 22
Harvard University 17, 32–33, 51, 157, 172, 181, 185
Haskell, Arnold 84

"Hawaiian Night in Dixie Land" 81
Hawthorne, Nathaniel 3, 10
Haynes, Lemuel 101–6
Haynes, Lemuel, Jr. 105
Healy, James A. 133 n21
Heartman, Charles F. 187–95
Hegamin, Lucille 96
"Hello Ma Baby" 68
Hemenway, Robert 43, 176
Hemings, Sally 161
Henderson, Fletcher 96
Herford, Oliver 15
Hesitation tango 66
"Hey-Hey" 90
Hickerson, John A. 124–26
Hickey, James 117, 118, 119, 122
Higginbotham, Evelyn Brooks 33, 181
Higginson, Thomas Wentworth 12
*High School Girl* 178
Hildeburn, Charles R. 163
Hill, Robert 110
Hill, Robert A. 113, 115
Hill, Wesley 22
Himes, Chester 20, 178
Hine, Darlene Clark 181
Hinkson, G. Duncan 116, 126
*His Honor the Barber* 64
*The History of My Songs* 153
*A History of the Negro Troops in the War of the Rebellion* 158
Hobsbawm, Eric 55
Hogan, Ernest 59, 69
Holly, James Theodore 133 n21
"Honolulu Belles" 59
Horn, Mother Rosa 152
Horne, Frank S. 179
Horsmanden, Daniel 191
Horton, George Moses 13
Hospital for Joint Diseases 85
Houseman, John 20–21
Howard, Bruce 21

Howard University 17, 124, 161, 183
Howard University Law School 118
Howard University Medical School 178
Howe, W.T.H. 3
Howells, William Dean 16
Howley, Haviland, and Dresser 70
Huggins, Nathan I. 171, 184
Hughes, Albert 29
Hughes, Langston 18–20, 23, 35, 37, 41, 52, 79, 95, 160, 174–75, 177
Hunter, Alberta 94
Huntington Library 163
Hurston, Zora Neale 20, 37, 43, 176–77
Hutchins, Julia 152

"I Don't Care Girl" 58
"I Don't Like No Cheap Man" 56, 60, 69–70
"I Have a Rendezvous with Life" 172
"I Want to be the Leading Lady" 56, 71
"I Wants Ma Honey Boy Now" 68
"If the Man in the Moon Were a Coon" 67
"I'll Keep a Warm Spot in My Heart for You" 63
"I'm a Little Blackbird Looking for a Bluebird" 83, 84
"I'm Craving for that Kind of Love" 79
"I'm Simply Full of Jazz" 79
Imani Temple 117, 118, 119, 120
Imes, Elmer 35, 174
Imes, Nella Larsen. *See* Larsen, Nella
*In Dahomey* 61–62

*In Search of Zion: The Spiritual Significance of Africa in Black Religious Movements* 117
Independent Catholic Church of Ceylon, Goa, and India 112
Independent Old Catholic Church of Los Angeles 120
Indiana University 183
*Infants of the Spring* 177
Institute for Church History, University of Copenhagen 115
Institute for Commonwealth Studies 115
International Composers Guild 89, 90
International Labor Defense Fund 23
International Liberal Catholic Church 127
*The Interne* 178
Irwin, Wallace 15
"I'se Your Little Nigger if You Wants Me, Liza Jane" 69
Isham, John 59
"It's Hard to Love Somebody When Somebody Don't Love You" 63
*I've Known Rivers: Lives of Loss and Liberation* 47–52

Jack, Edwin Macmillan 125
Jack, Sam T. 59
Jackman, Harold 38
Jackson, Andrew 105
Jackson, George 26
Jackson, Tony 78
James, C.L.R. 20
Jefferson, Thomas 159, 160–61
Jessye, Eva 21
Jigaree 66
Jocelyn, Simeon S. 4
*John Brown's Body* 8
John the Baptist 64
Johnson, Charles S. 20, 179

# Index

Johnson, Georgia Douglas  179
Johnson, Hal  23
Johnson, J. Rosamond  61, 64, 69
Johnson, James F.  96
Johnson, James Weldon  18, 39, 40, 56, 90, 92 n7, 161–73
Johnson, Morris R.  115
Jolly, Donald L.  120
Jolson, Al  81
*Jonah's Gourd Vine*  176
Jones, Absalom  108
Jones, Charles P.  153
Jones, LeRoi. *See* Baraka, Amiri
Jones, Martin  19
Jones, Oliver  157–58
Jones, Robert Edmond  22
Jones, Sissieretta  57
*Justice and Expediency, or, Slavery Considered with a View to its Rightful and Effectual Remedy*  6

Kahn, Mrs. Otto  90
Kahn, Otto  92 n8
Kaluschines, Mrs. J.L.  21
Kane, William  120
The Kangaroo  59
Keats, John  18, 172
Keith, George  163–69
*The Keithian Schism: Controversy in Early Pennsylvania*  163
Kellner, Bruce  39, 40, 172
Kelly, Abby Foster  13
Kemble, E.W.  11
Kenyon College  110
King, Alexander  21
King, Carol Weiss  24
King, Franzo W.  116
King, Marina  116
King, Martin Luther, Jr.  9, 120
Kingsley, Charles  11
"Kinky"  63
The Kinky Girls  63
Kite, Nathan  168 n2
Kite, William  168 n2

Knight, Charles R.  193
Knopf, Alfred A.  36, 173, 175
Knopf, Blanche  37
"Koonville's Koonlets"  72
Kristof, Civet Chakwal  127
Kummer, Clare  70

Lafayette Players  94
Lafayette Theatre  94
Lambert, Constant  82
Lane, Roger  72, 113
Lanfers, Ramer  127
LaPoint, James Amos LaFord  126
Larsen, Nella  35–41, 173–74
Lashley, James Francis Augustus  123, 126, 127
Latimer, Catherine Allen  46
Latino, Juan  160
Lawrence, Jacob  179
Lawrence, Margaret Morgan  48
Lawrence, Merloyd  51
Lawrence-Lightfoot, Sara  47–52
Lawson, Robert C.  152
*Leaves of Grass*  175, 195
Lee, Ivy  15
Leeming, David  33
"A Legend of the Lake"  6
Lemonier, Thomas  71
Lenox Library  163
Leslie, Lew  80, 82, 86, 90
*Levee Land*  89, 90, 91
"Levee Song"  90
Lewis, David Levering  37, 172
Lewis, Philip  128
Lewis, Theophilus  85
Liberal Catholic Church  127
*Liberator*  4
*The Liberty Bell*  13
*Liberty Chimes*  13
"Liberty Further Extended"  102
*Liberty or Slavery: The Great National Question, Three Prize Essays on American Slavery*  13
Library of Congress  161, 183

Licht, Robert 51
Liddell, Alice 3
*The Life of Langston Hughes* 174
Lightfoot, Charles 48
Ligon, Richard 53
*L'il Gal* 16
Lincoln, Abraham 7, 97
Lincoln Theatre 93–97
"Lines on Reading of the Capture of Certain Fugitive Slaves Near Washington" 6
"The Lion and the Monk (Die Trying)" 63
Lisle, George 105
*Little Mr. Thimblefinger and His Queer Country* 15
Litwack, Leon 181
Live Ever, Die Never Church 125
Lloyd, F.E.J. 126, 132 n21
Locke, Alain 17, 173, 177, 178
Long, Huey 124
Long, Vicki R. 120
Longfellow, Henry Wadsworth 13
*Loose Canons* 29
Loring, Ellis Gray 14
"Lover's Lane" 16
Lowell, James Russell 6, 12, 13
*A Lucky Coon* 59
Lyles, Aubrey 79
*Lyrics of Love and Laughter* 16
*Lyrics of Lowly Life* 16

Mack, Cecil 71, 72
Maclean, George 21
Maguire, Elizabeth 31
*Maid of Harlem* 95
Mailer, Norman 67
"Mammy's Little Pumkin Colored Coon" 69
Mandrake, Ethel Belle 177
"Mandy, Make Up Your Mind" 83
Mann, Horace 10

"March of the Wooden Soldiers" 83
Marchenna, Richard A. 126
*The Marcus Garvey and Universal Negro Improvement Association Papers* 113
Marino, Eugene 120
Marsh, Edward 26
Martin, Charles D. 161
Mason, Charles H. 153
Mason, Lelia W. 153
Massachusetts Anti-Slavery Fair 13
Massachusetts Anti-Slavery Society 13, 14
Mather, Cotton 167
Matthew, Wentworth A. 125
Matthews, Edward 21
Matthews, Edward M. 127
Maultsby, Portia K. 183
Maxixe 66
May, Samuel J. 4, 13, 14, 161
Mayer, G.H. 189
McBrien, Richard P. 119
McClendon, Rose 19
McGoings, Florence 131
McGoings, Robert 151
McGuire, George Alexander 107, 110–13, 117, 122, 132 n15, 132 n19, 132 n21
McKay, Chris 154
McKay, Claude 18, 20, 59, 179
McKnight, James 153
McPherson, Richard C. *See* Mack, Cecil
*Men of Mark: Eminent, Progressive and Rising* 158
"Menelik's Tribute to Queen Tai Tu" 63
*The Merry Widow* 63
The Messenger 124
Methodist Episcopal Church 130 n6

# Index

Metropolitan A.M.E. Church, NYC 93
Michigan State University 181
Mille, J.D. 11
Miller, DeWitt 11, 15
Miller, Flourney E. 79
Miller, Joseph 183
Millersville University 183
Mills, Florence 56, 60, 77–87, 89–92, 93, 97, 171
Mills, Maude 78
Mills, Olivia 78
*Mingo and Other Sketches in Black and White* 15
*Miss Dinah of 1933* 94
"Miss Hannah from Savannah" 56, 60, 71, 73, 77
Mitchell, Loften 22
Mitgang, Herbert 25
Mittelholzer, Edgar 44–45
Moore, George H. 163
Moorland, Jesse 161
Morgan, Robert 132 n15
Morris, Samuel 124
Moser, James H. 15
*Moses, Man of the Mountain* 177
Mother AME Zion Church, NYC 85
Motley, Willard 20
*Mr. Lode of Koal* 64
*Mulatto* 18
*Mules and Men* 176
Mullins, Mazie 96
Murray, Daniel A.P. 161
"My Black Mammy Did, Did She?" 68
*Mystery Developed* 104
Mythen, James G. 110

*Narrative of James Williams, an American Slave Who Was for Several Years a Driver on a Cotton Plantation in Alabama* 5
Nash, Gary 183

Nathan, George Jean 85
National Anti-Slavery Bazaar 13
National Anti-Slavery Society 4
National Association for the Advancement of Colored People 18, 19, 40, 161, 173, 178
National Council of Catholic Bishops 119
National Council of Churches 154
*Native Son* 24
*Negro America, What Now?* 173
Negro History Week 157
*Negro Life in New York's Harlem* 177
"The Negro Speaks of Rivers" 175
Nell, William Cooper 13
*The New Negro* 178
New Thought 124
Newman, Richard 113
Newton, Edward 193
Nickelette 93
*Nig* 36
*Nigger Heaven* 175
*Nights with Uncle Remus: Myths and Legends of the Old Plantation* 14
Nijinsky, Vaslav 56
Nine Abyssinian Maids 63
19th Street Baptist Church, Washington, DC 122
"Nobody Knows the Trouble I See" 69
North American College, Rome 117
*North American Negro Poets* 194
North American Old Roman Catholic Church 126, 127
North Carolina Central University 161
North Star 113
*The North Star: The Poetry of Freedom by Her Friends* 13

*Not Without Laughter* 175
*Notes on Fruits* 9
Notre Dame University 119
Nugent, Richard Bruce 56, 64, 179
Nurse, Gladstone St. Clair 113
Nybladh, Carl A. 112

Oblate Sisters of Providence 121
O'Connor Patrick 171
*Octoroons* 59, 60
Ogeltree, Charles 49
Ogilby, John 158
Ohio State University 183
Okeh Records 95
*An Old Ballad Retold* 172
Old Catholic Churches 107–29
*One Way to Heaven* 172
O'Neill, Eugene 21–22, 95
*Opera News* 171
"The Operatic Keleidoscope" 57
*Oranges Are Not the Only Fruit* 45
*Oriental America* 59
Orthodox Apostolic Church of America 126
Orthodox Catholic Church in America 126
O'Sullivan, Seumas 17
Ottley, Roi 20
*Our Nig* 33
Overton, Moses 56
Overton, Pauline Whitfield 56

Page, Oran "Hot Lips" 96
Paget, Gen. Sir Arthur 62
Paget, Lady 62
Paige, Billy 96
Palace Theatre 84
Panama Cafe 78
Parham, Florence 94
Parker, Dorothy 22
Parmlee, Ashbel 105
*Passing* 36, 174
Passon, A.J. 5
Pastor, Tony 57

Paton, Alan 25
Patrick, Archimandrite 110
Patterson, Janie 23
Pavilion Theatre 84
Peabody, Elizabeth Palmer 10
Pekin Theatre 66
Penn Charter School 164
Penn, William 164
Pentecostalism 149–54
Peter Ignatius III 112
Petersen, Ernest Leopold 126
Peterson, Diana 168 n2
Peterson, Dorothy 39
Petro, Pamela J. 187–95
Petry, Ann 20
Philadelphia Athenaeum 163
Philadelphia Yearly Meeting 165
Phillips, Wendell 5, 12, 13
"Phoebe Brown" 64
"Pickaninny Nigs" 69
Pimenta, Silverio Gomes 133 n21
Pinchback, Pinckney B.S. 175
Plantation Club 80, 84
*Plantation Review* 80–81
Plato 8
Platt, Warren C. 113–14, 129 n4
"A Plea for Captain John Brown" 9
Poe, Edgar Allen 3, 187, 191
*Poems on Various Subjects, Religious and Moral* 159
*Poems Written During the Progress of the Abolition Question in the United States between the Years 1830 and 1838* 5
*The Policy Players* 59, 60, 69
Polish National Catholic Church 111, 117
Ponceforte, Lord 77
Poole, Mattie 152
*Porgy and Bess* 21
Porter, Dorothy B. 194
"Porto Rico" 65
Pound, Ezra 3

# Index

"Previous Condition" 25
Prince George 84
Prince of Wales 62, 84
Procope, Russell 96
Prophet Jones 152
Protestant Friends of Irish Freedom 110
Provincetown (RI) Ladies' Anti-Slavery Society 13
Providence Playhouse 21, 94
Prudhomme, Phyllis 116
Pushkin, Alexander 160
"Put Your Arms Around Me, Honey" 68

Quakers. *See* Society of Friends
*Quicksand* 35, 173
Quincy, Edmund 13

Raboteau, Albert 119, 122
Race records 96
Rainey, Ma 93, 94–95, 96, 97
Ralegh, Sir Walter 8
Rampersad, Arnold 174–75
Randolph, James 78
Razaf, Andy 20
*The Red Moon* 64
Redman, Don 96
Redpath, James 9
Reed, Ishmael 29
"Refugee in America" 19
Remond, Charles Lenox 13
Republican Party 6
"Resistance to Civil Government" 10
*La Revue Nègre* 171
"Rhapsody in Blue" 89
"A Rich Coon's Babe" 56, 61, 70
Richards, David A. 122
Roberson, Warren 125
Roberts, James Pickford 127
Roberts, Robert E. 153
Robertson, Lady Constance 65
Robertson, William E.J. 127

Robeson, Paul 22, 25, 80
Robinson, Richard 113
Robinson, William 104
Rodrigues y Fairchild, Emile F. 120
Rogers, Alex 60, 64
Rogers, Hubert Augustus 127
Rogers, James Hubert 127
Roman Catholic Church 117–23, 131 n10
Rose, Ernestine 40
Rosenfeld, Paul 90
Rukeyser, Muriel 19, 23–24
*Rules for a Society of Negroes* 167

Sadler's Wells 82
St. Augustine's Cathedral, Brooklyn, NY 127
St. Avvakum Old Orthodox Church, San Francisco 116
St. Bishop the Vine 124
St. Denis, Ruth 65
St. John Divine Bishop 124
St. Martin de Porres Church, Washington, DC 122
St. Mary's Academy, Norfolk, VA 122
St. Paul's Church, New Haven, CT 126
*Saint Peter Relates an Incident of the Resurrection Day* 173
St. Teresa of Avila's Church, Washington, DC 117
St. Thomas Episcopal Church, Philadelphia, PA 113
St. Thomas Liberal Catholic Church, New York City 127
Salem Methodist Church, New York City 37, 172
"Salome" 65
Salt, Henry J. 9
Sanchez, Sonia 26
Sargent, George H. 193
Sarton, May 19

Saunders, Gertrude 29
Schiesler, Toni 49
Schomburg, Arthur A. 160, 161, 162, 173, 191, 194
Schomburg Center for Research in Black Culture 3, 35, 149, 161, 173
Schuyler, George S. 20, 179
Scott, Temple 193
Scottsboro case 23–24
*Scottsboro Limited* 175
Seamon and Hurtig 59, 60
*Selections from the Writings and Speeches of William Lloyd Garrison* 13
*Self-Determining Haiti* 173
Seligman, Emma 36
Senegambian Carnival 59
*Seraph on the Suwanee* 177
"Services for the Death of a Martyr" 8
7 Ginger Snaps 94
Sewell, Samuel 14
Seymour, William J. 152–53
*Shadows Move Among Them* 45
Shahn, Ben 11
"Shake That Thing" 95
*Shake Your Feet* 94
Shakespeare, William 23
Shapiro, Bernstein and Co. 72
Sharpshooters 95
Shaw, Stephanie J. 183
"She Kissed Him for His Mother" 68
"The Sheath Gown in Darktown" 62–63
Shepperson, George 114
Sherwood, Cyril John Clement 132 n21
Sherwood, R.E. 189
"She's a Sweet Little Snow White Blossom" 68
Shieks of Harlem 94
Shiffman, Frank 97

Shipp, Jesse A. 22, 59, 60, 64
Shooting the chute 59
*Shuffle Along* 79–80, 81, 86, 89, 93
Shyne, Gerard 44
*The Signifying Monkey* 29
"Silver Rose" 84
Simmons, William J. 158
Sinnette, Elinor DesVerney 183
Sissle, Noble 79, 89, 93
*Sister Jane, Her Friends and Acquaintances* 15
Sisters of Compassion 116
Six Dixie Vamps 81
Slaughter, Henry Proctor 161
Sleeper, J.R. 4
"The Sleeping Hills of Tennessee" 81
Smart Set Co. 64
Smith, Ada "Bricktop" 78
Smith, Albert 160
Smith, Bessie 94, 97, 171
Smith, George Totten 71
Smith, Lucy 152
Smith, Mamie 95–96
Smith, Nannie 125
Smith, William Gardner 20
Snow, Ophelia 93
Society for the Propagation of the Gospel 165
Society of Friends 163–69
Society of the Divine Saviour 122
Socrates 7
Soledad Three 21
"Some Sunny Day" 81
*Sons of Ham* 60, 71, 77
"The Soul's Errand" 8
Southern drag 66
Southern Enchantment Co. 64
Soyinka, Wole 25, 32
Spartas, Reuben 108
Spaulding, Martin J. 131 n10
*Speech on the Subject of Slavery, Delivered in the U.S. Senate on Thursday, March 7, 1850* 13

*Index*

Spencer, Anne 43–44, 179
Spingarn, Arthur B. 19, 161
Spiritual Baptists 128
Spoor, John A. 6
Stanford University 183
Stanley, Christopher 127
"Stanzas for the Times" 14
Starkey, Cyrus A. 127
State Historical Society of Wisconsin 182–83
Steamboat Bill 125
Stein, Gertrude 20–21, 37
Stein, Shelah 39
"A Steinian Catechism" 25
Steloff, Frances 19
Stern, Joseph W. 69, 71
Stern, Madeleine 195
Stevens, Aaron 8
Stewart, Jeffrey 183
Still, William Grant 89, 91
Stokowski, Leopold 95
Stone, Lucy 13
*The Story of Aaron* 15
Stowe, Harriet Beecher 10–12, 70
Strout, A.P. 16
Stuart, M.S. 114
Stuart, Moses 13
Sumner, Charles 6, 7, 12, 26
Sunny Land Cotton Pickers 96
Swaffer, Hannen 81
Swan's bend 59
Swarthmore College 51
Swedish American Church 112
Sweeting, James Stafford 122
Swift, Job 104
Syrian Orthodox Church 112, 122

Tacitus 8
*Tamerlane* 3
Tanguay, Eva 58
Tanner, Henry O. 160
Tappen, Lewis 4
*The Tar Baby and Other Rhymes of Uncle Remus* 15

Tate, Mary Magdalene 153
Teasdale, Sara 17
"Tell Me, Dusky Maiden" 69
*Tell My Horse* 177
Tennessee Ten 78–79
Terrell, George 15
Texas Southern University 194
Thackeray, William Makepeace 3, 11
"That's Why They Call Me 'Shine'" 56, 65, 72
Theatre Owners Booking Association 94
*Their Eyes Were Watching God* 177
*Theory of Flight* 24
Theosophy 127
"Thirsty After Thee, O Lord" 153
*This Was Harlem: A Cultural Portrait (1900–1950)* 172
Thompson, Arthur Terry 113
Thompson, Charles 57
Thompson, Louise 177
Thompson, Ulysses "Slow Kid" 78–79, 80, 89
Thompson, Virgil 20–21
Thoreau, Henry David 8–10
Thoreau, Sophia 9
Thornton, John K. 183
"The Three Little Kinkies" 57
Thurman, Howard 118
Thurman, Wallace 176, 177–78
Tilzer, Harry von 71
Toklas, Alice B. 37, 40
Tolson, Melvin B. 171
*Tom* 11
*Tomorrow's Children* 178
Toomer, Jean 175–76, 177
Toscanini, Arturo 90
Transvestism 75 n35
Tribble, Andrew 93
*A Tribute to William Lloyd Garrison at the Funeral Services, March 28, 1879* 13
*A Trip to Coontown* 59

Trotter, Joe 183
Tucker, Sophie 96
Turkish Orthodox Church 127
Turner, Henry McNeal 109, 129–30 n6, 131 n10
Turner, Nat 191
Tuskegee Institute 16
*Twenty-Five Years in the Auction Business and What Now?* 189
"The Two Real Coons" 57
Tyarks, William 126, 132 n21
Tyers, W.H. 69

Umoja Temple, Washington, DC 122
"Uncle Remus at the Telephone" 14
*Uncle Remus; His Songs and His Sayings: The Folkklore of the Old Plantation* 15
"*Uncle Remus*," Joel Chandler Harris as Seen and Remembered by a Few of His Friends 15
*Uncle Remus Returns* 15
"Uncle the Bamboo Tree" 69
*Uncle Tom's Cabin* 10–11
Union of Utrecht 111
United African Movement 121
Universal Negro Improvement Association 107
*Universal Salvation* 104–5
University of California 181, 183
University of Copenhagen 35
University of Florida 149
University of Gottingen 158
University of Grenada 160
University of Halle 157
University of Jena 159
University of Leyden 159
University of Massachusetts 183
University of Michigan 35, 182
University of Michigan Law School 173
University of Virginia 183

University of Wittenburg 159
Unwin, T. Fisher 16
Urban League 161

Valentine, Robert Arthur 114
Van Vechten, Carl 18, 20, 21, 22, 25, 36, 37, 39, 56, 63, 90, 161, 173, 175
Varese, Edgar 90
Varse, Mary Heaton 24
Vatican Council 111
Vernell, Rose 121
Verra, Michael E. 126
Victoria Theatre 65
Victory Mutual Life Insurance Co. 114
Vilatte, Joseph René 112, 122, 123, 132 n16
Vodery, Will 80, 81
Vogt, Francis Arthur 113
Voris, Gregory Michael David 120

W.E.B. Du Bois Institute for Afro-American Research 33, 181, 185
Waddles, Mother 152
Walker, Aida Overton 55–75, 77
Walker, Alice 176
Walker, George W. 55–75, 77
Walker, Jonathan 6
Walker, Madame C.J. 32
Walker, Margaret 20
Waller, Thomas "Fats" 96
*The Walls of Jerico* 178
Walrond, Eric 179
Wanamaker, John 11
Ward, T.M.D. 129 n6
Warford, Amanda 5
"The Warmest Colored Girl in Town" 68
Washington, Booker T. 16
Washington, F.D. 153
Washington, George 103
Washington, James M. 101

*Index*

Washington University 183
Washingtonians 96
Wasserman, Edward 35–41
Wasserman, Edward, Sr. 36
*The Waste Land* 3
Waters, Ethel 37, 94, 95
Waugh, Evelyn 84
Wayne, Beatrice Robinson 21
*The Ways of White Folks* 175
*The Weary Blues* 175
Weaver, Robert C. 37
Webster, Daniel 13
Wegelin, Oscar 191
Weiss, Harry B. 188
*The Welcome Table* 33
Weld, Theodore Dwight 13
Wells, Gabriel 193
West, Cornel 33
West, Michael 115, 133 n24
West Philadelphia Imani Temple 121
West Syrian Jacobite Church of Antioch 112
Weston, Anne Warren 13
Wetmore, Judson D. 173
Wheatley, Phillis 159, 183, 188, 191, 194
*When Harlem Was in Vogue* 172
"When They Straighten All the Colored People's Hair" 72
Whipple, Mrs. E.P. 5
White, Gavin 113
White, Lily 93
White, Richard "Mr. Clean" 153
White, Walter 20, 39, 92 n7, 173, 179
Whitman, Walt 3, 195
Whitney, Tutt 22
Whittier, John Greenleaf 4, 5–7, 13, 14
"Why Adam Sinned" 56, 61
Wilberforce, William 26
"Wildfire" 64
Wiley, Stella 57

Wilkie, Herbert F. 127
*William Dorsey's Philadelphia and Ours* 113
Williams, Bert 55–75, 77, 82, 94, 97, 158
Williams, Detroit 153
Williams, George Washington 158
Williams, John A. 20
Williams, Lottie 69
Williams and Walker 55–75
Williams Temple COGIC, Gainesville, FL 153
Wills, Cheryle 49
Wills, David W. 129
Wilson, Arthur "Dooley" 94
Wilson, Edith 81
Wilson, Harriet 33
Wilson, Joseph T. 158
Winfree, John 77
Winfree, Nellie Simons 77
Winfrey, Oprah 120
Winter Garden Theatre 80
Winterson, Jeanette 45
Wittingham, William Rollinson 109
Wolfe, Thomas 31
"Women and Scottsboro" 23
Women's Ordination Conference 121
Wood, Peter 183
Woodlawn Cemetery 85
Woodson, Carter G. 157–58
Woolf, Cecil 25
Woolf, Virginia 3
World, Joe 125
*Worlds Apart: Relationships between Families and Schools* 51
Wright, Ada 23
Wright, Elizur, Jr. 13
Wright, Richard 20, 24–25, 99, 176

Xavier University 194

Yacob, Bishop  125
Yale University  20, 32, 39
"The Yankee Girl"  5
*A Yankee in Canada, with Anti-Slavery and Reform Papers*  9
*Yearbook of American and Canadian Churches*  154
"The Yoke of Racial Inequality"  25
Young, Owen D.  3

Ziegfeld, Florenz  64, 82
Ziegfeld Follies  82, 158
*Zora Neale Hurston: A Literary Biography*  176

## About the Author

Richard Newman is currently Fellows Officer at the W.E.B. Du Bois Institute for African-American Research at Harvard University, where he was previously Managing Editor of the *Harvard Guide to African-American History*. Before that, he served as Managing Editor of Macmillan's *Encyclopedia of African-American Culture and History* project at the Center for American Cultural Studies, Columbia University.

He is the author or editor of over 200 books, articles, and reviews in the field of African-American Studies. Two recent books are *Everybody Say Freedom: Everything You Need to Know About African-American History* published by New American Library/Penguin Books; and *This Far by Faith: Readings in African-American Women's Religious Biography*, co-edited with Judith Weisenfeld and published by Routledge.

Richard Newman lives in Massachusetts with his partner, Belynda Bady.